Praise for Edward Ugel and **MONEY** *for* **NOTHING**

"Money for Nothing took me into a world I had no idea existed. For anyone who's ever dreamed of winning the lottery, this is a terrifying look at what really happens when someone hands you that huge cardboard check. Ugel's writing style is terrific—anyone who's ever found himself sobbing into a scotch glass at a casino at three in the morning is going to identify with the highs and lows of this compelling story."

—Ben Mezrich, *New York Times* bestselling author of *Bringing Down the House* and *Busting Vegas*

"Mr. Ugel's roller-coaster ride makes for dizzying, sometimes harrowing reading. Confessional, un-self-protecting and bitterly funny, it exposes the human failings of his customers, his colleagues and himself, in a personal memoir of greed and hope."

—*New York Times*

"[A] sordid—and highly engaging—tale."

—*Wall Street Journal*

"His tale is a colorfully written account by a self-proclaimed overweight, chain-smoking, Krispy Kreme doughnut–eating, fanatical gambler. . . . You will lick your chops, eager to hear the sordid woes of winners gone broke from

—*USA Today*

"A fascinating and rollicki on't know exists. Written with *Nothing* shows how being a gambler makes a good salesman even better, reveals the peculiar thrill of closing a deal, and most surprisingly, explains why winning the lottery is sometimes the worst thing that could happen to anyone."

—Alex Blumberg, producer, *This American Life*

"Ugel's natural showmanship makes for entertaining reading. He does little to pretty up his misdeeds (heck, they were legal) and offers comical vignettes of his rendezvous and run-ins with prospective clients while delivering a well-deserved scathing indictment of the government-backed lottery system."

—*Library Journal*

"A breezy, funny writer. . . . Maybe this eye-opening book will galvanize a movement. . . . By turns amusing and alarming."

—*Kirkus Reviews*

"Funny, eye-opening."

—*Details*

"A jackpot of sleaze and hilarity."

—*Oregonian* (Portland)

MONEY

for

NOTHING

One Man's Journey Through the Dark Side of Lottery Millions

EDWARD UGEL

COLLINS BUSINESS

An Imprint of HarperCollinsPublishers

HarperCollins books may be purchased for educational, business, or sales promotional use. For information please write: Special Markets Department, HarperCollins Publishers, 10 East 53rd Street, New York, NY 10022.

Designed by William Ruoto

First Collins paperback edition published 2008.

The Library of Congress has catalogued the hardcover edition as follows:

Ugel, Edward.
  Money for nothing : one man's journey through the dark side of lottery millions / Edward Ugel. —1st ed.
        p. cm.
  ISBN 978-0-06-128417-5
  1. Lottery winners—United States. I. Title.

  HG6126.U35 2007
  795.3'8092—dc22

                                                                    2007023895

ISBN 978-0-06-128418-2 (pbk.)

08 09 10 11 12   ID/RRD   10 9 8 7 6 5 4 3 2 1

FOR BROOKE
The best part of my life.
The best part of my day.

FOR SASHA
One day you'll understand
how much I love you.

FOR MOM AND DAD
For a lifetime of humor and love.

ACKNOWLEDGMENTS

THIS BOOK COULD NOT have been written without the patience and support of many people—a few of whom even *offered* to help. Others were dragged into my lair of self-doubts, needy rants, and at-gun-point reading sessions, whether they liked it or not.

I am particularly indebted to Jerry Oppenheimer, who knew this was a book long before I did. Mary Bralove was a soothing and encouraging early reader. Todd Pruzan read my proposal in its infancy and assured me it had legs. Elizabeth Sheinkman quietly and gracefully changed the momentum of this book. I am forever grateful.

Farley Chase is a loyal and insightful agent. He took a disjointed proposal by a neophyte writer and turned it into the foundation for this book. Farley is like salt. He makes everything better. My publisher, Marion Maneker, has an astonishing eye for what works and what's best left off the page. His skillful editing turned my story into an actual book. He's a magician. Thanks also to Kyran Cassidy, Genoveva Llosa, Chris Goff, Gretchen Crary, Angie Lee, Sarah Brown, and the rest of the HarperCollins team.

Writing this book had its share of legal issues. My attorney, Ben Feldman, has been a wise and calming guide throughout. Thank you for easing the pain.

Thanks to David Kestenbaum, who introduced me to the folks at *This American Life,* all because I made him laugh while making a toast at a wedding. It must have been a hell of a toast—or really strong champagne. *TAL* Producer Alex Blumberg was disarmingly funny and supportive from day one. Collaborating with Alex and the rest of the *TAL* crew was like going to raconteur fantasy camp.

Toby Oppenheimer read every word of this manuscript—mere moments after they were written. Toby's insight, support, and sense of humor were a daily elixir to the monotony and isolation of writing. Doug Green was an enthusiastic reader and supporter throughout this process. Aaron Gadiel had a tremendous impact on this book, as he has on my life over the past decade. Skip Holmes nursed me through this year, all but on call when I needed to leave my own head for an hour or two. Thank you to Megan and Keith for reading early drafts and allowing the book to monopolize so many of our conversations ever since. Uri Kushner was a supportive friend and fan of the book from day one. Still, he should stick to what he knows: fantasy football.

Karen Bralove, my courageous and unique mother-in-law, was an essential presence throughout the writing of this book. Mara Bralove could not have done more to support and encourage me this entire year. She is a cherished friend. Ari Fisher has been a trusted sounding board and the official IT Department for my website. Thank you for a thankless job.

To Nana and Pop, who have always made each of us feel like the most important person on earth. Although Pop is gone, a good name lasts forever. I am in awe of Nana's grace, dignity, and endless capacity to love each of us. And, even though I know she loves me the most, I promise I will never tell her other grandchildren and great-grandchildren.

Thank you to my siblings: Niki, Phil, Georgi, and Kami. Is there a richer source of love, support, *and material* than the four of you? I am proud of each of you. Sorry for talking so much at dinner. In particular, my sister Georgi was a devoted fan and supporter. I am extremely grateful. I'm listing the names of my nieces and nephews because I love them and I want them to like me better than their other uncles, none of whom have even *written* a book, much less mentioned Luca, Gigi, Coco, Dino, Dylan, Jono, and Pischer. *(Please remember this when I'm old and you need to drive me to the doctor.)*

My mom and dad stood behind me throughout this process, laughing and applauding me at various milestones along the way. My mom has a love of words which rivals that of any editor or bibliophile, a razor sharp sense of humor, and the grammatical recall of a sadistic English teacher. While writing this book I relied upon her opinion and advice at every turn. No matter how eloquent, words simply cannot convey the love and admiration I have for my folks. Thank you, and I love you.

To Sasha, my play date at work. You are too young to understand the pleasure you've brought into my life. Who knew that dancing, coloring, and making spaghetti out of Play-Doh could be a perfect break from writing?

Finally, thank you to my wife, Brooke, for your love, support, and patience. Living with me when I'm actually being paid to write about myself? You should be sainted. Thank you for being my partner in this whole thing. There is no warmer woman, no more loving wife and mother than you. You are my everything.

—*Edward Ugel*
March 16th, 2007

CONTENTS

"Money often costs too much."
—Ralph Waldo Emerson

INTRODUCTION

TIMING IS SOMETHING, ISN'T it? Sometimes, I wonder what would have happened had I never gotten involved with the lottery business. Sometimes, I thank God I found the business when I did. In a way, it saved me. Anyway, The Firm didn't turn me into anything. The seed was planted long ago. I was who I was long before I showed up at their door. The Firm just provided the right amount of sun and shade with which I needed to grow.

I'd do it all again, for the experience, and for the money. I'd be lying if I said the money wasn't great—addicting, but great. The money gave me options guys my age tend not to have. But things changed. The tail began to wag the dog. The money got me the big house. The big house came with the big mortgage. Suddenly, I *needed* my job. And, there's the rub. The day you realize that you, like every other schmuck in the world, *need* to work, you're an adult.

Why did I spend the better part of a decade chasing lottery winners? I could have done something else. But I had no earthly idea what else I wanted to do with my life. It's not as if I had big plans. And—did I mention my paychecks?—you should have seen my paychecks. I was clearing multiple six figures since I was twenty-eight. Don't be impressed, most of it's gone—just like with a lottery winner. It's as if I never had the money in the first place. I'm as jealous as you are.

I fell into this business ass-backwards, but it's an industry perfectly matched to my talents. If you are good at something that is bad for some people, does that make you a bad person? Try making heads or tails of that with your shrink.

Anyway, I'm writing this book because I know what really happens to people when they come into a lot of unexpected cash. Plus, the last decade has seen a paradigm shift in the nation's gambling culture, and I've been a big part of that story—from both sides. I've earned a good living off gamblers because I know them inside and out. I'm also emblematic of the gambling epidemic our country faces today. When it comes to gambling, I'm both the shark and the mark.

This book looks at the ubiquitous nature of casinos and gambling in our culture. We are raising a new generation of gamblers—and some, no doubt, will be addicted gamblers. Casinos are no longer distant fantasy worlds, a faraway Vegas or Atlantic City. Now, they're just down the street or the next town over. What's worse, anyone with an Internet connection has gambling options at his fingertips. It's a lot easier to sneak in a little gambling online from the den than it was for my uncle to find a little action back in his day.

The last decade has seen an absolute explosion in gaming technology. The Internet has altered the way individuals access all forms of gambling. And when the Internet fails to lure gamblers, television is there to pick up the slack. Poker is shown nightly on TV. When teens, and even preteens, turn on ESPN, they are just as likely to see Daniel Negreanu bluffing at a poker table as they are to see Kobe Bryant shooting a free throw. Instead of *Sportscenter*, they find the *World Series of Poker*, where young people—some no older than twenty-one—fight for their share of multimillion-dollar prizes.

These youthful, brash poker players are the new heroes of young American males. Everyone wishes he could be Tiger Woods, but few really think they could actually do what he does. Unfortunately, there are tens of thousands of people who are convinced that they have the chops to sit with, and beat, Daniel Negreanu. Moreover, if they can come up with the bankroll, they're welcome to have a crack at him. And, believe me, there's a lot more dumb money out there than real talent.

What does this mean for our youth culture? I believe that today's adolescents, some at least, will eventually look a lot like me. God help us all. Today's teens are growing up in a gambling society—entirely different from what it was even a decade earlier. And forget about nostalgia; we don't have to travel too far back in time to remember when things were different. I'm thirty-five, and I didn't even have an e-mail address in college. No one did. So we're not talking ancient history. Gaming is more socially accepted, and far more ubiquitous, than at any time in our history. What on earth will these folks act like when they are thirty, married, earners, and parents? This book contemplates that reality.

The fact that I worked with lottery winners while being a gambler myself makes for an interesting and valuable perspective into the greater gambling culture in our nation. And the work itself was certainly never boring. I worked in an industry that, among other things, sold money to lottery winners in exchange for a portion of their long-term annuities. It's a competitive and intense industry—not for the faint of heart. Yet, I've known it to be legal and legitimate in any and all of its dealings. The industry needn't play games with the law. There's plenty of money to be made playing it straight.

This is my true story. That is, the "me" part is true—insofar as how I experienced things. Still, I have a legal obligation to keep certain details of my employment confidential, which I fully respect. I've gone to great lengths to give all the people in the book their absolute respect and privacy. Among other things, I've changed every name, win amount, and win state, as well as certain descriptions of lottery winners with whom I've worked in order to protect their identity. Every detail has been changed so that actual people, locations, processes, and dates are unrecognizable. Every factual detail has been "fictionalized" so that no proprietary, confidential, or personal information is conveyed. I've done so in order to insure that the book violates no laws or third party rights. The people in this book deserve their privacy. I owe them that. I've made the same effort to protect the privacy of my colleagues in the company. This book isn't their choice; it's mine. It's my story; they all have their own. Let them write a book. It's a complete pain in the ass. Finally, everything I write about sales methods or strategies applies to salespeople in any industry.

I have no interest in causing any harm or discomfort to anyone in this book be they lottery winners, colleagues, former colleagues, or others. I have no ax to grind with my old company, its owner, old colleagues, the state lotteries, or, most important, lottery winners themselves. All of the above have been extremely generous in obvious ways (paychecks, promotions) and in ways far more subtle. They will never fully know how much I valued this time in my life, these people, and even this bizarre industry.

Firing me said, in the most absolute way, *we don't choose you.* That just about killed me. It took me a few months to get over it. Still, writing the book has been a surprisingly happy trip down memory lane. I find I'm a lot more mature and content a year later.

In the end, I'm trying to share a good story that gives people a laugh, and perhaps the occasional wow—nothing else. The business gave me more than I could have asked for, so many years ago. I wish them nothing but good deals and safe roads. I just want to write a good story, well told. I just want to write books.

You are all safer that way, too.

—*Edward Ugel*

1

GONZO GOES FISHING

August 1997: Southeast Florida

I am watching Tommy roll another joint, one-handed, while driving his new boat straight out of the inlet into the Atlantic Ocean. I'm laughing so hard it's making me even more nervous, happy, sad, stunned. I just made a serious commission off this guy and he's taking me out fishing, too. Forty minutes ago, we were at his bank notarizing the signature pages of his contract. Now, we're off the clock.

Thank God I left the contracts in the car. There's sea spray everywhere. They would be soaked, and I'd be beside myself—just beside myself.

Tommy's someone you like right away. Three years ago, he won a handful of millions in the Florida Lottery. Tommy swears he was happier before he won. I know he's telling the truth. That's one of the reasons he trusts me—because I *know* it's true. Two days ago, he called our office looking for money after seeing our commercial on *The Jerry Springer Show*. Within seconds I knew. This could be big.

Tommy's wearing nothing but a pair of cut-off jean shorts. He is tan, his skin leathered from a life on the water. This is not his first time in the sun. I, on the other hand, am fat and pale. A chain smoker, Tommy sounds like a young Wilford Brimley. I like him a lot. I just do. He's funny—and we both love to fish. But I can tell that he can be a mean son of a bitch. If he only knew...

The sun feels like it's thirty feet over my head. I'm burning everywhere. This is not the kind of boat where you go lathering yourself up with SPF 45. I imagine Tommy would not be inclined to rub the lotion into my tough-to-reach areas. I will burn like a man. I hate being manly. I want a Diet Coke. All we have is Budweiser.

I'm sweating. Tommy yells something to me. I hear nothing over the screams of the two huge engines mounted on the back. One engine would definitely be enough for this boat, but we have two ... lucky us. Typical lottery winner, the *nouveau riche* of the *nouveau riche*. They buy two of everything when one will do.

Tommy looks back and hands me the lit joint. He says something. I can't hear him over the goddamn engines. I'm pretty sure he said something about the money. I laugh as if to infer that I both heard him and agree with whatever he just said. At this point, it's best to just agree.

I'm in no mood to smoke, but I'm not about to refuse his offer. I take a long, deliberate drag on the joint. I close the back of my mouth so I look like I'm toking away. The smoke gets sucked into the engine exhaust before I inhale it. Tommy doesn't notice. Lesson 101 in sales: If a customer offers you something to drink or eat, you accept. It's just good manners and it puts the other person at ease. It's good for business—any business.

It's 3:45 in the afternoon and I'm faking a joint with a client. Why? Because he wants to, and I'm here to make him comfortable. Not a typical day at Smith Barney or Goldman Sachs. It is, to be sure, closer to car sales—very expensive cars.

Tommy is going this fast to (a) test me, (b) scare me, or (c) impress me. He has actually done (d) make me want my nana. I'm too numb and hot and happy about the deal to be truly scared. But deep down, I know I'm in a tight spot. At the very least ... the *very* least, I'm not exactly acting like the son my father raised. Pretending to smoke a joint with a lottery winner just after signing a deal with him is not quite the career my dad had in mind for me.

I think Tommy just said something about his lawyer reading

a copy of the docs. Goddamn engine noise. It doesn't matter now. The deal's signed. I nod and smile. All I can think about is holding onto any part of the boat that is bolted down—and not dying. The skin cancer I'm bound to get is a longer-term issue. Falling out of the boat, three miles out to sea with a stoned multimillionaire, is a more pressing concern.

Tommy has no idea how we make our money. They never do. He thinks we're fishing buddies. I wish we were. I will be sorry to disappoint him—that part always stings. But, in the end, more times than not, these deals are one-night stands. He offered to put me up at his house, for Christ's sake. He didn't even want me to check into a hotel. He can roll a goddamn joint with one hand. I like Tommy. I could use a friend like him in my real life.

In two weeks, he will threaten to kill me. He will mean it. And I will deserve it.

What kind of job makes all this possible, necessary even? To see the lump-sum business for what it really is, to understand that it has next to nothing to do with finance and numbers, you have to appreciate the kind of folks that win the lottery and the kind of guys who wait in the weeds for them to surface.

Tommy's first call to The Firm surfaced late in the evening, when decent folks were already home. I was with Ben at the bar, for a change. We were both still in our work clothes, as we'd come straight from the office—four hours ago. We were still working, in a sense, as our cell phones kept ringing with sales reps from all over the country calling in to give us (Ben, really) updates on the status of their deals. So far that night, over a handful of cocktails, we'd both made money as two deals had been signed, all while we guarded our favorite bar stools.

We were both in khakis and golf shirts with The Firm's logo on the breast pocket. The only real difference in our attire was that, for now, I'd managed to avoid spilling ranch dressing on the front of my shirt. Ben had not been so lucky. He wasn't too eager to clean it off, either. After a few hours, the dressing now looked more like bird shit, keeping me and several of the bartenders amused.

The night had started out as happy hour, but that was long ago. I was doing the delicate dance between getting looped with Ben, my boss, and trying to keep just a hair more sober than he was. A few more drinks and ten-to-one odds say he'd *strongly suggest* that we go to a strip club downtown. By now, I knew his drinking rhythms. They were not dissimilar to my own. Ben is a few months younger than me, a fact he loved. We were both young, successful, and highly paid guns for The Firm. He was just more successful and more highly paid. Ben is also disarmingly charming and likable. He is unbelievably talented and equally tough. Basically, I hated him.

The best way to describe Ben is to tell you about the first time we went drinking together. It was my second day working for The Firm. I was still living in my parents' basement, so I wasn't exactly running home—even on a Tuesday night. Ben had a black belt in holding his liquor. I had no clue. I figured I'd teach him a thing or two about the real world once we left his turf, the office, and hit a neutral playing field—a bar. Little did I know. He slid into the stool like it was a hot bubble bath. You could almost hear his body say, "Ahhhhh." A look of calm and comfort covered his face as he lit a Marlboro Light. Dark lighting, stiff drinks, a fresh pack of smokes—Ben was home for the evening.

We knew a few of the same people from high school. It was nice. I was relieved. There was instant chemistry. We liked each other. He was bright and had a decidedly blue sense of humor. He got my jokes, which I consider a sign of intelligence. He was trying to impress me, and he did. I was trying to impress him, too.

With the infamous bladder of a pregnant woman, I was off to the john every few minutes. During one of my bathroom breaks, Ben paid a bartender to go across the street and buy a pack of Depends for me. It was actually quite funny, especially from a guy you hardly knew. He was beside himself. I relaxed. I'd known Ben for two days. We were on a hell of a first date.

A few cocktails later, Ben went to light a cigarette. Striking the stick against the flint, the match caught just as it flung out of Ben's drunken grasp. As if in slow motion, the lit match tumbled head over heels like a baton, landing gracefully in the long, curly hair of the woman seated directly to my left. Instinctively, I swiped at the poor woman's igniting head, landing what must have seemed like a violent and unprovoked karate chop to her smoldering perm. She was stunned. I was stunned. Ben was thrilled. Half the bar looked at us, wondering what the hell had just happened. We giggled like boys caught with a *Playboy*. We were quite amused. The woman's boyfriend was not. We'd had four or five drinks, and lit matches were flying out of our hands and landing in people's hair. It would be hard to argue that the guy didn't have a point. Nonetheless, at that moment I saw a preview of Ben's dark side—one that I would get to know quite well over the next few years.

Ben went from laughing to dead serious, scary serious, in a split second. I'll admit that we should not have been lighting women's hair on fire—that's a given. But the boyfriend picked the wrong guy to make that point with. Instantly, Ben shot out of his stool and pushed the guy's chivalrous intentions out of the room. I was stunned. I was scared of him. I was impressed. I was mortified. Ben was *quick,* too. Not knowing him, I wasn't sure what the hell was happening, or what I was supposed to do. I don't exactly have a long history of bar dustups on my résumé. This, in fact, was my first, and I just wanted to become invisible. I was also ashamed of Ben, almost rooting for the other guy to knock some semblance of good manners into him. Thankfully, it didn't matter. The poor couple threw down a few bucks and scurried off into the night. I wanted to go with them.

I slept at Ben's condo that night. I was in no condition to walk, much less drive.

He was already up when I opened my bloodshot eyes. To his credit, there was coffee brewing. Apparently, Ben was human. He couldn't wait to tell me that after the second round of cocktails the night before, his bartender friend had been giving him ice water instead of vodka tonics every other round. I was outdrinking him two to one. He was just tickled with himself. That's when I realized that he was no ordinary boss. Still, Ben, like vodka, was intoxicating. I couldn't resist him.

This night, just before Tommy called, Ben and I had gone out for a few drinks. I'd wised up to "just a few" with Ben. We still went out; I just never got into the kind of shape I was that first night. It's work hanging out with your boss socially. At least it was with mine. Still, when given the choice between staying in the office cold-calling lottery winners until 9:00 P.M. or drinking with Ben, I'd hide my keys and head to Uno's.

After an hour or so, I was ready to head home. I stopped back into the office to grab my keys. Just as I was turning off the office lights, my phone rang. It was late for business calls, but lottery winners aren't known to keep banker's hours. Plus, it could have been someone on the West Coast. We did a lot of deals out West, and I was always taking some sort of late-night sales call or doing damage control with a West Coast winner. I rarely went to sleep before two or three in the morning. I answered on the final ring. It was a Florida winner named Tommy Holmes asking "how does it work?" and "what's the catch?" These are typical questions for midday but a sign of a serious need for cash at 11:00 P.M. I was on to him right away. He needed money or this call could have, *should have,* waited until morning. He was waving the financial white flag. The drool started creeping down my chin. Blood was in the water. It was time to go fishing.

I did my best to pretend that it was normal for me to be in the office at this hour. Despite the vodka and buffalo wings brokering a delicate peace in my belly, I went straight into sales mode. I was in no mood, but for lottery deals, you get in the mood. A winner could call me at two in the morning—collect—and I'd take him through the sales cycle before I even realized what I was doing.

Before finding them in the database, you have no way of knowing if the person on the other end of the phone is a fraud, just a *simple* million-dollar winner, or a major whale. A whale can make your year. A whale can make the company's year. I was a whale hunter. Actually, I was a closer. They brought me in when a deal was big enough that signing it or not was the difference between a profitable quarter or year. What does a whale-size deal look like? You know when you find it, and right now, it looked like it could be Tommy Holmes.

I quickly looked at the map of Florida on the wall. We were not on the phone more than twenty seconds before I'd told Tommy, with all the *aw shucks* surprise that I could muster—what a coincidence it was that he was calling from West Palm Beach, Florida, as I was headed down to Jupiter the very next morning! West Palm and Jupiter are maybe fifteen miles apart. He bit.

Appointment setting is an art form. Do it right and deals fall into your lap. That first move—immediately setting an appointment—was my signature play. I did it every time. If it worked, bingo. And, if it didn't . . . well, it always worked. It just went down too early in the conversation for a winner to even pick up on it. My ability to set appointments had made The Firm millions. It got me out of debt, too . . . twice. The strategy is so simple, it's cheap to call it a "close." It's more like a perfect opening. Before they even knew my name, they heard, out of the corner of their ear—before they were even listening—that I was already headed to their area. Typically, the comment was dismissed as an aside, said only to make small talk. Hardly. They may not have known why they called, but I did.

It took about twenty seconds to find Tommy's lead sheet in the database. I now had every conceivable bit of information about Tommy Holmes at my fingertips: his win date, what he did for a living, where he lived, his family situation, how many payments he had left, if he'd ever called us before, everything he had said to The Firm each and every time we cold-called his house. We knew what cars he owned and we knew his win amount. Our database was everything.

When I first started at The Firm, we kept all of our sales contacts on paper. In order to get something updated, you'd have to submit the information on paper and wait for one of a half-dozen researchers to manually enter the data onto master paper leads. Sometimes it would take weeks to get the lead back, just to get the winner's cell-phone number copied into our notes. Now, we were far more sophisticated. We have a computerized database.

Our research department spent their entire workweek looking for data on lottery winners. They did searches in every conceivable database, online, offline, physically at courthouses, submitting FOIA (Freedom of Information Act) requests to each state on a monthly basis—whatever it took to keep our database topped up. Additionally, we advertised on TV and through direct mail. We dropped mail to each winner once a week and we were on television every day. The commercials and direct mail made the phones ring (when they worked). Every time a winner called, we went through the exact same process. The winner was asked a myriad of questions. Every detail was recorded into the database. Before the winners even knew whom they were talking to, we had enough data to track them wherever they went, like it or not. They could try to go underground, but once we had certain key pieces of data (social security number, driver's license number), they were ours.

I saw in the data that Tommy was a big winner. This one had potential. And the hook was already set. So far, we'd been on the phone for less time than it takes to order at the drive-thru and I knew everything about him. Plus, he already thought I was headed to his neck of the woods in the morning.

I saw in notes that he was a fisherman.

"Say, Tommy, you're not a fisherman, are you? You used to run a boat?! No kidding? Do you know I never fly to Florida on business without bringing my travel pole. *(True.)* When? *Tomorrow?* Well, it would have to be late, because I have another meeting in Jupiter. *(False.)* But hold on. Let me look at something. *(ESPN. com.)* You know what, I may be able to push my Jupiter meeting back to Friday because the people I'm meeting are free all week. *(There are no people.)* They're older, and we're just meeting to sign contracts. *(False.)* They are already about to get their money. *(There is no money.)* If you want, we can hook up tomorrow and fish—maybe talk about your cash situation. *(True.)* Well, yeah, sure. You can pick me up at the airport. I was going to rent a car, but I can do that up by you because you and my other meeting are practically in the same city . . . I know, this *is* a weird coincidence! *(It's no coincidence.)*"

I feel like a faith healer who knows that the old lady up on stage with him has shingles because one of his informants followed her to the doctor in town earlier that afternoon. Hardly a miracle there, and definitely no coincidence that Tommy and I just so happen to have fishing in common. I *do* love to fish. But if I didn't, I'd learn to love it.

There is no magic to the way I set up the appointment. It's common sense cut with enough guts to jump right into the water. If you tell a Florida winner that you are getting on a plane and flying out for the *sole purpose* of coming to see him about buying all of his lottery payments, you are going to scare the hell out of him. Odds are, by the time you show up, the winner will be hiding at the mall, waiting for you to get lost. Countless deals never amount to anything because of winners getting cold feet about a poorly set-up meeting. Rather than face the rep outright and risk embarrassment or the pressure to sell from a real closer, many winners simply duck away.

Lottery winners are a fragile lot. Their phone rings off the hook, everyone wants something, no one's just stopping by to say "hi" anymore. Friends, coworkers, family, lump sum salesman; everyone's got an angle. It's no surprise that so many winners skipped out on meetings with us. But, with so much money at stake, there was ample reason for a salesperson to wait it out. What were we waiting for? Anything. Action. A shot at some precious face time with a winner that we *knew* needed to do something about his finances.

Tommy and I were not on the phone for more than ten minutes. The appointment was set for as soon as I could get there. I would have left right away except that it was pushing midnight and there were no flights out that night. It killed me to let a dozen hours pass for this guy to rethink his options or, worse, call a competitor. Anyone in this business would know exactly how hot this deal was. Plus, odds are that someone in the industry would give Tommy more money than we would. One call to a competitor could easily kill this whole deal. I was already stressed beyond belief about what could go wrong, and ten minutes earlier I didn't even know this guy existed. Welcome to the lottery business.

I always kept a travel bag with a few days' worth of clothes in the back of my truck so when deals like this came up, I was ready to go. Sometimes, there was such a race to get to a winner who was ready to sell that there was absolutely no time to stop home to pack. Once, one of the reps I worked with jumped on a nonstop to Seattle to meet a winner who'd called in and told us that she had another meeting with a competitor *that night* for dinner. She was giving all the right buying signs, and we knew that whoever got there first would sign this deal. We priced it and realized that the deal had a good amount of money in it. The competitor was flying up from West Palm Beach, and we figured that he would likely have a layover somewhere in the middle of the country. So we took a chance and flew our rep out to Washington with nothing but the contracts, an advance check for $10,000, and the clothes on his back. If we were lucky, we would literally fly over the competition somewhere en route and poach the deal.

Our rep got there and signed the deal a half-hour before the other company's guy was to arrive for supper. All lottery deals need to be notarized, so the Seattle winner and my guy drove to a Kinko's to notarize the docs. When they pulled back into the winner's driveway, our competitor was sitting there waiting, docs in hand. The beauty of it all is that there is no rescission period in the state of Washington. In other words, once the winner signs the docs, the deal is irreversible. Moreover, this other rep would be breaking the law by trying to get her to sign a deal with his company now. It's called *tortious interference,* and it means that you cannot interfere with another firm's contract as long as it's legit and notarized. Tortious interference is one of the rare legal road blocks that everyone in the industry respects. Once a deal is signed, if there is no rescission period, it's done. To the victor go the spoils.

I had yet to price Tommy's deal, but at this point, I was sure it had major potential. For a deal like this, we would go into attack mode. How do you do that just before midnight? The first thing you do is call Shannon. Shannon was a sales assistant. She was beautiful, loyal, and crazy about me. She was also an incredible assistant. She lived in the sticks, about an hour away from our downtown address. I called her and she answered on the first ring.

"Don't even think about it," she yawned.

"Do I even get a hello?" I purred, doing my best Barry White impression. Flirting is okay, even recommended, when you are asking someone to drive to the office at midnight so that you can make a big payday.

"*Hello. . . .* Can this wait till dawn, Ed?" she pleaded, already knowing the answer.

"I'll buy you lunch for a month," I said. I already bought her lunch most days. She was not impressed. Still, she agreed to come in and made me swear that there would be coffee on when she arrived. I promised, and then forgot. All I could think about was my whale. I wanted to get to him now, and coffee was not going to get me there any faster. Shannon needed to come in because she was the only one who knew how to actually create the documents that we used to sign the winners. The entire operation would come to a grinding halt if she quit, but somehow we still paid her only a $36,000 salary. I could make twice that on this deal. She knew it. I knew it. I still forgot her coffee.

The docs took well over an hour to complete. Making matters worse, we didn't have Tommy's social security number, which is essential for the contracts to be considered valid by a judge before granting us a court order. The court order officially consummates the sale of the lottery prize from the winner to The Firm. We could always go back and get the docs re-signed, but this creates a possible out for the winner. Any savvy competitor (they're all savvy) knows that contracts must be legally binding in order for the warm protection of tortious interference to come into play. I'd never tell a winner about the loophole but someone else could, thus making me quite a treat for Shannon to deal with so late in the evening. I was worried, so I did what came naturally at this point—I blamed Shannon. Finger pointing is fruitless, and Shannon told me in a very succinct way to go fuck myself. Touché.

I put us both out of our misery, thanked her, and headed home, now hours sober and more than okay to drive. At home, I quickly checked the baseball scores before passing out. I completely forgot that I had money on Baltimore and The Mets. Baltimore, loser. Mets, loser. Ed's bookie—winner. Always a winner, that guy. Football season can't come soon enough. Betting baseball is one small step above buying a lottery ticket. Lose, and you hate yourself for betting. Win, and all you feel is relief from dodging a bullet that you had no business messing with in the first place. I didn't know what I was doing and the Vegas wise guys had been eating my lunch all summer. Plus, there are baseball games on all day long from the end of March deep into the fall. Day games, night games, late games on the West Coast. It never ends. If you gamble too much, and you bet on baseball, it's a long, hot summer.

Having a bookie is like having a mistress with expensive taste. Sometimes, I felt like I worked for him. I'd probably paid the guy over $20,000 and I'd never even seen his face. When I owed, and I always owed, I gave my payment to a guy in my office. It was *his* bookie. If he were smart, he would just take my action himself and cut the bookie right out. These days, I was good for about a grand a week. I wished *I* were my goddamn bookie.

I got what sleep I could before it was show time in the morning. If I closed this deal, it would make up for a lot of shitty baseball bets. I'd be flush with cash for football in the fall, too.

My flight was uneventful. I was dressed in typical travel attire for a lottery deal, khakis and a forest-green golf shirt. You would *never* show up to a meeting with a lottery winner in a suit and tie. Big mistake. Lottery winners aren't real business-attire folks. They put the *blue* in blue collar. One of our biggest challenges in the lump-sum business was to make the winner feel at home with us. We were inherently intimidating. Showing up at their door looking like an attorney was not the first impression we were after. So, khakis and a golf shirt it was. Sometimes, even that is overkill. That was the case when I landed at the airport to meet Tommy.

I told Tommy to look for the guy holding a travel fishing-rod case. I walked out of the security area waving the long plastic tube like I was leading the rest of the passengers into the Olympic opening ceremony. Sure enough, Tommy was there waiting for me. From our phone conversation the night before, I wasn't worried that he wouldn't show. With his money issues, I imagined he was more concerned that I wasn't on the plane.

Tommy's shoulder-length strawberry-blond hair flapped about in his Jeep, as he opted for windows rather than air conditioning despite the fact that we were driving up I–95 in late August. It was 700 degrees outside. And it wasn't a dry heat. But what was I going to do, complain that my hair would get frizzy? Why not just wear a T-shirt that says, "*I'm a big finance pussy from out of town?*"

Make no mistake, Tommy's a bright guy. He was trying to get a read on me from the start. What did he want to know most of all before signing the deal? The interest rate? The amount of money we were making off his prize? How long it would take for him to get his money? The tax implications of doing a deal? No, no, no, and no. He wanted to see if I was smart enough to know that he needed to break bread and have a few drinks with me before even discussing the deal. He wanted to fish with me, drink with me, laugh a bit, to make sure that I was the real McCoy. He was a sure thing. I knew it and so did he. However, Tommy still wanted to be treated with respect. If I played my cards right, this deal would sign itself. If I rushed things, I'd have a fight on my hands.

The first thing Tommy did was take me to his place so I could drop off my stuff. He also said that I could change clothes if I wanted. Perhaps the sweat dripping off my face tipped him off. Tommy was hoping that I'd change into some shorts, as we were off to his local beach bar, and sitting with a schmuck in khakis and a golf shirt was akin to sitting with a cop. *Know your audience, my friends.* I'll never forget standing in his guest room asking myself if I should really put on my Tevas and a regular pit-stained T-shirt. Admittedly, I vacillated a bit. I had a deal in my briefcase worth hundreds of thousands of dollars. I walked into his living room in my beat-up sandals, my pasty legs flapping along. Tommy took one look at me and grinned.

"Let's get drunk and eat some fish," he said. He was relieved.

"You're buying," I said. "I'm about to make you rich."

That was the last time we spoke about his deal for two days. What did we do? We drank, we cooked, we talked shit, we spent time with his kids. I met his friends, we ran errands, we smoked cigarettes. It was fun. I liked him. I even liked his kids. Everything was going great. Then we went fishing together for the first time.

The First Time on the Boat

Tommy can't believe what I just did. That makes two of us.

We are drifting. Waves knock against the boat's hull. The current is pushing us back toward the coastline. We're a good five miles out. Ostensibly, we are still fishing. There's bait in the water, but the fish are no longer biting, and the mood on the boat has definitely turned. It's as if the fluorescent lights just popped on at last call, instantly killing the bar vibe. Neither of us can handle the brightness.

Tommy's at the bow. I'm tucked so far into the stern that I'm practically hanging off the back. It's hard to hide on a boat. For the first time in hours, days even, we are quiet. I'm wracking my brain for something to say. I've got nothing. It dawns on me that I don't really know this guy, and no one knows where I am. No one.

I've been fishing my entire life. Moreover, I've been talking to Tommy about fishing since the first time we spoke on the phone. I practically made myself out to have gills. So, after two days of doing little other than remind him how much I love fishing, two days of selling *me*, two days of bonding, it's time to fish.

Ninety-nine percent of the fishing I've ever done has been off the beach. Deep-sea fishing is only a distant cousin to the surf fishing I grew up doing—a detail I should have thought of before. The biggest difference is the equipment. Most deep-sea fishermen use "conventional" reels. For my entire life I've used "spinning" reels. The only thing the two have in common is the fact that both are used to catch fish. Other than that, I'm clueless. It's akin to driving a car with a manual transmission versus an automatic. And here I'd been bragging about what a good driver I was. It never occurred to me that the car I'd get to show my stuff in would be a stick shift.

Mix that with a few rare afternoon beers and, I'm wholly unprepared to *fish* on this fishing trip.

We're near Tommy's favorite area for drift fishing. Within
minutes, we stumble upon a massive school of bait fish. There are
seagulls everywhere. The surface boils as mahimahi crash through
the foaming blue water, attacking the bait fish in a powerful frenzy.
The entire scene came out of nowhere. This is the kind of thing
fishermen bullshit about, but rarely see. It's amazing . . . right until
Tommy starts yelling like we're under attack. Yes, it's intense, but he
becomes some sort of fishing madman, which makes me nervous.
They're *just fish*, for Christ's sake. Once Tommy began yelling, it
occurred to me that I was in a bit of a pickle.

I had a bit of a meltdown.

Tommy hands me a rod just as things started going nuts. There's
a bucktail lure tied on as bait. No problem; I grew up fishing buck-
tails with my dad. Tommy points to the school of bait fish, now
foaming over with attacking mahi, and says, "If you can't catch fish
here, you're just a dumb-ass." Truer words have never been spoken.

I grab the rod in my right hand, instinctively wedging the
reel between my middle and ring fingers, as I've done a thousand
times. I pin the line between my thumb and the rod, in order to
keep the spool tight. I flip the bail, eying a nice little target maybe
twenty yards into the bait school. I cock my arm back and flick
my wrists forward, just like a pro. The bucktail lands within inches
of my target. Bull's-eye. Unfortunately, the rest of the rod and the
$200 reel land about six feet behind the bait, the entire ensemble
promptly sinking to the bottom of the Atlantic Ocean. I'd thrown
everything into the water—everything.

There are no words.

The birds go silent. We are strangers again, just like that.

The look on his face . . . It wasn't anger. Not at first. The scene
was so beyond the realm of what he expected to see, what either
of us expected to see. I was as stunned as he was. He stood there

squinting, trying to figure out if I really just threw his fishing rod off the side of his boat.

The boat could not have felt more claustrophobic. I knew he wasn't going to kill me. He was broke, and I had the money he needed. The only difference now was that I owed him a new rod. Big deal. For this fee, we'd have bought him a boat.

The first time I ever told Tommy how much his lump sum was worth, we were on our way to the notary to sign the docs. That, boys and girls, is called controlling a deal. Here was a man that I'd known for less than a week, who was about to sell me millions of dollars' worth of lottery paper, and he had yet to ask me what I was paying him for it. Why? Because I'd spent the last three days building a relationship with him and he trusted that I knew what I was doing. I did. Now, if I'd tried to drag him to the notary the day I flew into town, you can be damn sure things would have been different.

Did I want to spend three days goofing off with a lottery winner in Florida? No. There are lesser gigs—this much is true. But, believe it or not, I had a life and I preferred to get back to it ASAP. Still, those three days of what seemed to be nothing but drinking and playing grab-ass were actually essential to the deal. Spending that kind of time with a winner *is* the deal. (Yet another reason why this job was best suited for single people, or those with extremely understanding spouses.) Can you call this *wining and dining* a client? Yes; lottery style, but yes.

It takes a certain breed of cat to take a job that requires this kind of travel. Tommy's deal just happened to be in South Florida. Clearly, there are worse places to go on business. Occasionally, deals take you to great cities or beautiful beaches. But it's more likely that days spent building rapport with a winner will take place in tiny little towns, where the only fish are the ones in the frozen-food aisle of the Winn-Dixie. If a deal takes you to the big city, odds are that it isn't a city you'd want to visit, at least not on *that* side of the tracks. The vast majority of winners live in locations far less appealing than a Florida beach town.

It's hard to describe how it feels to actually close a deal—when you're literally at the table getting the documents signed. It is a very powerful feeling. Now, there is a big difference between closing a deal worth $50,000 and one worth $500,000. Still, getting *any* deal signed is a high. And, like so many highs, this one is quite addictive. And the rush of signing a deal and the financial payoff that accompanies it was right up my alley.

The body releases endorphins when you do certain things that cause pleasure or fear—or both. When I saw a winner take that pen into his hands and start signing page after page of *my* contracts, when he was doing what I told him to do, when I had successfully imposed my will upon him, when I was getting what I wanted—what I came for—it was a rush. It was akin to those precious few seconds leading up to an orgasm, the exhale of a drag on a joint, driving too fast in Montana, an ace dropping on top of a king at the blackjack tables, or bluffing a major pot at a poker game. Those were my rushes. For some it might be snorting cocaine, jumping out of an airplane, fighting in a ring, or skiing down a mountain. The latter are thrills I'll never know. Skydiving, fighting, and skiing can generally be placed in one category—things Jews don't do. At least not this Jew.

Signing seems like the high-five moment. But you're not done there. Getting a winner to actually go to the notary is like taking the dog to the vet. They know what "going for a ride in the car" means, no matter how high and squeaky your voice gets. Winners get that same, "Oh no!" look in their eyes, as if it's dawning on them for the first time who you really are and what you're doing there. You can just see it in their eyes as they start to do the math. They give you the "Hey, this isn't the way to the park" look. Things can get serious pretty fast. Deals often crumble right there. Those hurt the worst, like losing a game in overtime.

Normally, the best way to actually get the winner to the notary is to be nonchalant about the whole thing. If you don't get all worked up about things, with any luck the winner will act in kind. In sales, it's called the assumptive close—as if you simply *assume* that this is what the winner wants and that heading to the notary is the next logical step. If there's any resistance from the winner you ask, "Isn't this what you want?" Doesn't he want to pay off that debt? Buy that house? Start that business? Isn't that why he called you in the first place?

If things get really wacky, there are two ways to play it: You can either soft-shoe the entire situation or you can go for the jugular and scare the crap out of him. Now, if you get bold and it works, you're good-to-go. But if you try to strong-arm the winner and he pushes back, nine times out of ten your deal is dead. There is very little left to fix if you piss all over the place and the winner doesn't take too well to it. Thus, enter at your own risk. Almost without exception, the best way to handle a deal going sideways, at least at first, is to back off and let the winner feel like he is in control again.

Sometimes, however, a winner needs to have the shit scared out of him in order to keep things together.

A few years back, James, one of my best sales reps, had to go to the airport in Boston to sign a deal. He was meeting a Texas winner who was flying in, on our nickel, for the sole purpose of signing his deal. We had him landing at noon and flying back to Dallas on a 1:45 flight. That left precious little time for the "getting to know you" stuff. You pretty much had to get him off the plane, sit him down, sign the docs, get them notarized at the Hyatt attached to the airport, and say goodbye. If the winner was lucky, he'd have time to grab a sandwich and take a bathroom break before boarding the return flight.

These airport deals were strange. It was odd closing a deal by the Cinnabon at gate C–14. There was never any time to build rapport. The winner felt rushed. We felt rushed. With so little time, there was no room for error, and no room for the dance that you'd always have to do to actually get a deal signed. And, God forbid the winner forgot a document or there was an error in our docs (something that happened about 90 percent of the time). If a typical lottery deal was making love, airport closings were a quickie. We hardly stayed around to cuddle.

James is a wolf in sheep's clothing. He looks like a big, pudgy kid, not a day over twenty-one. For a while, he led a life centered around food, drink, and gambling—most of which he financed with commissions from lottery deals. He was such a jolly disheveled mess that winners thought he was too much the outsider to have bad intentions. Winners almost pitied him as he signed them into a deal, all the while a wide, benevolent smile stretched across his second chin.

So, James sat our Texas winner down at the airport Hyatt to sign the docs before the winner had to hurry back to the gate. About halfway through the signing, the winner started questioning the terms of the deal. Suddenly, he told James that he wasn't sure he even wanted the money at all. Without blinking, James snapped the partially signed contract binder closed, grabbed the winner's return ticket (boarding pass and all), and put out his hand to thank the winner for his time. The winner—stunned—asked James why he took the plane ticket. Without a care in the world, James told him that we pay all travel expenses for people with whom we are actually *doing* deals. Since the winner had changed his mind (which James reminded him was absolutely fine), James was no longer authorized to pay for the winner's return flight. "Company policy," he said as he slid the binder and the ticket into his briefcase and stood up. James was about six steps toward to door when the winner caved.

The winner was just trying to sweeten the terms of the deal. He got cute with the wrong guy. A rookie sales rep would have lost it, calling in to the office, begging for help. Not James. Meekly, the winner asked to sign the rest of the docs. James, gilding the lily a bit, told the winner that he would have to call me to make sure that I was comfortable with the risk in that the winner was not entirely on board. Tex said that it would not be necessary. He was, assuredly, there for the money. James sat down and finished the deal.

For years, I'd tell that story to every training class that came through our door. I'd watch their reaction as I told them. You could tell who got it and who was thinking that they may have made the wrong career choice. I did my level best to get rid of the ones who didn't see the beauty in it. They wouldn't last anyway, so it was better not to waste time and money training the saints that slipped through our interview process. Those who stayed knew full well what they were getting themselves into.

Two Weeks Later . . .

Once I flew back from Florida, all hell broke loose on Tommy's deal. Ben decided to sit on the file rather than fund it right away. Why? I'm sure he would tell the story differently, but it can be summed up in one word: greed. Ben wanted to wait and see if we could sign Tommy's friend to an identical deal, thus doubling our fee, as she'd split the initial prize down the middle with Tommy. When they won, the winning ticket was actually worth $14 million. Splitting the money avoids dealing with a lot of legal and psychological issues that typically act as a relationship trip wire for new winners. In states that allow it, multiple winners have the prize legally split into two. One winner has absolutely nothing to do with the other.

The country is littered with court cases involving married couples, friends, co-workers, and family members who thought splitting the lottery prize up front was unnecessary. Much like those of a prenuptial agreement, the issues surrounding how a prize is claimed are riddled with emotion. Going in, when "life-changing" money has just fallen into their laps, when fresh winners see nothing but good times ahead, when they believe that they can finally stop worrying about money, winners make foolish decisions regarding how to claim their prize. They may seem insignificant at the time, but these decisions have a massive impact on their lottery experience and what happens when things go bad.

Sometimes, new winners—or their friends, family, even co-workers—have ulterior motives from the start. New winning lottery tickets are a lightning rod for incredible, downright stunning lawsuits. If nothing else, news of a winning ticket has a way of bringing people's worst qualities, their worst behavior, their most true selves to the surface. Some of the stories are heartbreaking. Some are astonishing. Some just make you thank the stars above that, to date, you've never been "lucky enough" to win.

Connie Parker, then seventy-four, of Melville, Long Island, was hit with cupid's lottery arrow when she won a $25 million jackpot on Valentine's Day 2003. Ironically, at the time she purchased the winning ticket, she'd been out looking for a Valentine's Day card for her husband, Kenneth, who was three years her senior. They'd been married for sixteen years. Sixteen years of marriage, a couple in their mid-seventies, a lottery lump-sum payment worth nearly $7.4 million after taxes. One would think they'd be over the moon and ready to bask in the glow of a well-funded journey through the golden years.

Think again.

Three months after Connie won, good old Kenneth went ahead and filed for divorce . . . yes, divorce, at the ripe old age of seventy-seven. (Perhaps he wanted to see other old people?) Of course, Kenneth wanted half the lottery prize, as he claimed that Connie had used *his* $20 bill to purchase the ticket. Adding to the drama, Kenneth was pushed into the courtroom in a wheelchair, oxygen tank in tow. In order to put the ugly divorce behind her, Connie agreed to a $1.8 million settlement.

Then there's Juan Rodriguez of Queens, New York. A Colombian immigrant then forty-nine years old, Juan had never been much of a saver. A midtown Manhattan parking attendant making $28,000 a year, he was so deep in debt that he'd filed for bankruptcy just a month prior to winning a $149 million Mega Millions jackpot. Records show that at the time he won, Juan owed various collectors nearly $44,000. Bankruptcy documents stated that he had only $.78 in his bank account when he bought the winning ticket during a break from working a double shift at the parking lot.

Juan chose to receive his winnings in a one-time lump-sum payment of $88.5 million before taxes. Just before he won the lottery, Juan and his wife of seventeen years, Iris, reconciled after she'd thrown him out of their home, largely because of his financial woes. Newly reunited, Juan and Iris appeared together at the lottery press conference. But only ten days after claiming the prize, Iris filed for divorce, seeking half the lump sum. She was awarded a significant portion of his prize. *Ain't love grand?*

Ben is inherently more risk tolerant than most, definitely more than I'll ever be—outside of a casino. In a casino it's a different story altogether. But in the lottery game, I leaned more toward the bird-in-hand side of the field. Ben had guts no one else even thought of having. In many ways, that's what made him great at his job. And while people could criticize his methods, no one could say a thing about his results. He was right a lot more than he was wrong. Truth be told, I can't think of another time that he made the wrong call on a lottery deal. Just *this* one, which cost me thousands of dollars.

At the end of the day, Ben was willing to bet that the rapport and goodwill that I'd developed with Tommy would translate into another deal with the friend. I wasn't, but my vote didn't count. It was a rabidly aggressive move, though not necessarily incorrect. The problem was, it was the wrong move at the wrong time. For years I held it against him. Ben had played God with *my* money, and I'd had no say in the matter. Still, having been a manager who spent nearly six years making calls just like that with other sales reps' commissions on the line, I now see the situation differently.

From a funding standpoint, we would have made a lot more money had we been able to bring our investor both sides of the prize. The investor wants bigger payment streams. Tommy didn't want to wait for his money, and we couldn't very well tell him why we were stalling without looking like assholes. So, I had to dance and stall and dodge calls and take a lot of shit from Tommy. He felt betrayed by me. I felt betrayed by Ben. Ben thought we were both a couple of babies.

The laughs on the boat were a world away. The beers, the fishing, the trust, the bonding . . . gone. What remained was a lottery winner who felt like he'd been abandoned by a lump-sum company he was foolish enough to trust.

Within a few weeks, I got word that Tommy had signed with one of our competitors in Florida. They promised to pay his legal costs to get him out of his contract with The Firm. Plus, they gave him more money than we had agreed to pay on our deal. He jumped at the chance. He had nothing to worry about. We were never going to take him to court. A handful of months later, Tommy got his lump sum, and somewhere in the swamps of Florida, there's a sales rep with my commission in his bank account.

... 2 ...
LOTTERY FOR DUMMIES

TO FULLY APPRECIATE HOW powerful and entrenched lotteries in America have become, we must first examine their origins. I *worked* in the lottery industry for the better part of a decade. Still, I was wholly unaware of the lottery's genesis, its place in the development of our culture, and in fact, the development of our nation itself.

Setting out to write this book, I was only vaguely inclined to research the lineage and proliferation of lotteries across the nation. It felt like ordering a side salad along with a Big Mac and chocolate shake at McDonald's. The salad isn't the most exciting item on the tray, but you eat it because it's good for you. It helps digest the rest of the meal and you won't feel like such a fat-ass digging into a sandwich so popular that it has its own theme song. However, the research I was dreading and its relevance to the basic premise of this book hit me with a thunderclap. The origins of lotteries—and, on a broader level, gambling in our society—is more relevant than I had imagined. Lotteries and gambling have been part of our culture since before our nation was born. In fact, the history of civilization, not to mention the history of the United States, is tethered to gambling. Our nation, like so many others, was built on the shoulders of lotteries.

Lotteries in one form or another dotted the globe as far back as written historical documents. The Bible itself refers to the use of lotteries in ancient times. In Chapter 26 of *The Book of Numbers*, Moses used a lottery to decide which of his flock would win a plot of land by the River Jordan. (Personally, I see the Jews as more of a bingo crowd.) The last century B.C. saw Julius Caesar incorporating lotteries into the daily lives of Rome's citizens, raising money for both the war effort and construction at home. During the same century, halfway around the world, China's Hun Dynasty financed the construction of the Great Wall through lotteries. More than a millennium passed before lotteries were publicly introduced to the Western world. Although undocumented, smaller "numbers games" are believed to have existed since biblical times.

Throughout their history, lotteries were understood to be voluntary, thus less oppressive than taxes mandated by the government. Ironically, today's lotteries are viewed largely through the same skewed lens. The middle of the fifteenth century saw a wave of lotteries spread across Europe. According to the National Gambling Impact Study Commission, "The first recorded lottery to distribute prize money was held in 1466 in Bruges, in what is now Belgium, for the announced purpose of providing assistance to the poor."[1] Concurrently, other countries at the forefront of Western culture (England, France, and Italy) began incorporating lotteries into their governments' fund-raising methods. Taxes were about as popular with citizens then as they are today. Any enterprise that could successfully raise capital without uttering the word "taxes" was received with open arms. Lotteries quickly gained popularity as a way to finance national projects and expansion into new territories without imposing new taxes.

Lotteries came to the New World along with the funny hats, bad beards, and bland food brought by the first wave of European settlers. Without lotteries, our nation's early development, our benchmark moments, would be entirely different, and we would not be the same country today. Understanding that many colony members fled England largely to escape exorbitant taxes levied on them by their governments, leaders of the colonies didn't have the courage to raise taxes so soon after their arrival. Alternatively, the colonies implemented various forms of lotteries in order to raise the necessary capital to develop things like 7–11s, Krispy Kremes, and Starbucks. They were instrumental in financing and capitalizing infrastructure in all of the original colonies. In 1612, the first colonial-era lottery raised nearly 30,000 pounds for the Virginia Company's Jamestown Settlement. The same period saw lottery proceeds throughout the colonies used to build everything from churches to roads. Eventually, even buildings at Harvard and Yale would be financed by lotteries.

Simply put, our forefathers were gamblers. If not shakers of the dice themselves, they were most certainly willing to provide the forum by which others could gamble. The big names—Washington, Hancock, Jefferson, Franklin—were each heavily involved in the implementation or promotion of lotteries. In 1768, George Washington unsuccessfully attempted to use lottery funds to connect either side of the Blue Ridge Mountains. John Hancock operated a lottery to rebuild Faneuil Hall in Boston. According to the National Gambling Impact Study Commission, "Benjamin Franklin sponsored an unsuccessful lottery to raise funds for cannons to defend Philadelphia against the British. In the year of his death, 1826, Thomas Jefferson obtained permission from the Virginia legislature to hold a private lottery to alleviate his crushing debts. Held by his heirs after his death, it was unsuccessful."

Though an essential part of our financial and social history, lotteries and gambling remain the black sheep of our cultural heritage. They are the wealthy but unkempt cousin in our nation's family photo, whom the rest of us pretend not to see. In fact, lotteries, whatever your position on them, are as American as Thanksgiving and baseball.

Lotteries and other games of chance go hand-in-hand with the idealized portrayal of the American frontier, the Wild West, imperialism, growth, expansion, conquest, and advancement. Still, the United States was not built by the gambling set alone. On the one hand you had puritanical, God-fearing moralists who fled their homeland to worship as they saw fit, without fear of persecution; on the other, gun-slinging, for-profit, land-grabbing, build-it-bigger, buy-it, borrow-it, take it folks. (Today, we call them Republicans.) Each side played a fundamental role in developing our national image, both here and abroad. After all, we are a mutt of a nation, a mixed breed, part Puritan lap dog, part frontiersman pit bull. And, like any parents, save perhaps in Appalachia, our intertwined heritage makes us our interesting, unique selves.

The first century following the Revolutionary War saw the proliferation of gambling across our growing nation. Card and dice games, most notably poker and craps, made their way through our land, gaining particular popularity in southern states and the western frontier. The images of a sordid lot hunched over a card table in a saloon or on a riverboat are as iconic as anything Norman Rockwell ever painted. Gamblers, while reviled in certain circles, were also part of our developing American vernacular, the newly formed lexicon used to conjure our collective identity. Having a "little gamble in you" was all but a prerequisite to the manifest destiny that willed people to seek their fortunes in America, and ultimately, to push our nation's borders as far west as possible.

For better or worse, gambling was a mainstay of American society right through the Civil War. Only after the North and South fought the bloodiest war in our history did the government turn its attention toward gambling:

"Most gambling, and all lotteries, were outlawed by ... several states beginning in the 1870's, following massive scandals in the Louisiana lottery—a state lottery that operated nationally—that included extensive bribery of state and federal officials. The federal government outlawed use of the mail for lotteries in 1890, and in 1895 invoked the Commerce Clause to forbid shipments of lottery tickets or

advertisements across state lines, effectively ending all lotteries in the U.S."[2]

It was almost another century before New Hampshire opened
the first modern-day lottery in 1964. Does that mean there were
no lotteries or games of chance in the United States for the entire
period? Hardly. Like Prohibition's effect on alcohol sales, gambling
never stopped; it just moved behind closed doors. For the vices so
many enjoy, it takes a lot more than Uncle Sam signing a piece of
paper to stop a person from having a shot of rye or a roll of the
dice. The private sector was more than willing to fill the void left
by the government's ban on lotteries and gambling. However, New
Hampshire's 1964 reentry into the lottery world brought gambling,
and lotteries in particular, back into the government's hands.

Once other states saw an angle to infuse revenue into their own
pockets, the dominoes began to fall. New York's lottery was introduced in 1970. Within the next five years, another ten states legislated
lotteries. The growth has yet to subside. Today, there are thirty-nine
state lotteries, plus a high-impact group of multi-state lotteries (Powerball, Megamillions) whose jackpots can shoot into the hundreds of
millions of dollars. Of the thirty-nine states that have a lottery, twenty-
five are assignable (allowing for the assignment of lottery annuities to
third parties) and fourteen are non-assignable (no legislative language
allowing for the assignment of lottery annuities).

For necessary political cover, every state that contemplated
introducing a new lottery held a public voter referendum in addition to a traditional legislative vote. No politician would implement something as divisive as state-sponsored gambling without
being able to hold a mirror up to the citizens if they ever cried
foul. Not surprisingly, the public in each state, save North Dakota,
voted for the implementation of a lottery. Of course there were
portions of the population that opposed it. Still, on election day,
voters were decidedly in favor of a lottery.

Each of the thirty-nine states that now have a lottery used the same basic strategy to convince voters to approve. The idea that closed the deal was always the same—*painless revenue.* A Princeton study states, "A key element in winning and retaining public approval is the degree to which the proceeds of the lottery are seen as benefiting a specific public good, such as education."[3] Obviously, voters want their states to spend more money on things like education, security, roads, and infrastructure. Of course, they aren't thrilled by the idea of paying more taxes to capitalize these projects. Predictably, citizens lined up to vote "yes" on a ballot that had been marketed to them as something for nothing, an alternative to taxes. (More money for schools without the guarantee of a tax bite? Where do we sign? How many of us can fit in the voter booth at once? Can we carpool?)

Perception is reality when it comes to voting for lottery legislation. Logic dictates that the idea of "painless lottery revenue" would be a hotter seller in states that are in a cash crunch at voting time versus states that are flush. If residents hear rumblings about cuts in publicly funded programs, *lottery revenue* has a nice alternative ring to it. Still, the likelihood of lottery legislation passing in a state is not necessarily determined by the state's financial position at that time. In this sense, it appears that the public's approval of lotteries rests more on the *idea* of lotteries reducing the potential tax burden on the general public than it is on any specific instance of relief.[4]

No state has ever abolished its modern lottery once it arrived. Do citizens play enough to keep the lotteries going? Umm . . . yes. In states that have lotteries, 60 percent of adults report that they play at least once a year.[5] However, it's not the players alone that keep the lotteries thriving year after year. It's also the special interests and their lobbyists:

"In addition to the general public, lotteries also develop extensive specific constituencies, including convenience store operators (the usual vendors for lotteries); lottery suppliers (heavy contributions by suppliers to state political campaigns are regularly reported); teachers (in those states in which revenues are earmarked for education); state legislators (who quickly become accustomed to the extra revenue), etc."[6]

Many who oppose state lotteries do so largely on moral grounds. They believe that states have no business in the "vice trade" in the first place. They see states providing residents with a forum to gamble in the same manner as the governor selling weed out of her mansion. Even if you favor lotteries, it's hard not to find the entire enterprise just a bit creepy, or, if nothing else, unfortunate. "Whatever the impact on revenue and illegal gambling may be," Bernie Horn of the National Coalition Against Legalized Gambling wrote, "the benefits of the lottery are more than offset by its expanding the number of people who are drawn into gambling. Worse, lotteries are alleged to promote addictive gambling behavior, are characterized as a major regressive tax on lower-income groups, and are said to lead to other abuses. Even more troubling, however, is the general criticism that the state faces an inherent conflict in its desire to increase revenues and its duty to protect the public welfare."[7]

Unbeknownst to the majority of the public, the proliferation of state lotteries has had another bizarre consequence. Over the past fifteen years, a cottage industry worth hundreds of millions of dollars has developed around lotteries and lottery winners.

The lottery lump-sum finance industry began back in the late eighties, when a practicing attorney saw an incredible business opportunity. He had a client who'd won a jackpot in an eastern state. As winners are wont to do, this one found himself broke. The lawyer assumed that the winner could sell off the annuity on the secondary market for cash, albeit for less than face value. He was wrong.

At the time, most state lotteries had a provision prohibiting the assignment of a lottery annuity. If their statutes did not overtly prohibit the transfer of an annuity, it was because they never contemplated a sale in the first place. The lotteries weren't expecting someone to show up at their door waving a contract, demanding their cooperation.

The lawyer had little trouble finding an investor interested in purchasing a safe, secure, government-backed fixed asset. The annuity was guaranteed by the full faith and credit of the lottery state itself. Odds were quite good, all but absolute, that the asset itself would not default. After all, what would happen to the public's faith in the lotteries if a state defaulted on an annual payment? The lotteries rely upon the public's trust that, on the off-chance that they win, they won't have to chase their windfall around the state. Any state would let a lot of other bills pile up, or go unpaid, before they'd dream of defaulting on a lottery payment. The public relations impact on the lotteries would be catastrophic.

The first person to finance a lottery deal was a private businessman. The terms that the parties agreed upon is unknown. Still, it's safe to assume that they didn't go to the trouble of fighting for the state's cooperation without a tidy sum hanging in the balance. The lottery kicked and screamed. They dragged the issue to court. They did whatever they could to dissuade the winner from pursuing the transaction. But, in the end, the lottery played ball. The winner was able to sell his annuity. The lawyer, ever the showman, went so far as to have a jumbo check made for a photo op. To this day, that photo sits prominently on his office wall, just as it should. In the picture, the winner looks relieved. The lawyer looks like the Cheshire Cat. I didn't smile that much at my wedding.

That lawyer was Ethan, founder of The Firm. Ethan, a good lawyer but a brilliant businessman, knew his client couldn't be the only winner in the state, not to mention nationwide, who found himself in need of cash. He figured that if he could do it once, he could replicate the transaction again and again. Thus, The Firm and an industry were born.

Ethan struggled like any new entrepreneur. Later, he would fondly recall The Firm's first few years and how he'd battled to close deals. I ate it up. Ethan *really* did something special. He'd created an industry all by himself. We're not just talking about a few successful restaurants, either. The guy was a pioneer. A lot of the people who turn up their noses at the inelegance of the industry would jump at the chance to have accomplished what he did. I sure would.

Early on, Ethan, a salesman trapped in a lawyer's body, would drive around knocking on winners' doors. Cold-calling is a tough gig on a good day, but imagine knocking, uninvited, on a lottery winner's door, in the middle of *nowhere*, and pitching him to sell his annuity. The activity can be hazardous to your health. On the few occasions where I did a cold-door knock, when I was really freaked out by the house or the neighborhood or the guys on the stoop looking at me like I was dinner, I'd ring the bell and instantly step to the side the way they do on *Cops*, just in case the winner decided to answer the door by blowing a hole through it with a shotgun. Where do you put that gem on your résumé?

Today, the industry makes millions of dollars a year, yet it's largely unregulated by the government. Virtually any other financial services industry (mortgages, trading, banking) adheres to strict federal regulations. Sure, a mortgage guy can twist the knife a bit and get a less savvy customer to agree to a higher rate or a bunch of add-on fees. Banks can dig you with this fee and that charge. Every business has its angles—regulated or not. Being regulated does not mean that companies can't make a lot of money in their field. What it does mean is that there are certain levels, or depths, to which a regulated industry can take a transaction. A subprime mortgage company could have the world's biggest knucklehead willing to take a home loan at 31 percent interest. The mortgage officer might even be creative enough to make the customer believe himself lucky to be getting such a competitive rate. But, in the end, Uncle Sam has determined what rates are fair and which are downright usurious in that industry. Whatever the size of the fish on the hook, sometimes, for the sake of fair play, the government makes businesses cut the line. Not so in the lottery lump-sum industry.

Typically, in a broker-model business (buying the deal for x and immediately selling it to an investor for y), we know going in what the resale rate (the discount rate for which the investor is willing to buy the annuity) will be. The only real variable is the price for which a winner will sell his prize. The investor rate is basically predetermined. Therefore, the fee that The Firm gets on a deal is predicated on the amount of the lump sum the winner receives. The investor's profit is more or less set. So, regardless of the size of the fee to the broker, the investor is still due to get the same dollar amount—over time.

It should come as no surprise that some state lotteries do not love the lump-sum industry. The industry is seen as a thorn in the lotteries' side, forcing them to deal with our paperwork, inquiries, and legal issues. Moreover, from time to time, winners are known to complain to the lotteries about the industry's sales and marketing tactics. The lotteries are stuck between an obligation to work with lump-sum companies and protecting their winners from some of the industry's worst, most aggressive practices. Remember, too, that lottery workers are government employees making civil-servant salaries. Not only are they surrounded by strange, demanding lottery "millionaires" but they are accosted by adroit lawyers and fast-talking salesmen from the lump-sum industry, some of whom make more money in a month then the lottery's office staff does in a year.

In *assignable* lottery states (those that allow winners to sell their annuities), the industry is more nails-on-a-chalkboard than boot-in-the-groin. Winners are permitted to assign their prizes and, like it or not, they do—in droves. There are everyday closing issues such as tax liens, child support, divorces, or bankruptcies, but at the end of the day, the assignable lotteries work in partnership with the lump-sum industry, generally getting along with us, whatever they may say behind our backs.

In *non-assignable* states (those that *specifically do not* allow winners to sell their annuity), the lump-sum industry's relationship with the lotteries is far more complex. Just because a non-assignable state prohibits its winners from selling their annuities doesn't mean that their winners are any less likely to need money. And then what? Should the winners simply stay broke? Should the lump-sum industry pass up the opportunity to do business with a winner who needs its services? Is it fair that Florida winners can sell their prizes but a winner five miles over the state line in Georgia cannot?

Today's lottery system has next to nothing in common with its early cousins. Lotteries have always invoked passionate "what if" daydreams among its players. Still, technology has taken lotteries from quaint raffles to big-business, big-dreaming, life-changing, unfathomable jackpots. Beyond the size of the prizes, the history of lotteries is a cautionary tale. No one, be it Ben Franklin, Julius Caesar, or the people lined up to buy tickets for the first modern-day lottery in New Hampshire, could have foreseen the innovative games, the mind-boggling jackpots, and the "daydream for a dollar" that lotteries provide. And yet there is a darker, sadder truth tucked underneath. Like bamboo, lottery growth has spread far beyond where we had originally intended. Today, no matter how hard we fight to trim it back, its roots are too deep. We cannot control the state lotteries. Doing so would take local and state politicians who were willing to commit career suicide. And even if we found such leaders, they would be powerless to uproot the gambling culture that flourishes today.

...3...
EVERYTHING YOU'LL WISH YOU NEVER KNEW ABOUT WINNING THE LOTTERY

"I wouldn't wish winning the lottery on Hitler."
— FLORIDA LOTTERY WINNER

Misery Loves Company

Sometimes—often, in my experience—fantasy far exceeds reality. What if you really *did* win the lottery? Okay, day one—week one, even—would be a whole lot of fun. Personally, I think I'd take a bath in warm butter. But, what then? If you think that life would somehow get back to normal, that you'd still be you, just a lot more relaxed, think again. Sure, some lottery winners go off the deep end right away and cause themselves a lifetime of hurt as a result. But the vast majority of winners want nothing more than to have their old life back. More than anything else, they want their anonymity—something they never bothered to covet—returned at once. Along with that, they want to lose the feeling that everyone expects something from them, that they are somehow responsible for the happiness and financial lives of so many friends and family members. While millions dream of winning big, few ever contemplate the notion that lottery winners are akin to animals in a zoo or freaks at the circus. Do some winners put that spotlight upon themselves? Absolutely. But it's far more likely that new winners have a lot of help, from unexpected places.

Lottery winners deserve better treatment from a lot of people.

Better from the lump-sum industry? Sure. But the lump-sum industry is a legitimate business, after all. It never claimed to be the Red Cross. The lump-sum industry has the same right to exist as the hundreds of credit-card companies or thousands of fast-food outposts that thrive today. It has no more responsibility to protect lottery winners than credit-card companies do the hundreds of millions of Americans who carry credit cards, or the fast-food industry does for the millions of Americans who eat their meals out of a box each and every day.

Does the fast-food industry have a hand (or a leg, or a breast) in our nation's obesity epidemic? Of course. But they still have every right to exist. Businesses are not in charge of looking after their customers' well-being. This may not sound good, but it's true. Just ask the tobacco industry. Say what you will about some of the business practices of any of these industries; you'd be hard pressed to find an argument from me. Whatever the public may think, however right they may be, none of these industries works outside the parameters set by state and federal law. Each industry may give you the willies, but they are all legal.

What *should* make us uncomfortable is the intensity with which these industries go about generating new customers. Each acts as an enabler, tapping into the need, weakness, naïveté, and lack of other options of their target market. And each uses masterful marketing strategies to seize upon those very vulnerabilities, locking in revenues for state coffers or shareholder dividends, all while generally making the lives of their customers worse than they would be without them.

If sales is all about finding a customer's need, then what better product to sell than something that a portion of the population believes they must have rather than simply want? When we *want* something, we may or may not actually go out and buy it. When we *need* something, we grab our keys and head for the car. Nothing can stop us. We are our own worst enemy.

Each industry shares an unquenchable thirst for new clients. The fast-food industry not only wants you to keep lining up at their feed troughs, they also want your kids, ASAP. The sooner your little Timmy associates the golden arches with fun, french fries, and games, the better it is for the long-term health of the industry. The credit-card industry constantly advertises easy access to credit or cash, regardless of whether accessing that money is in the consumer's best interest.

If more consumers qualified for credit at prime plus *something reasonable,* the credit-card industry as we know it would cease to exist. And if lottery winners could sell their annuities directly to a bank, if their annuities were considered liquid instead of illiquid assets, if the federal government regulated the lump-sum industry, protecting winners from having to match wits with the sales and negotiating experts that live in the lump-sum world, the industry itself would be wholly different. While no one is holding a gun to their head, winners in need of capital are, in fact, often forced to sell their annuity payments to the secondary market because the industry is the only option they have. Today, most *new* winners have the option to receive their prize in a lump sum directly from the state lotteries at the time of their win. However, once they elect to collect their winnings over time, the only place they can go to change their minds is the secondary market: the lump-sum industry. Imagine a fresh winner, one who can barely fathom what just happened to him, one who was pushing a broom at the mall a day ago and is most likely in shock at the reality of winning millions of dollars. Within a month this neophyte has to decide how he'd like his millions delivered to him. Will it be over time, or in a lump sum? The decision has massive legal, tax, investment, and social ramifications. Still, winners are asked to make the call with little guidance or counsel from the lotteries. Anyone else they approach for advice—friends, family, attorneys, accountants, financial planners—has an agenda. After all, if *you* are not lucky enough to win the lottery yourself, who better than someone you love, like, or with whom you have an hourly billing arrangement?

A Wolf in State's Clothing

The ones who *really* harm winners are the state lotteries themselves. Lotteries market players into believing a myth. Then, when the player defies the odds and wins, the lotteries hang their winners out to dry, leaving them exposed to the vultures and hangers-on. New winners are entirely unprepared for this, but the lotteries are well aware of what's coming at their new millionaires. They don't go out of their way to prepare new winners for what is about to happen to them, despite the fact that the state lotteries are the *one* group that actually knows what new winners can expect. There are virtually no new-winner assistance programs, no classes or seminars held by the lotteries themselves. Instead, lotteries push the myth, snap the ever-important marketing photos, and go back to what they were doing before yet another in an endless line of "millionaires" walked through the door.

In reality, the state lotteries facilitate the misery of their winners. The fact that people win *very publicly* is what the lotteries care about most. They need to make sure that everyone hears that *someone* won before next week's drawing. Lotteries need a steady flow of jackpot winners in order to remind the public that people win *all the time*. Who wins, and what happens to them after the big day, is far less consequential.

Winning the lottery is stunning and a "once in a lifetime" experience to almost everyone but the lotteries themselves. The lottery departments are, to say the least, desensitized to the miracle. They know the man behind the curtain too well to be impressed by all the special effects. They *are* the man behind the curtain. But worse than their simple indifference to what's in store for new winners is that lotteries know better than anyone else—even me—

how insane things are about to get. Nonetheless, the jackpots keep growing. Billboard, TV, radio, and newspaper ads continue telling us how good life is for a lottery winner. It doesn't take long until new winners know better.

Trust Me, I'm with the Government (and Other Failed Lottery Marketing Campaigns)

In 2002, state lotteries spent nearly $466 million on advertising.[8] The lottery marketing machine is a well-fed, relentless, and shrewd monster. State lotteries live off of their ability to generate consistent and growing revenue stimulated by new game concepts, effective marketing strategy, seamless product rollout, memorable advertising, and positive publicity. In the stunning first chapter of the 1989 book *Selling Hope: State Lotteries in America,* authors Charles T. Clotfelter and Philip J. Cook assess the line crossed by the lotteries' ever-increasing marketing and new product development:

> Viewing the lottery debate simply in terms of paternalism versus tolerance . . . misses the most prominent feature of lotteries as they currently exist. The states now offering lotteries do not simply make a product available in order to accommodate the widespread taste. Lottery agencies . . . are engaged in a well-focused quest for increased revenues. The state lottery agencies have in fact evolved into a new breed of government agency created in the mold of the modern corporation with its eyes firmly fixed on the bottom line. With businesslike efficiency these state enterprises have combined their monopoly position, their high built-in profit rates, and the techniques of modern marketing to generate new revenues for state governments. But by choosing to stimulate rather than merely accommodate

demand, they have thrust the state into an unaccustomed role, one that may be inconsistent with other functions of government. To succeed in increasing sales, lottery advertisements must either encourage existing players to buy more tickets or entice non players to begin playing, neither of which is consistent with the traditional government policy of not inducing citizens to gamble. The manner in which the lottery agencies have advertised also has come into question. Some have charged that the agencies are less than forthcoming in explaining the low probabilities of winning or the manner in which prizes are paid out. Others are troubled by the message of lottery advertising. The columnist Andy Rooney asks, "How can we teach kids that hard work is the way to success if they hear radio commercials paid for by their government suggesting that the way to get rich is to bet money on a horse or a number?"[9]

Why do the state lotteries knowingly take advantage of their own constituents? They need the revenue. It's their job to find it. Lotteries are the only state agencies run like for-profit corporations. And while states dabble in other consumables such as liquor sales, the lotteries are their largest foray into the business of selling to their citizens. According to Illinois's first lottery director, "The lottery agency itself was designed to be operated as a business. It was broken into three conventional business divisions—operations, finance, and marketing—each with its own deputy, who took on the role of a corporate vice president."[10] A *Chicago Tribune* article notes, "A new lottery director appointed in 1987 promised to 'keep up the hype' in order to keep sales going."[11] When we think of our state governments, "hype" shouldn't be the first thing that jumps off the page.

I'm not implying that the word "lottery" carries some benevolent imagery. But the word "state" should. Individual states are not responsible for the welfare of their citizens. Yet, the state should look out for their residents' best interests. I have no false conceptions that my state is doing anything in particular to enhance the quality of my life; I'm far too jaded to imagine the governor sitting around his mansion jotting down ideas for how to make *my* life happier. Still, I'm not so cynical as to imagine him listing ways to harm me, either.

If You Build It, They Will Come

Technology is a hell of a business partner for the state lotteries and other gambling venues. In the "old days," lotteries didn't have the money, the muscle, or the reach that modern lotteries do. Yes, lotteries have always advertised and always made money, regardless of the era. In *Selling Hope: State Lotteries in America*, Clotfelter and Cook write that in the early nineteenth century, "advertising by lottery offices was as vigorous as it was common. Newspapers carried daily inducements to buy tickets, with slogans like 'Now is the time to fill your bags!' Even the names of the shops, such as Kidder's Lucky Lottery and Dean's Real Fortune, were designed to appeal to the potential player."[12] But how much reach did a lottery realistically have before such things as billboards, radio, television, and the Internet? The town crier is a lot less powerful than a thirty-second TV spot during *American Idol*. As is further noted in *Selling Hope*, "Day in and day out, probably the most visible sign of the lottery agency is its advertising, about half of which appears on television."[13]

Bookies used to be the only means to place a bet on tonight's game. Now, a sports bettor can log onto one of hundreds of online sites that have, for all intents and purposes, replaced the corner bar bookies of yesteryear. Not long ago, casino gamblers had to travel to Vegas or Atlantic City in order to get their live casino fix. The physical distance alone created a safety zone for gamblers. In order to gamble in a casino, players needed to make the same kind of travel plans they would for any other vacation. One didn't go to a casino on a whim. Today, there are exponentially more Americans who have a real casino within driving distance of their home. Often, the casino is just down the street. "Powerball" and "The Big Game" multi-state lotteries have dwarfed most individual state lotteries by offering massive jackpots against which states simply cannot compete. None of these developments that drive modern gambling would be possible without recent technological advancements.

If It Looks Like a Casino and Smells Like a Casino . . .

Beyond advertising dollars, lotteries seek to increase the number of users through product innovation. More than ever before, today's lotteries are introducing new, more addictive, more interactive, more "casino-like" games. All state lotteries start out with a few modest games. But once the curiosity dies down, once the monopolistic state lotteries feel the pressure of competing with gambling alternatives, lotteries have little choice but to design new, more complex interactive games. The ongoing expansion of the industry is driven by the relentless pressure for revenue.[14]

When state lotteries began to emulate casino-style games such as video poker and keno, they lost their right to be compared to anything other than casinos. Video poker alone has single-handedly changed the face of lotteries. Robert Hunter, director of the gambling treatment program at Charter Hospital in Las Vegas, believes that "lawmakers need to factor into their analysis something that has received little attention thus far: that video gambling machines are 'the crack cocaine' of gambling because they are so addictive."[15] Several state lotteries have made the video poker machine (the most addictive form of gambling in the world) available in thousands of locations throughout their states. Gamblers, especially addicted gamblers, living in those states are being put in a dangerous situation.

Early on, lotteries flew under the radar while doing their best to keep citizens gambling *with them*. Presently, they have no such cover. As noted by the National Gambling Impact Study Commission, "Revenues typically expand dramatically after the lottery's introduction, then level off, and even begin to decline. This 'boredom' factor has led to the constant introduction of new games to maintain or increase revenues."[16] Is this any different than McDonald's periodically introducing new sandwiches? In the end, how many Big Macs can you eat before you just get tired of them? McDonald's figures that if you haven't tried their new and delicious chicken club sandwich, maybe you'll try it instead of seeing what Burger King has to offer. The business of lotteries is no different. And the trend is far from over, as "it appears that the primary instrument for converting moderate or inactive players into active players is product innovation, rather than advertising."[17] Lotteries overtly need players. Players have more gambling options than ever before. Therefore, it is only logical for the states to find alternative methods to keep their customers interested. That's just plain old good business.

Wanna Play Monopoly?

State lotteries are, in fact, big businesses, built like any other. They are highly financed, multimillion-dollar *for-profit monopolies* that prey on the vulnerabilities and addictions of their own residents. Modern lotteries camouflage their hard-core business practices by promoting the idea that lottery dollars fund major education, health, and housing initiatives. The states have made an art of hiding behind the "lottery as benevolent hobby" flag. Each year, they remind us of the millions of dollars they contribute to education and other public works projects, making any negative social issues that arise as a by-product of the lotteries minute in comparison. However, in recent years, criticism that the public's perception of inaccuracies as to where the lottery-generated money is going has increased, along with accusations that the public is being deliberately misled.[18]

While the vast majority of states earmark lottery funds for specific purposes, some states have the moxie to put lottery proceeds right into the state's general fund, allowing elected officials to determine where the money goes. (God knows state elected officials *never* have their own agenda.) Moreover, the entire concept of earmarking, created to make this type of wink-wink insider decision-making completely transparent, is not nearly as benevolent as it seems.

Oh, Please, Please Think of the Children

The lottery PR departments spend countless hours coming up with creative ways to remind their customers of the millions of lottery dollars that go directly to education and other worthy causes. They aren't lying. The money does indeed go right where it's supposed to, as promised. The lotteries probably have video of an oversized check being made out to "Little Timmy's Future" with a bunch of gushing, appreciative parents flanking the lottery director. These folks know from their PR. However, what the lottery folks don't mention is that the millions of dollars the lottery gives to education is *not* in addition to the states' budgeted amount. The total dollars given to education *does not increase* as a result of the lottery's contribution. We are just given the impression that the lottery is making a net positive difference in the community. In fact, nothing could be farther from the truth.

Imagine that a state is budgeted to spend $500 million in a given year for public education. The next year, the lottery arrives and, with all the fanfare it can muster, distributes $75 million to the state's public education fund. *(Insert applause here!)* We are led to believe that the $75 million would be over and above the $500 million already allocated in the budget. But once the lottery signs on to kick in the $75 million, the state actually *decreases* their total contribution down to $425 million. The total dollars awarded to your child's education doesn't go up at all; the only thing that changes is who's signing the check. A *Money* magazine study finds that states *without* lotteries spend a greater portion of their total budget on education than do states with lotteries.[19] Gary Landry, spokesman for the Florida Education Association in the late 1990s, said, "We've been hurt by our lottery ... The state has simply replaced general revenues with lottery money—at a time when enrollments are increasing. It's a big shell game."[20]

The perceived utility of tying lottery proceeds to popular causes such as education is so great that real abuses have occurred. For years following the introduction of Virginia's lottery in 1988, for example, lottery spokesmen and state officials publicly touted the benefits to the public schools stemming from lottery revenues. This linkage was emphasized in advertising and in public statements by state and lottery officials. But the proceeds of Virginia's lottery have always gone directly into the general fund, and were earmarked for education only in 1995. And, according to S. Vance Wilkins, Jr., then the minority leader in the Virginia House: "There's absolutely no point in earmarking except for fooling people into thinking we were doing something for education when we didn't do a thing ... It didn't change the budget one penny. It's a sham."[21]

What remains is hundreds of millions of dollars of profit to the states every year. In terms of gross revenues, lotteries rank first among the various forms of gambling. Lottery sales in 1996 totaled $42.9 billion. In 1982 gross revenues were $4 billion, representing a 950 percent increase over the preceding fifteen years. Lotteries have the highest profit rates in gambling in the United

States. In 1996, net revenues (sales minus payouts, but not including costs) totaled $16.2 billion, or almost 38 percent of sales. They are also the largest source [of] government revenue from gambling, in 1996 netting $13.8 billion, or 32 percent of money wagered, for governments at all levels.[22]

Taking Your Lumps, if You Can

Many lotteries now offer new winners the option of receiving their prize in either a discounted lump sum or the traditional long-term annuity. Today, the majority of new winners who have the lump-sum option take it. So many potential customers forever disappearing from a business is tantamount to a nuclear bomb going off. States' offering the lump-sum option themselves eliminates any need for winners to *ever* deal with the tough lump-sum industry. With the vast majority of new winners going by way of this option, the entire dynamic of the lump-sum industry has changed. One would think that the industry would simply fold. Except for one point, it could have.

Even with the majority of players lumping out with the state, the lottery lump-sum industry, while nothing like its former self, is still alive and quite well. Why? There are still thousands of "old" winners who never had the chance to take a lump sum from the state. Additionally, certain states, and certain types of lottery games, still don't offer the lump-sum option.

The majority of new winners who make their way into the lump-sum industry's databases are instant or scratch-off winners from Massachusetts and Texas. While both states offer the lump-sum option to their traditional winners, neither state offers it to scratch ticket winners. Therefore, the lump-sum business thrives in those locations. Moreover, nationally, a small percentage of new winners still elect to receive their payments over time. *These* folks keep the industry going. But, as you can imagine, the feast that was once the lottery lump-sum industry is now more akin to a continental breakfast: Everybody still eats, but no one is raving about the meal. Consider, too, the effect of losing the majority of its potential market has on competition in the industry.

Ironically, the lump-sum industry did benefit (in a small way) from the lotteries' decision to offer the lump-sum option directly to winners. By offering the option themselves, the lotteries have validated the secondary market's practice of discounting jackpots back to their present value. For the majority of my time in the industry, the hardest part of the job was explaining to winners why we were able to pay them only roughly half the face value of their prize. Invariably, winners would be convinced that the lump-sum industry simply kept the "other half" of their prize as profit from our transaction. Of course, in reality, there is no "other half" of a winner's prize. It doesn't exist.

Using formulas, factoring programs, and investor parameters, the lump-sum industry can approximate the value of future payments and discount them back to present value (today's dollars). Discounting lottery annuities is a science. Pricing the deal effectively and selling the present value of a prize to a stunned winner interested in a lump-sum transaction is pure art. The fact that states now offer the lump-sum option to new winners has devoured much of the secondary market. Ironically, it has also legitimized the methodology by which the lump-sum industry prices its offers to winners. At once, the states offering the lump sum became the industry's biggest competitor *and* its best marketing tool.

4

GO WEST, MY SON

I'M BAD AT MATH. I can barely add. I even got a "D" in algebra and had to retake it in summer school with a bunch of freshmen. *Good times.* Still, let me posit an equation that should give you a quick understanding as to why I had to leave Portland, a city I love dearly and that to this day is full of the closest friends I have. Regardless, it's best for everyone if I stay out of the state.

X = **Ex-girlfriend**

Y = **Dead-end job**

Z = **Oregon Lottery video poker machines**

Z(x + y) = **Start Packing the U-Haul**

Sometimes, all you can do is cut your losses and run. After nearly four years of pretending that I could make it living in Portland, it finally dawned on me that I needed to call it what it was, a disaster, and head back east. If it weren't for the Atlantic Ocean, I'd still be driving.

Looking back, there were three factors that contributed to my heading home. Like so many sad songs, the natural place to start is with the girl. Often, in one way or another, it's about a girl.

X = The Girl

Lisa and I ran with the same crowd in college. I spent the first three years in school avoiding her. We had only two things in common: cigarettes and our mutual disdain for one another.

I joked my way into her bed. Joking your way into sex is hard to pull off with a stranger, so I've dated a lot of girls with whom I was friends first. I'm *the funny friend*. I've picked up a girl at a bar only twice in my life, and I'm convinced that they were both paid for by my sympathetic buddies. For you to really get a good sense of me, I've got to grow on you for a while. Lisa and I were not friends. She'd known me for years and found me utterly repugnant. Yet she was still drawn to me, as to a stinky cheese.

One boozy, bar-hopping night early in our senior year we found ourselves back at her place. We could hardly stand one another, yet somehow I found myself ripping open a condom with my teeth. It had been so long for me, I was just happy that I remembered how to do it. I put the condom on and went inside this beautiful, crazy woman. On my way in, *upon insertion*, I came. It happened too fast to even be called premature. It was like being full before dinner. Here was this girl I'd known for three years, who was close to all my friends, who didn't even *like* me, and I'd just set the bar for the shortest sexual encounter in the history of Boulder, Colorado. What to do, what to do?

Sell. When in doubt, sell.

Just like every time I find myself in a bind, I started talking, hoping my lips could cover for me while my mind searched desperately for a thought that mirrored the delicacy of the situation. Without missing a beat, I looked into Lisa's soft brown eyes and said the only thing I could think of that would distract her from my little situation.

"I think this is going too fast."

She looked at me and uttered the most romantic thing anyone has ever said to me.

"Bullshit! Did you just come?"

Ah, young love! We were together for four years. We broke

up several times, but it never stuck. Once, about two years into the relationship, I built up the nerve to sit Lisa down and *really* end things once and for all. We were living back east after a short stint in Sonoma County, California. I wanted to move out to Portland and live with a few friends who had just moved there. Lisa listened to my news and thought it through for a minute. Her response was short and to the point. "No," she said. Instead, Lisa decided that she'd move to Portland, too. I had not anticipated her reaction and found myself with little in the way of a snappy convincing counterpoint. "Um, okay . . . but, well . . . okay, I see your point."

Two weeks later, we moved across the country together for the third time. It was a long drive.

Nothing changed in Portland except for the quality of the beer. You bring your baggage with you in life. I brought my baggage *and* her baggage out west. It rained for three years straight.

We arrived in Portland in late August 1995. Armed with my undergrad degree in film studies, I did not exactly have offers flying in the door. My college roommate Doug was working as a bartender at a sports bar named Claudia's. Claudia's was built in the fifties and had the era's workmanlike sense of architecture. It was nothing more than a brown brick box. It looked exactly like a bomb shelter. The bar's clientele was almost 100 percent male, all the time. The mere sight of a woman walking through the doors was enough to make tongues wag all over the establishment, even if she was just delivering the mail. Gay bars have more women in them than Claudia's ever did. Doug was able to get me a job befitting my upper-middle-class background: short-order cook. You can imagine my parents' pride at bridge night.

Y = Dead-End Job

I have always thought it should be mandatory for anyone in management, no matter the level, no matter the compensation, to do a six-month stint as a short-order cook. It offers the greatest time-management training I know. I've been cooking all my life. From the time I was eleven until I was sixteen, I took serious cooking classes from Jacques Blanc, the 1980 Chef of the World. I absolutely love cooking, and I'm good. Still, making dinner for the family, or for a handful of friends, has next to nothing to do with cooking in a restaurant. They both involve food; that's it.

You want to know chaos? You want to see how someone handles pressure? Don't put him on the floor of the New York Stock Exchange. Don't make him run a fifty-person sales meeting. Instead, give him an apron and let him handle the lunch rush at a local greasy spoon. Watch him as the first ticket starts spitting from the computer printout. Watch him as the next five come in all at once, followed by another, then another. Watch him as he prays that the bells attached to the front door don't ring again.

What makes short-order cooking such excellent training for corporate management? On any day, at any time, you have no idea what to expect, but you know that action is imminent. Restaurant cooking is guaranteed insanity. So, too, is managing people, projects, or companies. It's the promise that everyday you will make hundreds of decisions, keep track of twenty things at once, and ultimately be responsible for the results, no matter who screwed up.

The average weekday lunch is enough to show a person's true colors. One lunch at Claudia's, I watched a new cook yank off his apron and walk out the back door because he couldn't find the veggie burgers. That was it. He was overwhelmed, and the veggie burger was as good a reason as any to leave the chaos behind.

The problem with cooking lunch in a restaurant is that everybody wants to eat at basically the same time. You serve 85 percent of the lunch crowd from noon to 2:00 P.M. After that, you're hanging out doing the crossword puzzle. But up until then, the kitchen is for adults only. Imagine, in the middle of the rush, with twenty different meals in various stages of preparation, an order for six comes into the kitchen. The six folks who just ordered could care less about your problems in the kitchen. They have problems of their own, and this is *their* lunch hour. They order the following:

- One burger, no lettuce, with fries (side of ranch)
- One bacon-cheeseburger, no tomato, no onion, extra mayo, with onion rings
- One medium pepperoni pizza
- Two chicken gyros (one with no green peppers)
- One Greek salad, with chicken

You can see that my pub wasn't exactly Nobu. We're just talking about burgers, salads, and pizzas. Still, when do you start cooking the hamburger patties? How long will the pizza take to prepare? How long does it take to bake a medium pizza, anyway? Did I remember to preheat the oven? Do I bake the pizza and *then* throw the burgers on the grill? What about the chicken gyros? What *is* a chicken gyro, anyway? Does it take chicken longer to cook than a burger? How do I avoid giving this entire restaurant salmonella? What *is* salmonella? Could I have it right now? I bet I have it. I bet I'm going to die because I play with raw chicken all day long. *I've got to go to grad school.* Can I kill someone if I undercook the chicken? Am I insured if I kill someone while cooking at a bar in Oregon? Am I insured at all? Oh God, what about the buns? Did I remember to butter the buns? There's not enough room on the griddle for the goddamn buns! What am I supposed to do with the buns? Oh SHIT! The salad. Who the hell comes to a sports bar to order a salad anyway?! There's *no way* I can make a salad right now . . . no WAY. There's no Greek dressing . . . what am I supposed to do now? I'm *not* making Greek dressing right now. I can't. I have forty things to do! I don't even know *how* to make Greek dressing. If they think that I'm going to sit back here burning the hell out of myself for $8.65 an hour, worrying about the fact that there is no

Greek dressing, they are insane. I hope they all get food poisoning. Can't they see I'm in the weeds?

Suffice it to say, it gets a little stressful in the kitchen. Yes, we're only talking about cooking bar food. Still, I'd rather have a guy running my company who lived through these moments on a daily basis than someone who read all about it in business school. Not to mention, I like the idea of hiring salespeople who *had* to work in bars, kitchens, or the mall, or mowing lawns, while growing up. I'm not interested in the ones who lived off of their parents' name or money. No, that does not mean I'd hire the fry cook from Wendy's over the next big thing out of Wharton. And, yes, I *was* rejected from Wharton, for all the conspiracy theorists out there. I will tell you, however, that I'd hope the Wharton grad paid her way through school slinging hash somewhere. I'd like her more that way.

I'm deeply insecure about not having gotten my MBA, or some other graduate degree. There is not a lot one can say about my lack of a master's degree that I haven't already thought about myself, or heard from my mother. My colleagues at The Firm, all lawyers—mostly Jewish like me—used to say that I was the only Jew they knew without an advanced degree. I would always respond by threatening to throw my wallet at them. Yet, privately it *killed* me. I did get accepted into the Georgetown MBA program, but at the last minute, I chose not to go in order to join an Internet start-up three minutes before the tech bubble burst. I spent my entire savings, at the time $250,000, to verify that four guys who knew next to nothing about either the health-care industry or the Internet should, in fact, *not* start an Internet-based health-care firm. *(I am available for business consulting gigs.)*

The pay for cooking at a pub is crap. Financially, the best thing about the job is that you eat for free. Plus, at the end of your shift, you get two free pints of beer. Of course, once you get to know all the bartenders, the two-pint limit goes out the window.

Then, work becomes one long Oktoberfest. My problem, however, wasn't drinking too much of the house ale during or after my shift. It was the five Oregon Lottery video poker machines flanking the back wall.

After a few months of doing nothing but cooking, the owner, Marty, started to give me bartending shifts, too. Clearly, bartending has a certain cachet that short-order cooking does not. Still, this bartending gig wasn't exactly akin to Tom Cruise in *Cocktail*. This was nothing but popping bottles of Bud and pouring pitchers of Olympia to the local blue-collar drunks and sports bettors who flocked to Claudia's on a daily basis. I'd also clean ashtrays, a job I found particularly disgusting and demoralizing. Bartending was better than cooking in the back, but it could hardly be considered a promotion.

In many ways, I was a good bartender. I think the owner was just happy to have an educated guy who he figured wouldn't take cash out of the till and would show up on time. I was good at building rapport with the customers. I'd schmooze the patrons, dish rag over my shoulder, clever line on the tip of my tongue. They would show their appreciation by leaving me incredibly small, borderline-insulting tips, if they left anything at all. Blue-collar, sports-betting drunks are the wrong demographic to rely upon for income, unless they've just won the lottery. . .

In other ways, my white-collar, private-school upbringing betrayed my "regular Joe" act, exposing the fact that I had no business behind the bar. For example, to this day I still can't tap a keg of beer. As a bartender, in a beer-and-wine-*only* pub, not having the ability to tap a keg is like being a veterinarian afraid of dogs. It is an obstacle toward long-term job growth. I believe that tapping a beer keg is terrifying for any Jew. We were not made to tend bar. Plus, beer makes us feel bloated and it doesn't go well with brisket. We are more of a wine-drinking people.

Throughout my life, every time I've tried to tap a keg, beer foam has sprayed everywhere, uncontrollably, until a real man came and rescued me. I did try to do it a few times at the bar (being a *bartender* and all that), but it was an absolute disaster. The kegs were housed under the bar, in a refrigerated storage unit. Once, I pulled a dry Budweiser keg out, disengaged the tap, and rolled a full replacement keg into the cooler. Then, I just went for it—figuring that doing it quickly was my best shot, like ripping off a Band-Aid. Bad call. Foam started shooting out of the keg, except now it was filling up the expensive refrigerated cooler with sticky beer. As I was the only bartender working at the time, there was no chance I'd be saved by Superman, or any man for that matter. Instead, I just helplessly let the keg run out of pressure, like a first-grader pissing down his leg at recess. I made a mess and all I could do was stand there.

I pulled the now useless keg out of the cooler and rolled it back into the larger storage unit where we kept the dozens of kegs the bar went through every week. From that day forward, when one of the fifteen different beers the bar had on tap needed replacing—a daily occurrence—I'd simply say we were out of that brand and leave the empty keg for the poor guy taking the next shift behind the bar. Some kegs—the porters, hefeweizens, or the grand old man, Guinness—took a long time, weeks even, to run dry. There were other beers—Budweiser, Miller Lite, the local Olympia—of which the bar went through a keg on an almost daily basis. So, for me to tell a regular, who had been coming to this bar since before I was in high school, that we were out of Budweiser was often met with a raised eyebrow or, at times, the call of "bullshit."

Z = Oregon Lottery Video Poker Machines

There are no casinos in the city of Portland. There is, however, something far worse: video poker. The Oregon Lottery runs the poker machines, meaning that the cash goes right to the lottery, the same as when you buy a lotto or scratch ticket. The lottery's video poker machines are everywhere. Virtually every restaurant, bar, or pub has them. The rule is a maximum of five machines per establishment and, would you believe it, every place has ... five machines. Basically, the government has turned the entire state into a small chain of loud, creepy casino-bars. At least you have to go to a market or a gas station to actually purchase traditional lottery tickets. With the poker machines, you can't get away; they find you. Wherever you go, there they are, like a bad ex. There is no need to interact with a dealer or other players; no one judges your play or how much you've won or lost. Video poker is easy to learn, gives you your privacy, and is just as welcoming to women as to men. In short, it's lethal. Moreover, video poker is known to be the most addictive form of gambling out there, casino or not. In 1996, when I was neck deep in the Oregon Lottery's video poker obsession, revenues from video poker and keno grew a stunning 41.8 percent nationwide in that year alone![23] I'd like to think that I contributed only a few percent of that number on my own. Still, misery loves company. I'm glad it wasn't just me.

Consequently, being a bartender in Oregon also meant that you were a mini-casino cashier. All video poker tickets were brought to the bar, scanned into a computer terminal, and paid out in cash by the bartender. There was a special lottery cash register with which we'd pay out winning tickets. Depending on the day, there could be anywhere from two to five thousand dollars in cash sitting in that drawer. So I'd spend my day watching patrons shove $20 bills into the poker machines, living vicariously through their wins and losses. If they lost, I'd think, 'Better them than me.' If they won, I'd steam with jealously and pay them *my cash*. I kept an eye on those machines at Claudia's all day long. And they watched me right back.

It was quite a paradox, being a hard-core video poker player myself and acting as a lottery cashier during bar shifts. I saw firsthand the addiction that those machines created. I saw the same sad people, day after day, month after month, shoving their futures into the waiting insatiable mouth of the Oregon Lottery. I was being paid to sit behind that bar and watch their losses pile up, watch their false sense of hope when they cashed a winning ticket, only to take everything I gave them and put it right back into the machines. They were hopeless. They were helpless. So was I. The lottery owned these people and, I imagine, it took most of their hope along with their cash. Try telling me, or any other serious video poker player in Oregon, that there's no difference between buying a lottery ticket for a dollar and spending hours on end shoving $20 bills into an interactive game. If it looks like a casino, smells like a casino, and acts like a casino. . .

There really is no difference between a casino and any bar in Oregon. The poker machines eat residents for breakfast, lunch, and dinner. And who's behind it? Who profits from the addictions of these Oregonians? Who makes it that much easier to gamble anywhere, anytime? The state. The Oregon Lottery found a way to take their product far beyond the convenience stores. They put *gambling* machines in bars, where people go to drink, to loosen up, to get a buzz, to *lose a little control*. From a business perspective, it's brilliant. But last time I checked, Oregon is *not* a casino and those at the wheel—the governor, the house, the senate—are not elected to answer to the investors regarding quarterly profits and new platforms to generate gambling revenue in the same way the CEO of Harrah's must. The state is . . . well, a state, with police and laws and school buses and the promise that your tax dollars are going to a better way of life for *all* who live there, even the gambling addicts.

You walk into a casino at your own risk. You'd better know what you are doing because they have mastered the art of marketing, of making you play more than you should, of relaxing you, of distracting you, of pumping you full of sounds, colors, and lights to the point where you forget the bills, your responsibilities, your kids. Still, you went to a casino, so what did you expect? But people with a gambling problem living in Oregon cannot go for a beer, a burger, or a coffee without the lottery beckoning them to "give it a go." Anyone who thinks this a bit dramatic should spend an evening at any bar in Portland—any bar. Is it really any different from a crappy little casino?

Making my life even more ironic, at night, once the bar closed, the bartender was responsible for opening up the five machines, taking the cash out, and counting it before putting the money in the office safe. Typically, you'd pull eight to ten grand out of the machines on any given night. Then you'd sit there in this poorly lit bar, full of windows where anyone could see what you were doing, with a crappy little bolt locking the door, and count out the money. Bars like mine got robbed all the time. I think we got hit twice while I worked at Claudia's (never on my shift). Honestly, it was petrifying. There was a lot of cash moving around this joint every night, and a half-drunk bartender making minimum wage plus tips was responsible for all of it. It's amazing the bars don't get robbed more often. It's equally surprising that Oregon bartenders don't rob their own bars.

Beyond the fear of being killed while working in a Portland sports bar, and the subsequent questions it would bring up in the alumni magazine at my fancy high school, the most interesting part of the whole bartending gig was emptying out those poker machines every night. I spent hours, weeks, seasons filling the machines with my own cash. I was bonkers for the video poker in Oregon. It controlled me. I was unable to stop. Still, several times a week, when I pulled the closing shift at the bar, I'd change sides and act as "the house," counting out tens of thousands of dollars a week from poor addicted gamblers just like me. No matter the time of year, the weather, or the proximity to a holiday, if the bar was open, the poker machines were full of cash. Some days were lighter than others, but not by much. A Saturday night was a given, but real gamblers, the addicts, prefer more privacy than a weekend night provides. The hard core played mostly during the day, when the bars were empty.

It was amazing to watch the "regulars," the everyday poker players who were sometimes waiting for us to open the doors at 10:00 A.M. so they could hit the machines. On the one hand, I'd shake my head in disapproval at their obvious addiction. On the other, I'd envy their bankroll or their day off, both allowing them to do the one thing I really wanted to fill my time doing. Still, I found plenty of time to play.

Eventually, my life in Portland spiraled down to the point where I did little other than play video poker and avoid people I knew. Toward the end of my four years in Oregon, I was a mess, an absolute disaster. I had finally broken up with Lisa. The split was anything but clean or final or healthy or normal or tolerable. Yes, it was one of *those* breakups, filled with jealousy, fear, pettiness, and insecurity. And that was before it got bad. Lisa started dating a bouncer, whom she later married, and I took to sitting in my room wondering what he was doing to *my* girl. By then, we couldn't stand one another, but I couldn't handle the idea of someone else being with her, either. Interesting, the male mind. I didn't want to go out with the gang, because the gang was happy and having fun. The bastards! I'm relatively sure I was mean to anyone with a vagina, which is a lot of people, something like half the state.

Toward the end, the one thing I did that made me "happy" was play video poker. I hid in some creepy places—strip clubs mostly, all over the city, where I knew my crowd would never think to go. All I did was play those poker machines, and they played me right back. Portland has more strip clubs per capita than any other city in the country. Strip clubs cover the entire metro Portland area. They are as ubiquitous as McDonald's or 7–11s. I was so paranoid about someone seeing me pull into a club, or recognizing my truck, that I never went to the places close to home. Instead I found the fringe joints, clubs literally on the other side of the tracks, and eventually set up camp there. I'm not going to pretend that I didn't enjoy being in places full of naked women. I did. I still do. But the girls weren't the attraction. The strip clubs were the places where I had the smallest chance of bumping into someone I knew. My crowd wasn't a strip-club crowd. If they were, I'd be sitting here trying to explain why I started going to techno clubs or biker bars. I was after privacy and anonymity. I'd take it where I could get it. Boobies were just a nice bonus.

Sadly, that's how I remember Oregon—not for the fresh air, the mellow people, the river fishing, my excellent friends. I remember Portland for the lonely, depressing days spent shoving one $20 bill after another into those machines, sneaking a glance at a naked day-shift dancer, both of us wondering why we were there. Both of us knowing that this was not the way we had intended to live our lives. Both of us lost. Both of us really into the Rod Stewart blaring through the speakers.

I imagine the preceding pages are sufficient explanation as to why I moved back east. It's hard to love any town when you are in such a dark place in your life. As great as Portland was, as many good friends as I had there, anyplace but there was bound to be an upgrade—even my folks' basement, which is where I ended up going. I'm surprised my parents didn't pick me up from Portland themselves. I'd become too odd, too addicted, too reclusive, too broke. It wasn't Portland's fault. It was all me. I was twenty-six years old and I moved to the only place that would have me, or that I could afford. I went back home.

Let me describe what it feels like to move back into your parents' house at the age of twenty-six. The shame of it, the reality of it, sinks in only once you've unpacked and settled in for a week or two. It's amazing how we fall back into familiar patterns, especially with family. There I was, having lived on my own, all over the country, for the past decade, and I suddenly found myself passing up happy hours with old friends because I felt I should be home for dinner.

My parents are great. They are open, welcoming, supportive, funny people. They avoided rules per se, perhaps at times to a fault. I grew up with a real come-and-go-as-you-please, all-are-welcome kind of a structure—one I appreciated then, and still do now. However, there was one thing my folks always demanded. Unless you were stuck under something heavy, you were expected to eat dinner with the family. It was hardly an unreasonable request. Not to mention, my family knows how to cook, how to eat, how to really enjoy food. Most days, it was in your best interest to be home for dinner because it was more than likely going to be something good. I never really knew how superior the cooking was at my house until I was old enough to eat at friends' houses. I'd just assumed that everyone's family (or housekeeper) knew how to cook. Not so. I think I stopped being friends with one kid because his mother made terrible crab cakes. Yes, the food's good at Mom and Dad's house. It's also good at various truck stops around the country and I don't want to live there, either. Once reality set in, I opened the classifieds—fast.

I don't know where you found your job, but I bet for a lot of you, it wasn't in the classifieds. When's the last time you looked around in there? It's depressing. How the hell do normal people, people without connections, without an education, get a job that they don't hate, where they can actually make a few bucks? I tried. I lowered my standards. I went to a few interviews. It's not that people didn't want to hire me; I got a few offers. Even back then, I could handle an interview. I just wasn't interested in any job that was interested in me. I truly did want to work. I was desperate. Was I slacking a bit here and there? Of course; I still do. Don't you? But I wanted a job.

I was willing and ready to enter the corporate world. I'd go kicking and screaming, but I'd go. There would be no scenes like when my mom dropped me off for the first day of kindergarten. This time, I would not wedge myself between the front and back seats. I would willingly let go of the door handle. I would not let my body go limp as Mom extracted me from the back of her station wagon, causing a scene in the drop-off lane. This time, I would be a big boy. A big boy who lived at home, but, a big boy nonetheless.

Those first few weeks back home were just like high school. I spent a lot of time trying to convince my folks that I was working hard. We'd play the usual game of cat and mouse. They'd head off to work; I'd get stoned. They'd call the house; I'd avoid the call. But I did make sure to eat dinner with them. Dinners usually consisted of me doing anything to keep the conversation away from my day.

One night after dinner, I went out to the patio to have a cigarette and finish off a joint I'd started that afternoon. It was early August. On the East Coast, that means intolerable heat and humidity, even in the evening. I was instantly clammy. I finished the joint and the cigarette, then headed back inside. I plopped down on the sofa in the basement and threw on a baseball game, expecting that to be it for the rest of the night. Then, the phone rang.

The call changed my life.

It was Julie Gold, a friend of a friend from Portland. Originally from Minneapolis, she'd moved east for a job in politics. Julie and I had hung out a few times since I came back to town. She was smart and far better connected than I was, even in my hometown. She was as energetic as I was lazy. She was employed; I was not. She worked out every day; I watched a fair share of porn. Julie, good. Ed, bad. She was becoming a true friend and she believed in me at a time when few did, myself included.

On the phone, Julie said that she was at a new restaurant that had just opened in town. She was with a guy named Ethan; he owned a finance company, he was hiring, and he wanted to meet me. I still had pot in my lungs. I had not shaved for days. The game was tied in the bottom of the eighth. I was getting more stoned by the second. I declined.

She would not take no for an answer.

"But I'm filthy."

"Take a shower."

"I have a three-day beard."

"Who cares?"

"I just got high."

"Trust me, you'll be right at home."

"JULIE!"

"Ed. Get dressed. Get in your car. Meet us for a drink. We're waiting."

The line went dead. She'd hung up. Left with little choice, I did as instructed and made myself all beautiful and drove to meet the man for whom I'd work for the next seven years.

... 5 ...
THE FIRM

DESPITE MY PRAYERS, THE restaurant had not caught fire and burned to the ground when I met Julie there. In fact, it was packed.

I was miserable the moment I got out of my car. Young, manicured beauties were everywhere, eager to be seen, displaying their bodies like mannequins in the windows of Macy's. The crowd spilled out of the bar, fanning three deep into the more sedate restaurant side. The music thumped with too much bass. It could be heard well down the block. Club music felt out of place pulsating in the affluent city night. The place smelled of lamb, cigarettes, and chickpeas. It had that physical musk of too many people packed into a bar on a summer night. Twenty minutes ago I'd been at home, in sweats, with a buzz and the ball game on TV. I wasn't even wearing underwear. Now, this.

I felt familiar, self-conscious pangs hit my stomach like a sucker punch the moment I reached the door. I was overwhelmed with anxiety. Where was the *air* in this place? I felt like a foreigner, not someone who grew up two miles away. You want to see me at my worst? Watch me walk into a crowded bar. It's my kryptonite. I get the feeling that every set of eyes in the place is looking at me, knowing me, whispering about my double chin, my love handles, my secrets, feeling my discomfort, plotting against me. *Can you say, Paxil, anyone?* What's worse, I walked in alone. It took every fiber of my being not to do a U-turn and speed home.

Julie and Ethan were sitting comfortably around a tall circular table toward the back of the bar. By the looks of them, they'd gotten a head start on drinks. Ethan was surprisingly young—thirty-five tops. He was not what I'd expected. Within minutes, he had ordered the table two rounds of tequila shots, neither of which I wanted. This was not your father's version of a CEO.

I was drawn to Ethan from the start. Perhaps it was just that I had people to talk to, a destination, a life raft of sorts, a table that was expecting *me*. But Ethan had an air, an aura about him that was absolute, tangible, intoxicating. It was apparent that he was successful, but not flashy; there was no "bling" reflecting the recessed lighting into my eyes. Rather, he had the demeanor, the inner peace, the confidence that money often brings. What's more, he was engaging and very interested in my favorite subject: me.

I had left my cigarettes in the car, as showing up high and unshaven seemed enough of a reach for our first meeting. Still, with the tequila burning my throat, I wanted a smoke and I almost jumped for joy when Ethan asked me if I had a cigarette. I laughed, and told him the truth—that I had left my pack in the car, that I wanted to make a good first impression. Ethan popped up from his stool and went to the bar to buy smokes. I looked at Julie and winked with the swagger that only two shots of booze in ten minutes can provide. "I like him," I breathed into Julie's ear.

"You're drooling," she popped back.

"I bet I have an offer by the end of the night."

"And, if you're wrong?"

"My kingdom."

"You live with your parents."

"Then, *their* kingdom. Either way, you're covered."

Ethan returned with Marlboro Ultra Lights—my brand. I was so star-struck, I even thought *that* was a sign. We smoked and drank and relaxed. With all the tequila, the heat, and my desperation to find something to believe in, I'm lucky Ethan wasn't a Scientologist. I was his no matter what.

In Portland, I had surrounded myself with a lot of folks who, at the time, were not reaching very high in their careers, their goals, their aspirations. Portland was where you went to *be*, not to *become* something more than you were upon arrival. Most of us were part of that whole Generation X paradigm. I had not been around someone as impressive as Ethan since professors in college. Sitting there with him, I knew that I wanted to surge, to take steps I'd not taken in years. I wanted to get out of my folks' basement. I wanted to hitch my future to Ethan's.

Whatever it was that happened that night, why we clicked—or moreover, why he had such an impact on me—it changed my life. I had met my mentor. I'd met the man who would allow me to make several million dollars over the next handful of years. I'd met the savviest businessman I'd ever known. I'd met a man as charismatic and driven as any I'd ever heard of or read about in books. I'd met Dr. Jekyll. I never thought about Mr. Hyde. Major oversight.

I lost my bet with Julie. There was no offer that night, nor the next three. If they were icing me, like a kicker before a field goal, it worked. I was going mad waiting for Ethan's call, or, perhaps, for the man himself to swoop into my driveway—on a white stallion, or at least in a Lexus—and deliver me to my new corner office. Perhaps he'd even offer to help me move out of my folks' basement. Maybe he had a van?

I had lobbed the prerequisite follow-up call into Ethan's office the day after we met. Still, nothing. I wasn't exactly sure what his company did, but I knew I wanted to do it too. Finally, the call came. It wasn't Ethan, but the caller ID said "The Firm," and that was good enough. Ethan had forwarded my voice mail to his young rising star, Ben Keller, and asked him to handle things from that point forward. Ben asked me—scratch that; Ben never asked, he *told* me—to meet him for lunch the following day at Austin Grill. For Ben, this was just another meeting with another young guy that Ethan wanted to vet for a sales gig at The Firm. For me, it was the biggest meeting I'd ever had.

At least he told me to dress casually. If not, I'd have shown up in a suit. The one suit I owned at the time was heavy wool and looked like it was ten years old, largely because it was. As it was late August, and we were—for some ridiculous reason—dining al fresco, the suit would have brought on the sweat and the sweat would have preceded the panic attack, neither of which would have made the best first impression. Instead, I wore khakis and a new green polo shirt. I was still sweating by the time he showed up, a solid fifteen minutes late. I mean, who wants to eat outside in the middle of a clammy East Coast summer anyway? Who was this guy?

I wouldn't have believed the man-child approaching my table with a toothy grin and John Wayne swagger was Ben were it not for the company's logo stitched onto the breast of his dark blue shirt. He looked like a kid—a cocky, intimidating kid. It was clear from his handshake that he didn't lack confidence. He was friendly, too friendly, *salesman* friendly. I knew the type. I knew what he was doing. Between the two of us, there were more teeth being displayed than at my dentist's office. He didn't apologize for being late, something I'd get used to over time. But he did his best to make a little small talk and relax me, which worked. *I just could not get over how young he was.*

Ben was handsome. He was short and rough around the edges, but he was stunning to look at. Later I'd come to understand that the roughness was directly related to his love of drink. He had that look, that just-got-out-of-bed-but-I'm-still-beautiful thing because, well, most days, he *had* just rolled out of bed after what was invariably a late night. He had unexpectedly fair skin and blue eyes. Looking at him, I was reminded of that famous photograph from *National Geographic*, the one with the Afghani girl staring into the camera. They shared the same eyes. They were striking.

Ben wanted to make a specific impression at lunch. His message had two main themes. First, he was the big gun in the office, making tens of thousands of dollars a month. Second, if I was lucky, I could have the honor of working *for* him. What did I have to do? Anything he said. I also think he was looking for someone to believe in him as much as he did. He was looking for a lieutenant, a right hand, someone to assist him in his plan to take over the company and own the entire industry. Of course, I'm telling this story with the benefit of hindsight and a knowledge of what ended up happening to him, to me, to the industry. Looking back, that is exactly what he meant; he just wasn't aware of it yet.

A day later, via FedEx, the offer came. I know, whoopee . . . a FedEx! But at that time in my life, I'd received precious few items deemed important enough to merit overnight delivery. If I recall, the one before this was Grateful Dead tickets for their '91 spring tour. A package from a corporation, addressed to me, not from a collection agency or from Ed McMahon telling me that I may have already won ten million dollars, was news. The excitement lasted until I saw the offer. The bloom quickly fell off the rose.

The offer stipulated a ninety-day probationary period during which I would be paid a $30,000 base salary. That's $1,250 gross every two weeks. After deductions, you're looking at a net of about $875. The real kicker was that during this time, I would give all commissions I earned to Ben. I was to start in a new, entry-level sales position that Ben had created just for me. *What a mensch!* Parenthetically, this would allow me to come in and give the job a shot without exposing the company to much risk. I have another theory. I think Ben sold Ethan into hiring me into such a junior position for the sole purpose of earning my commissions for ninety days. Ben had, and still has, an incredible eye for talent. He *knew* I was different from the hacks he had up in that bullpen. I didn't know it at the time, but he certainly did.

The hours were set from noon to 9:00 P.M., Monday through Friday. Why work until 9:00 P.M.? Cold-calling. Salespeople have greater success calling customers when they are likely to be home from work, or whatever they do with their day. Why do you get those annoying telemarketing calls during dinner? Because the company on the other end of the phone wants to sell you something and they can't very well do that when you are at work or sitting in traffic on the highway.

So, to recap: bad compensation, terrible hours, and lots of cold-calling in my future. I suddenly yearned for the good old days bartending for minimum wage back in Oregon. This was not going to be as easy as I thought. I looked around my folks' basement and realized that I'd still be receiving my mail there for some time. I called The Firm, asked to speak to someone in human resources, and accepted the first and only corporate job I'd ever had.

Prior to this, my only office job had been working for my dad the summer after I turned fifteen. It lasted a week. Reading the tea leaves and refusing to let my own father fire me, I quit. We were both relieved. I don't think he took too kindly to my sitting around the break room confirming the nurses' speculation that he was a bit moody from time to time. "You should see him at home!" I'd whisper dismissively to the women. "He's just impossible." That was my last day at the office.

Walking into The Firm for the first time was excruciatingly intimidating. I was no longer the intriguing hipster doing shots at the bar with Ethan. I was the new junior salesman—a dime a dozen, the life expectancy of whom was never very long. If I were walking into a restaurant kitchen for the first time, this is where they'd hand me a potato peeler and a dish rag. My direct line to the boss was now a jigsaw puzzle filled with office politics and organizational charts. (You know, the *fun* stuff every job offers.)

The better part of my first day was spent signing forms I didn't understand and would not see again until eight years later when I was fired. As you can imagine, the forms were a lot more interesting the second time around. The documents basically made me promise that, in the event of my termination or resignation, I would never compete against The Firm, never spill The Firm's secrets, never work for a competitor, never love again, nor pass GO, nor collect $200. What the hell did I care?

My first week was spent in training, one-on-one with Ben. Back then, the company was too small to hire large groups of salespeople and train them together. Ben likes the sound of his own voice more than anyone I've ever known, other than myself. He got to talk for hours on end. He was thrilled. Training a salesperson is part science, part art, and part psychology. The interview process is hardly an exact science. Often, the prospect is on church behavior and the interviewer is desperate to wrap it up and get back to his real job. Sometimes a real dud sneaks in past you. You really don't know what you've got, who you *really* just hired, until you get that person in house and start training. Once officially employed, new hires tend let their hair down a bit. Sometimes, you're pleasantly surprised. Sometimes, you simply can't believe you hired a kid who asks moronic questions and says "dude" a lot. Most salespeople are pretty savvy to begin with, so you tend to have to really put it to them to see if they can handle themselves when up against a tough selling situation.

Ben had no such problem with me. I got it—right away. I knew what the industry was, and what it wasn't.

In the early years, sales training at The Firm focused on two main goals: First, make sure you know how to close deals. Second, make sure you understood the laws surrounding the industry. The Firm always took the law very seriously. When I came on board, it was catch as catch can . . . but never put the company in any legal trouble along the way. It came down to Ben telling others what to do, which largely meant doing it his way. He was the best, so doing it his way was typically a pretty good call.

Every new salesman needed to understand exactly what The Firm did, and equally important, what we didn't do. Everyone knew going in that we worked with lottery winners—which sounded exotic enough, but what did that mean? Did we invest their money? Did we sell them insurance or real estate? Did we give them tax advice? No. We specifically did not give any tax or investment advice. We did not sell insurance to winners. We sold winners money, at a discount, and nothing else.

The tenets of the lottery business are based around the following facts:

Imagine winning $1,000,000 in the lottery. You may have *won* a million on paper, but that's not how you're going to get paid. Not even close. Prior to 2000, winners were paid in long-term annuities, typically over twenty or twenty-five years. Before the lump-sum industry came along, they had no choice. When the winners needed cash—say, in April when Uncle Sam wants his cut and the annual payment's long gone—we'd buy some or all of their payments in exchange for a lump sum. Of course, The Firm takes a piece of the lump before it goes to the winner.

How big a slice does The Firm take? It varies. How do you make that decision? You sell. You pepper the winners with questions, probing into their lives, into their minds, revealing how they think, what they care about, what makes them happy, what problems need solving. You find their need, their pain, their problem, and you fix it, you make it go away, you clean up their mess. You solve problems that seemingly can't be solved. How? The old-fashioned way: with money.

Why would the lotteries pay winners over the course of several *decades* rather than at the time of their win? Why else? Money. Let's say that the jackpot for tonight's Maryland Lottery drawing is two million dollars. Imagine winning tonight's drawing and realizing that you are a millionaire—no, a *multi*millionaire. (Mazel tov, by the way.)

Let's jump past all the descriptions of what you'd do next: the phone calls, the rechecking of the ticket for the nineteenth time, the joy, the relief . . . we'll get to all that. Let's move on to you, the new winner, walking into lottery headquarters, family in tow, slapping the ticket down on the counter and calmly asking whom you see about claiming a $2,000,000 winning ticket. Again, let's jump past all the hoopla at the lottery with the obligatory photograph of you holding a jumbo check, made out to you in the amount of $2,000,000. We'll come back to that as well.

Imagine your surprise when it's finally time to cut your check, officially making you a millionaire, and instead, you are handed a check for $70,000. What then? Do you ask to speak to the manager? Perhaps the governor is available? You could ask, but odds are she's not seeing lottery winners today. Is there some mistake? Are you on *Candid Camera*? Aren't you missing the other $1,930,000? Did they accidentally give you the check for some poor schmuck who only won a measly $70,000? No, the check is made out for the proper amount. And, you lucky devil, will get another one just like that on this date every year for the next twenty years.

You do the math and see that $70,000 × 20 years = $1.4M. There are too many questions in your head, and one of the most recurring is "Does anybody have a gun?" Why $70,000? Why twenty years? Why not all at once? And, if they are paying me over twenty years, why did I just get my picture taken with a big check that had $2,000,000 written on it, not $70,000? What the hell is going on here?

The lottery gave you your first of twenty *identical* payments. You are to be paid $100,000 per year for twenty years. The lottery withholds both state and federal taxes, or their approximation of what you will pay in taxes, in this case 30 percent. So, your $2,000,000 life-changing payday has turned into one-twentieth the fun, with twenty times the questions. Not to mention, they are withholding a portion of the taxes right there in front of you— thus, the $70,000 check in your increasingly crestfallen hand. If you think you're upset, you should see the look on your relatives' faces. They had plans for your money, too.

Why play this game with winners and players? Why not just come clean about the way in which winners are paid? Why not just advertise the actual value of a jackpot rather than the inflated annuity value? The answer is marketing. The *only* reason lotteries have historically paid winners with long-term annuities is that doing so has allowed them to double the advertised jackpot amount. The bigger the jackpot, the more people are interested in playing. What sounds better: winning $1,000,000 in the lottery or $2,000,000? Do you think that more people would buy a ticket for a jackpot valued at $9,000,000 or one for $4,500,000?

A $2,000,000 winner really just won $100,000 a year for twenty years. Now, how does the lottery go about paying off the prize? The lottery buys an annuity that, upon maturity, will pay $2,000,000 in total, but, the $2,000,000 comes in slowly over twenty years. What is the cost of that type of annuity? Roughly half the face value of the advertised jackpot. Different states go about these investments in several ways. Some buy U.S. Treasury strips. Some buy government-backed securities. It really doesn't matter how they fund the long-term payout. What matters is that the cost is basically 50 percent of the face value of the lottery prize, no matter how much the winner "won." The truth is that he won only half the advertised jackpot amount in *today's* dollars.

Is the lottery lying by advertising a $10 million jackpot when the fine print discloses the lump-sum value at roughly half that amount? No more than Coke lies when they say that it's refreshing. It may be, but it's also rotting your teeth. Are the lotteries thieves? Well, no, not exactly. The lottery does in fact give the winner the total face value of the prize, as promised. It just takes twenty years. Is it a lie? No. Is it a crummy way to do business? Absolutely.

Making a bad situation so much worse, the lottery does not pay one red cent of interest on the money that they are "holding" for the winner. If I handed you an envelope with $70,000 cash inside, you would know how much it was worth today: $70,000.

Now, if I gave you the same envelope with the same $70,000 but told you not to open it for fifteen years, what would you have then? The envelope would have the same $70,000 in it fifteen years from today, true enough. But what would the $70,000 actually be worth in fifteen years? What was $70,000 worth fifteen years ago versus today? Fifteen years ago, you could buy a condo for $70,000. Today that same $70,000 is worth a lot less than it was in the early 1990s. Yes, the actual dollars are the same, but the value of what that money can buy is *considerably* less each and every year.

What does it cost to go to a movie today versus fifteen years ago? What did a gallon of milk cost in 1992 versus today? So, yes, the lottery will eventually pay you your entire prize, every penny, but every year that annual payment is worth less than the year before. The time value of the money is extraordinarily different based upon whether it is paid all at once or in little pieces. If the lotteries paid winners interest on their money or if they increased the annual payments a few percent for inflation every year, the lump-sum industry would cease to exist. If payments went up each year to compensate for the rise in the cost of living, winners would be smart to simply sit on their annuity. However, without any interest awarded or annual payments increased to compensate for inflation, any winner with his head on straight should sell his prize and get all the cash he can. Selling a long-term lottery annuity is the absolute correct decision. The problem isn't selling it. The problem is the people you have to sell it to. Example A: Ben. Example B: me.

How do you sell money to lottery winners? However you can. Whatever a winner needs, you provide. This sale is both need-based and impulsive. Winners don't want to hear a lot of investment advice. They don't care about terms like inflation or ROI (return on investment). What winners want to know is that the person on the phone or in their living room is giving them a fair price and has their best interests at heart.

Wealth and materialism are at the heart of the lottery culture.

Still, the vast majority of winners have no concept of what *real* wealth is. Many think that their lottery ticket has magically changed them and that the laws of finance or human nature no longer apply to them. Many lottery winners instantly see themselves as invincible.

Who are lottery winners? What are they like? Winners are often impulsive by nature. But, soon after winning, along with their impulsivity comes a sense of doom, of insecurity, of paranoia. Therefore, when winners contact The Firm because they *need* money, you're all but guaranteed an interesting show. Whether or not a deal gets signed, you're going to see their vulnerability, their humanity, in all its beautiful, ugly glory.

Release the Hounds

No winner was more full of contradictions, paranoia, and debilitating fear than Thelma Washington. While it would be over a year from the time I left training until I first laid eyes on her, she personifies the essence of what it really means to win the lottery.

Thelma Washington doesn't suffer fools. And if she did, it wasn't going to be some lottery "whatever-the-fuck name you call it—lumpin' me out—salesperson," as Thelma delicately described me at one point. No. Throughout this process, she planned on taking absolutely no crap from me—that point was made clear early on.

Thelma won nearly $6,000,000 in the Virginia Lottery. Mean as hell, she was also chin-deep in debt when I met her. The debts sanded down her rough edges. She needed help. She couldn't intimidate her bills away. She couldn't yell at them, or threaten them. She saved all that for me, the little sweetheart.

She called us; I hadn't cold-called her and wedged my way into her life. She wasn't even on our radar. Thelma was actually one of the few winners who'd slipped through the cracks. The research team had never been able to find much information on her. All the database notes indicated was that she'd purchased her winning ticket at a gas station in some town nobody had ever heard of. Other than that, we knew she was forty-eight at the time she won, making her something like fifty-three now.

The research notes didn't mention how tough she was—nor anything about her paranoia or her goddamn bloodthirsty dogs. On the phone, where she was in control, she told me about her no-good family, the "sons of bitches" at the IRS, and trying to keep her daughter focused on school "after Mama won so many millions." She talked a mile a minute—but never one word about those dogs. God forbid the sharpies down in research should tip me off about the fact that Thelma had a half-dozen toothy, drooling Cujo impersonators. No such luck.

Thelma lived near the Virginia/North Carolina border. Her Virginia is all but unrecognizable to the Virginia that's just a stone's throw from Washington, D.C. Down there, the vibe is more Tobacco Road than Embassy Row. I view the South as I do any other foreign country—with respect, cultural openness, and a modicum of fear. And, like any of the places in the five continents that I've visited, from the bustling streets of Bangkok to the intense bazaars of Morocco, my overall travel philosophy remains a constant— embrace the people but don't mess with the police . . . or the dogs.

Thelma didn't have a lot of options. If she was going to eliminate the debts she'd accrued since winning, she'd have to sell her annuity. She knew it. The question was, *would* she sell? Was she willing to tackle her debts? Some folks don't like taking medicine, even if they know it's good for them, even when they're sick. That was my challenge: Could I get her to take her meds?

Thelma lived so far down a dusty dirt road, I imagine even she got the willies a few times. Driving to her place at night would be a horrifying experience—one I'm not sure I'd have the guts to pull off even if it were absolutely necessary. The dirt road went on for several miles, protected on either side by thick, mature evergreens. Finally, deep into the Brothers Grimm forest, the road opened to a large clearing. The clearing was five or six acres. In the middle stood one lonely house: Thelma's house. I was reminded of the Overlook Hotel from *The Shining*. This place gave off that kind of vibe. There's a difference between "secluded getaway" and "creepy hermit lady in the woods." This place was Boo Radley's summer home.

The house was surrounded by a six-foot wooden fence. The fence, like the house, and the two cars indiscriminately parked in the driveway, was brand new.

I wasn't sure where to park. The driveway was sealed off by a gate that swung out from the fence. The gate was secured with a padlock. She wasn't kidding about this privacy thing. Was she a lottery winner or Greta Garbo? I pulled my car into a little gravel area just beyond the fence-line. Getting out of my car, I could see her peeking through the curtains. That happened a lot when you had as many meetings in people's homes as I did. But this felt different. Something was off; I could feel it.

It wasn't until I'd walked through the gate and bolted the door behind me that she let them out of the house. At first all I thought was, *Cool, dogs. I like dogs.* I even knelt down to say hi to them, wanting her to see what an animal lover I was. People love when you're nice to their animals. But these dogs weren't going to turn me into PETA's Man of the Year. Also, the "dogs" were more like wolves. For the sake of the story, they should be considered wolfish dogs—anti-Semitic wolf dogs.

They never bit me, but they surrounded me, yelping and growling at me like I'd already done something wrong. The worst thing they did—physically at least—was scratch me with their paws and get me dirty. The dirt unnerved me. I wasn't sure if it was my blood, their blood, or even feces (theirs, I assumed). But the worst part was that instead of calling them off me, Thelma just stood there on her steps—watching.

Suddenly, as if on cue, the dogs went silent. The queen wanted to address the dummy trying to shield his groin with his briefcase. "You got a number in mind?" she asked disinterestedly, as if the answer meant a lot more to me than to her. Under the circumstances, she had a point.

While she wasn't holding a gun, make no mistake, I was being held up. At least guns don't have the ability to bite off your penis. I'd happily have traded the six drooling dogs nipping at my groin in exchange for a gun aimed at my head. After all, Thelma wasn't going to *shoot me*. At least, I didn't think so. Meanwhile, I was concentrating on not peeing on myself. I imagined the scent of my urine could act as an *au jus* of sorts for the dogs, quite possibly tipping the scales toward a decision to eat me.

And, was she really talking to me about money like this—with her dogs pinning me up against the fence? Was she out of her tree? I was some kind of angry. Scared, too, but angry as hell.

"What?" I squeaked, my cracking voice betraying the casualness I was attempting to convey.

"Your offer," she demanded. "How much is it?"

Here's what was going through my mind:

She was seriously unhinged.
She was using the dogs to scare me honest. (It was working.)
This was the closest I'd ever come to knowing what it feels
    like to be a lamb chop.
If we were keeping score, she was winning round one—
    handily.
The dogs could eat me, and no one would ever find me.
I was about to start throwing money at her.
I'd have sold my soul for a box of Snausages.

No salesman could increase an offer without the prior blessing of a manager. This wasn't one of those *wink-wink* rules that no one really followed; this was etched in stone. Thelma's deal was locked in at $250,000 for a small partial purchase. In order to increase her offer I had to jump through a few hoops, the first of which was to call Ben. No one coughed up a penny until Ben said so. Still, under the circumstances, Ben was the least of my concerns. Without a moment's hesitation, I tossed another $12,000 into her deal. Why $12,000? Perhaps it was the *six* dogs multiplied by my *two* vulnerable testicles? That, or it was the first number that popped into my head.

"We've got you selling a small portion of six lottery payments for a lump sum of $262,000," I said.

The original $250,000 was a pretty good offer in and of itself. We weren't aiming for the fences on this deal. It was just a little partial, an ice-breaker deal. The $262,000 should have gotten her attention. It did.

She paused a moment, mulling it over. The dogs seemed to run the numbers themselves. As expected, the $262,000 was enough to end the scene in the yard. Thelma gave an authoritative whistle. In unison, the dogs turned around and trotted inside. Suddenly, she was all smiles. She put on her coat, grabbed her keys, and came outside to join me. She obviously didn't want me inside her house . . . not a good sign.

"I'd have done it for $255,000," she said with a wink and held out her hand. "We haven't officially met. I'm Thelma."

I shook her hand. *Officially met?* Who did she imagine I might have mistaken her for?

"We'll chop up the extra seven grand between the dogs," I said, trying to seem cool despite everything that had just happened. "*They earned it*," I muttered under my breath, wiping the dirt and drool and shit off my pants.

"Are we gonna sign this thing here or at the notary?" she asked. "You need a notary, right?"

"We do need a notary, but we can go over the docs here if you'd like."

"Nah, no need. Two hundred sixty-two thousand, right?"

"Right . . . $262,000."

Was she kidding? Just like that, everything was fine? Suddenly, we were off to the notary, no questions asked?

"Follow me. My bank's up the road. They've got a notary."

"Will do."

I hurried back to my car. Forty-five seconds ago, I was a hostage. Now, I was safely inside my car, ostensibly on my way to sign the deal. I followed her out of the clearing, back onto the dirt road.

I called Ben from the car and told him we needed to increase the offer by $12,000 because the deal was getting competitive. I could have told him the truth, but the story would have given him too much joy. Hearing about me getting out-negotiated by an entirely different species? By dogs, no less? Not even a chimp or an elephant? I just couldn't give him the pleasure. I'd never hear the end of it.

I was relieved to be headed away from the little kennel of horrors, but I sensed we still weren't on the same page, despite what Thelma had led me to believe. That dog thing was no joke. That's not what most folks consider an appropriate way to greet a visitor. And not letting me inside her house? What was *that* about? One minute she'd unleashed her dogs on me and the next, we're off to the notary? Something was off.

Pulling out of the dirt road, onto the street, I talked myself into not overthinking things. "We're on the way to the notary," I told myself. "Stop looking for trouble."

A few miles toward town, Thelma turned into a busy strip mall and stopped near a bank. She threw on her hazards, rolled down her window, and motioned for me to pull up next to her. "I don't want to go here if this one manager is working. He's in my business enough as it is. You go park and ask if Mr. Patterson is working."

I've done a lot worse chores for winners. Running into the bank was nothing. Without a second thought, I parked my car and went inside to ask for Mr. Patterson.

Ed to Teller: "Is Mr. Patterson working today?"

Teller to Ed: "Who?"

Ed to Teller: "Mr. Patterson . . . the manager."

Teller to Ed: "I'm sorry sir, there's no employee here by that name."

Ed to Ed: "Oh shit."

I didn't even have to look outside. I knew she'd be driving away. I turned around and saw Thelma speed out of the parking lot and turn onto the main road. I didn't chase her. What would I have done if I'd caught her? Instead, I walked into a Subway a few doors down and ordered some lunch.

In a way, I was relieved. Lottery deals get weird, sometimes a lot more so than some scared woman driving off on you. This was nothing. She'd just driven off. It's not like she sold her annuity to another company. This wasn't over. The deal still had legs. With lottery deals, you never know. Do this long enough and you end up taking odd moments like this in stride.

I put my cell phone on the table where I could see it. I knew she'd call me. I surely wasn't going to call her. She'd just ditched me at her fake bank. She needed some space. A novice would have called her right away. Having done this a time or two, I did not call. Instead, I ate a meatball sub. She was just freaking out a bit. If she'd only call me, I could tell her how many lottery folks lose it in one way or another. Deal or no deal, I could calm her down.

I was nearly finished with my sub when my phone rang. It was a local area code. She was at a pay phone. Interesting. Why not her cell phone?

"Hi, Thelma."

"Ed, I'm sorry . . ."

"Hey, it's okay. I had lunch next door. Have you ever had a

meatball sub from Subway? They're surprisingly good. Where are you?"

"Down the way. Look, I know I've only got thirty seconds, so let me talk."

"Thirty seconds? For what?"

"So you can't trace my call." Talk about someone who's seen too many movies. Not to mention, what an inflated sense of self-importance! Did she really think that we would trace her calls?

"Oh. . . . Do you think I'm tracing your call?" I heard a click. "Thelma? Hello?"

She'd hung up. Unreal.

Two minutes later, my phone rang once again—same area code, different number. She was at another pay phone. She was serious. This was new. I couldn't believe it, but she was actually jumping from phone to phone.

"Hello."

"I'm sorry, Ed."

"Thelma. Slow it down for a second. What are you sorry for? What's going on?"

"I just need some time, some space to decide what I'm gonna do." She was embarrassed. "I'm sorry I drove off. I just didn't know what to say to you."

"I'm not worried about it. Anyway, you could have just told me the truth. I could tell you weren't ready. I could see it."

She started rambling about Jesus and her family. It was hard to keep up. She was a real mess. The last thing I wanted to do was push her for another meeting.

"Thelma. Listen to me—"

The line went dead again.

Five minutes later, another thirty-second call from a different pay phone ending with her hanging up.

Two minutes after that—*ring ring*. Thirty seconds of manic chatter and click, end of call. This time I hardly got a word in before she hung up. Still, we *were* making progress as, by the third or fourth call, she was saying things like, "I'll call you right back," or "Don't go anywhere, I'm going across the street." She was nuts, but she'd recovered her manners.

I found the whole thing both humorous and sad. Having thirty-second sales calls seemed like a poorly conceived training exercise, especially since she was doing all the talking. I'd basically pick up the phone, say hello, and listen to her rant. But it was sad to think that this was the only way she felt in control, as tenuous as that perceived control might be.

The pay-phone calls kept coming. She was a bit eccentric, but she sure had staying power. Sometimes she'd call a bunch of times in a row. Sometimes I wouldn't hear from her for an hour or two. But she kept calling. I didn't call her once.

She still wanted the deal.

While the method was unconventional, we were definitely in deal mode. Sensing that she'd come around, I checked into a hotel, which allowed her to call my room—a local number rather than my cell phone, which was long distance. I could only imagine her calling-card bill. She appreciated the gesture.

Sporadically throughout the night, and once again first thing in the morning—ring, chat, hang-up . . . ring, chat, hang-up. It went on like this for two days. And, progress with the deal or not, I couldn't get her to stop, so I played along. If this was important to her—this feeling of control—if it got the deal done, so be it. A few times, she'd forget to hang up on me so I'd actually remind her to go ahead and kill the call. She always thanked me for reminding her.

The morning of day three, just before 9:00 A.M., she called . . . from her cell.

"Good morning, beautiful," I said.

"Let's go for a ride."

"Where to?"

"The bank."

"We robbing it?"

"No!" She laughed. "I'm ready."

"You downstairs?"

"Yes."

"Are the dogs with you?"

"No."

"You gonna drive off the second you see me?" I teased her.

"No." She chuckled. "You gonna act like a little bitch next time you see a dog?"

Touché. "No," I said. "I'll be right down."

I got dressed as quickly as possible. On my way to the elevator, I called her back on her cell.

"Thelma, let's take one car."

"Why?" she asked.

"Just in case," I said as I hung up my cell.

She was waiting for me in her blue Lincoln Navigator. I got in, gave her a hug, and locked my door . . . just in case.

This Is Not a Drill

In order to really understand what we did, in order to get good at it, great at it, you had to go out and do it. Hit the phones, travel, get in front of winners, sign deals, try different closing techniques, blow a few, win a few, learn a lot. That was Ben's plan for me. He stood to make a lot of money off me once I was producing. The more time spent in the conference room, the fewer lottery winners I'd have a crack at on the phones. He wanted me selling ASAP. Ben's plan was to give me just enough of The Firm's lexicon to get me on the phone—the sooner the better.

What was brilliant about Ben, my first sales management lesson learned from him, was that he was happy for you to hit the road and fail. Failing was part of any sales gig and with deals that were this complex, with the possibility of major fees, who cares if you swung and missed? Even when they failed, the guys who went out and took their shot were welcomed back to the office with open arms. If you closed every deal you traveled on, then you weren't traveling on enough deals.

You knew quite quickly who the real players were on the sales floor. The guys who traveled every once in a while, the ones who hit the road only on deals that were lay-downs—those were the weak ones. Those folks were just playing it safe, not wanting to take a shot at something that wasn't a sure thing or, God forbid, knock on a tough winner's door, popping in unexpectedly because the winner refused to meet with them face-to-face. The plants, the ones who sat at their desks and never moved, as if they had roots, cost you a lot of money—millions, maybe.

Why would someone stay put instead of traveling and try-ing to make deals happen on the road? Fear. Fear of failure more than anything else. Fear is, in and of itself, a brilliant motivator. I've accomplished more things in my life due to fear than because of any other factor. For me, fear of failing—of not being considered good at something, of not being the best, of not being able to pay my bills—that is what gets me out of bed in the morning. Fear has been my secret weapon since I was a kid.

Ben had me take a test at the end of my training. I needed to get a score of 80 percent or better to pass. Why 80 percent? Because Ben said so. My anxiety was diluted by the fact that I sat with him at a bar while he wrote the test. Ben invited me for drinks know-ing full well that I'd have to sit there and watch him think up the questions for *my* test. Boy, did this guy love an audience! We both did. I think I was the first sales rep to take a lottery test. Now that he was managing lottery sales, Ben wanted everyone to take it. As the guinea pig, I made sure Ben's glass was never empty the entire night. By question ten, I should have been given a ghostwriting credit. We wrote the thing together.

I passed.

Ben liked the *idea* of giving me a test, of being in the power seat, of being my teacher. Was the test necessary? Actually, yes. Begrudgingly I must say that, like so many of his gin-soaked ideas, this one was right on the money. From a legal standpoint, it was important for us to be able to say that everyone on the sales floor had a basic knowledge of the product and the legal lines that a sales rep could not cross. From a CYA (cover your ass) perspective, it was solid business. But, far more important, from a "scaring the crap out of a new sales hire" side, it was priceless.

For some sales reps, this test was approached with the same intensity as the medical boards for an aspiring physician. A lot of salespeople are not exactly delivered to the firm's door by the Ivy League. For this sales gig, we like them gritty and street smart. The test, coupled with the legitimate promise of a six-figure income, meant the world to most reps who came through our office. The *idea* of the test—its importance to their future income, which we stressed to no end during training, its implied value—that made the test invaluable.

I was dying to get out of training and hit the phones. Regardless of whether or not I had to fork over my commissions to Ben, I needed to start earning some money for someone. If I made Ben rich, so be it. Doing so would get me out on my own that much sooner. Like a circus freak or a sick dog, I had been sequestered in the conference room across the hall for the duration of my training. A few times a day, someone would poke his head into the room to get Ben's approval or signature on something. Invariably, the messenger would sneak a glance at me, the Elephant Man, doing his best to size me up or make nice, depending on the person. I'd do the obligatory, awkward head nod combined with the semi-wave to those who made eye contact. To the ones who played hard to get, I played right back—feigning a lack of interest in them, masking my desperation to make a friend or two before week's end. Each evening, I'd smile and say hello to one woman who was particularly kind, giving me hope for the rest of the office. On Thursday I realized that my new friend was not employed by The Firm. She was the building's cleaning lady. Two weeks earlier, I was doing shots with the owner. Now, I had the inside track on where to find extra hand soap.

Once I passed my test, I was allowed out of the conference room. I was still the new guy and very much the outsider, but I got a desk and a phone, which was all I needed. The Firm was planning a move to a bigger space, just across the street. Everyone made a big deal about how great it was going to be once we got there. In the meantime, space in the current office was tight. There were desks that wedged out into the hallway; virtually every office was shared by several people. It looked like a corporate refugee camp. The place was a fire marshal's nightmare. I took the chaos as a good sign. Things were happening here. The Firm was growing, which meant that somehow, despite the disorder and clutter, they were making money.

The first thing I did when I sat down at my desk was write out "$11,000" on a piece of paper, taping it to the dented wall I was wedged against. Eleven thousand dollars was the amount I owed the rest of the world. Ben's training was not what motivated me to close deals. I was broke, in debt, and living with Mom and Dad. If that doesn't get you hitting the phones, I truly don't know what will. If I had a shot at getting out of my folks' place, the debt had to go. I figured there was no point in hiding it from my new co-worker–office roomies. To what avail? If displaying my debt to the world was embarrassing, wait until they heard that I lived with my parents and that I'd just run home from Oregon because I was too crazy to control my video poker habit. The $11,000 scribbled onto a folded piece of paper was the least of my concerns.

In the center of the office was a "bullpen," which housed the sales force. The room was all glass and small, maybe fifteen by twenty feet. It had an intense sales-ish look to it. Think Jerry Maguire meets Hannibal Lecter. Old desks occupied every inch of the place. The room pulsated with energy. Smooth voices with overly polite come-ons bounced off the glass, a cacophony of pitches and promises—reminiscent of a racquetball court on a busy Saturday afternoon. The room reeked of salesmen. It felt as if Jack Lemmon would appear at any moment, begging Ben for better leads. From what I could see, the entire space shared one air vent.

I walked into the bullpen for the first time with a new "Associate" title hanging from my neck like an albatross. That title, and the junior status it afforded me, was manna from heaven for a bunch of cold-hearted, backstabbing, hilarious, brilliant, insecure salesguys. Ben might as well have hung a sign on me that said, "Make fun of this dipshit!" I'd have had more clout with a Buckaroo Card from Roy Rogers.

Five or six guys were pitching lottery winners, all at once, each one more full of shit than the next. A few of them sounded like amateurs, even to me. But there were two guys who you could tell right away knew what they were doing. They were in total control of their calls, asking question after question, painting their winners into corners, imposing their will on the poor person on the other end of the call. I was impressed. Still, it was a real boys' club, generally not my scene. Thankfully, fire codes determined that there was no way to put one more sales rep in the bullpen. While I was pleased not to have to jump right into "Boys' Town," there were few alternatives.

I ended up tossed among the research group, which also housed the two sales assistants. Putting a salesman into that scene was like dropping a chainsaw-wielding lunatic into a convent. Salespeople are different from the rest of the office. It's an absolute fact. They are loud, arrogant, difficult, troubled, exciting, schmoozing raconteurs. If they are not as described, then they likely are not good at their job. The stuff you *want* a sales rep doing all day long (talking on the phone, making travel plans, telling stories) is the same thing that gets Steve from accounting fired. The mere fact that salesguys are on the phone for hours on end is incredibly annoying to a bunch of people doing reports and data entry all day. It's just asking for trouble. Thus, the glassed-in bullpen.

Sitting among the research group meant having a captive audience of critics and Monday-morning quarterbacks. They were forced to listen to me pitch all day long, success or failure, from day one. We were right on top of each other, so they heard everything that came out of my mouth.

The first time I picked up the phone to actually call a lottery winner, I could feel the researchers waiting, listening, as curious as I was to hear what was going to come out of my mouth. They weren't rooting against me as much as they were just hoping for a good show, one way or the other. Odds were that I'd be handed my ass a few times right away and they would get to see it firsthand, living vicariously through my successes and my failures—especially the failures, as they were bound to be a lot funnier.

There is nothing quite like your first day out of training. I had just been told to go fuck myself for the first time (by a lottery winner). Over my shoulder, eight researchers were trying not to laugh *directly* in my face. I laughed, too—because it was really funny how mean this winner was to me on the phone. She said she was going to cut off my penis. The staff was good-natured enough about the whole thing. They were laughing because it was funny. They *should* laugh. Plus, in five months, they would all be working for me. That would be funny, too.

Unbeknownst to me at the time, a new buyer had never closed a deal during his first week on the phones, not even Ben. Normally, those early days were chalked up to wasted opportunities, nervous dialing, and flat-line results. The Firm was more interested in a buyer getting acclimated to the overall sales environment. Consequently, they took week one's results with a grain of salt. No one was expected to actually sign deals. The Firm was just happy for you to have a few conversations with real, live winners.

Lottery winners carry some cachet for those who don't know any better. For some, there's a real wow factor associated with everything "lottery." Occasionally, a new hire would get nervous just at the thought of talking to someone who'd won the lottery. It was as if they were getting on the phone with Robert De Niro. Give that same hire five minutes with an actual winner and this is no longer an issue. The romantic vision of lottery winners is the first thing to go once you hit the sales floor. You quickly learn the truth—winners are often tough, rude, unreliable, disinterested, and annoyed. How do you act when you answer the phone and a salesman is on the line? I'm sure you're as charming as I am.

The trick was to be able to talk to anyone, at any time, no matter the person's age, ethnicity, gender, or sexual orientation. I was fascinated by the randomness of it all. If I was cold-calling, anyone could pick up the phone. It could be someone interested in talking to me, who needs money, or someone talking to a competitor (indicating a red-hot deal). The person could hate my company, the industry, the world—which just wouldn't leave him alone since he'd won the lottery. It could be someone of any nationality and any degree of proficiency in English. Calling winners, or picking up the phone when they called you, was playing the lottery in and of itself. You never expected too much, but there was always the chance of a life-changing call.

My first day hitting the phones was a total bust. I was exhausted and humbled. I left at 9:00 P.M. with my tail between my legs. My ego was in the trash, next to my pride. I was sworn at, called names, and hung up on all day long. The research crew watched the whole thing.

Wednesday, my second day on the phones, was a whole different story. I'd been in the office for an hour when Shannon, new to me at the time, dropped a green lead sheet into my lap. She smelled like flowers, her perfume lingering for a moment after she left the room. Whenever she stood close to me, I felt like Lenny with the rabbits in *Of Mice and Men*. I wanted to pet her hair.

"This one's legit," she nodded, gesturing at the piece of paper with her chin, acting as if I'd done this a hundred times.

"Wait! What do I do?" I begged, not wanting her to leave my side, embarrassed to be so freaked out in front of such a pretty girl.

"Um, your job. Sell the deal," she said playfully. "Two million dollars, New York winner, $100K per year, twelve years left, divorced, lives in Richmond, line two."

"Which one's line two?" I stalled, forgetting everything she'd just said.

"The one that's blinking."

"How do I . . ."

Shannon looked back at me—eyebrows raised, head tilted to the side like a perplexed puppy—squinting, not believing the terror in my voice. "She called *us*. She *needs* money. Line two," she repeated calmly like my first-grade teacher convincing me to go down the big-boy slide. I took a breath and pressed the blinking button on my phone.

It took me a few seconds to get it together, but Shannon was right. There was nothing to fear. The winner, Sarah Baker, was more nervous than I was. Each of us was terrified. We both needed a hug.

Sarah had never seriously considered selling her lottery prize and had made a habit of hanging up on every lump-sum salesman who called her house over the last handful of years. Every now and then, she'd read our direct mail. She knew the deal, more or less. Immediately, she asked how much money she would get for selling her prize. Knowing that money is the *last* thing you want to talk about with the winner, I answered by giving her a long, disjointed response about how it all depended on where the fed posted interest rates the day we signed contracts. I added that until then, there was no way to know an accurate dollar amount. At the time, I knew as little about what I was talking about as she did. Honestly, I'm still not exactly sure how interest-rate movement by the federal government affects the lump-sum industry. That was always a back-of-the-house issue, and I tended to have my hands full up front selling the deals. The fed had *nothing* to do with our day-to-day pricing; I knew that much. But if *I* hardly knew why, odds were heavy that she didn't, either. She didn't question what must have sounded like an insightful, legitimate response. And that was the last time we spoke about the value of her prize for the remainder of the conversation. Bullet dodged.

It's a mistake to assume that the amount of money a winner would get in a transaction is the most important topic to cover on a sales call. Often, a deal hinges on something far more valuable than dollars: peace of mind. Granted, Sarah was looking to get a fair price on her deal, but that wasn't the major issue for her. For Sarah, the pain was a lot closer to home. She was petrified that her son would find out she was contemplating selling the prize. Lumping out would have cramped his style, as he had lived both with and off of his "millionaire" mother since the day she won. I could have offered her one hundred cents on the dollar—face value—which is absolutely unheard of, but unless I dealt with the issues surrounding her son, there would be no deal.

As a lottery salesman, once you understand that, you're on your way. I'd been doing this for two days and somehow, I cracked the code. If you solve the winner's problem, nine times out of ten you've got yourself a deal. Money is often of secondary importance. The winners may not even know that, but it is not *their* job to know, it's mine. I assured Sarah that her son had nothing to do with the transaction. It was her call whether she chose to tell him or not. I wasn't completely sure if that was true (it was), but I figured . . . solve her problem, right?

In this industry, you are not selling money; you are selling solutions to problems. Money is simply the tool by which you ply your trade. Most problems in lotteryland can be solved with money. The only variable is how much. It had just dawned on me to leverage the company's money—to use it as my paintbrush, my hammer, my olive branch, my friendship pin, my voice, my gun. As soon as I did, I was ahead of my peers. Most folks never saw it so clearly. The whole artist-tool-intellectual-psychological-selling thing, there was too much gray in it for a lot of my early peers. Most of these folks were real black-and-white *it is what it is* salesmen. That approach was a bit too artsy-fartsy for the boys in the bullpen.

Sarah was in a tight spot, as her annual check wasn't coming for another five months and she had serious bills that needed attention. She'd gotten behind on her credit cards and had to pay the first installment of her niece's tuition within two weeks. Through the years, you'd see this same situation play out over and over again. Once they got their annual check, winners would spend the first six months living high off the hog and the next six months trying to figure out how to make it to the next check.

My first directed question came right out of training, just as Ben had taught me a few days earlier.

"How much capital are you looking to raise?" I could hear Ben's voice in my head—a phenomenon that would continue for years.

"How much you got?" she joked.

"Me? I live with my parents. But The Firm's got more than enough."

"I need some day-to-day cash . . . like today. You got *that*?"

When I heard her say "cash" and "today" in the same sentence, I half expected to see Groucho's duck fall from the ceiling. My next thought was that Ben was just messing with me and that "Sarah" was really some girl from accounting who he had charmed into participating in a sick practical joke. *(It wasn't, but that happened*

*a lot over the years. It was mean, but too funny a joke not to pull on a
cocky new sales rep. We once had a new hire drive about three hours into
the middle of nowhere for a deal that he thought had almost a million-dollar fee in it. We planned on letting him in on the joke a lot sooner than we
did, but we just couldn't help ourselves. So, he got a six-hour drive through
the countryside to learn a bit of humility.)*

In fact, Sarah *was* willing to consider selling her entire prize.
The catch was that she needed money right away. If I could give
her a little advance, I knew I could sign my first deal. Protectively,
with all the paranoia of a con on the lam, I lowered my voice to
hide from the vultures in the bullpen. It was time to toss the bait
into the water.

"Sarah, if I can get out to Richmond tomorrow—with a
check for $5,000—would that help?"

"Do you know your way around Richmond?" she answered
before I'd finished my question.

Bull's-eye!

"Sure, I do business out there. What's your address?"

I'd never been to Richmond, but I knew how to buy a map.
I wasn't about to waste time having her give me directions. I got
the appointment and that's all I needed. Spending any more time
on the phone with her would only give her the opportunity to
change her mind. She confirmed her address, which we already
had. I told her I'd be at her place around ten the next morning—check in hand.

It was my second day selling, and a hot lead wanted to meet
me and a $5,000 check as soon as I could get out to Richmond.
It was 4:00 Wednesday afternoon. Could it be that easy to set up
a live meeting with a winner? Had I just done that? I realized that
the key to the entire business was getting in front of winners and
solving their problems. Do it right, and maybe they won't even
consider issues such as how much money they are losing or what
the tax consequences of selling their annuity are. You didn't need

to wait for a winner to beg you to bring a contract. All you needed was the green light to stop by the house . . . if that. This was beyond an epiphany. It was a moment of clarity.

I had no idea if Ben would give me a live check for $5,000 or fire me for asking. I went to his office, hat in hand, to ask about the five grand. I all but flinched when I told him, thinking he'd hand me my ass for doing something so aggressive without his thinking of it first. Instead, he practically kissed me. Sure, he found a way to spin it so that it was his idea, but I was going to Richmond—able to make good on a promise. I was going to close my first lottery deal with a very poor millionaire.

Ben priced the deal and Shannon put together contracts while I was busy trying not to pass out from nerves. The deal had something like a $90,000 fee in it for The Firm. That was a lot of money, but not considered a big deal back then. It was, however, a nice deal, and it was *my* deal, and I loved it very much.

The research guys were thrilled. I took their high-fives and nods of approval in humble stride. I demurred when they said that I was, in their own words, the man. I thought that I had made a big impression on them, but the truth was a lot more simple. They were rooting for me because their bonuses were 100 percent based upon sales results. They would have rooted for Bin Laden if he was traveling on a deal.

I tried to play it cool before leaving the office, hiding the fact that this was the first deal in which I'd ever been involved that didn't include the need for my father to co-sign the contract. I felt a bit out of my league. There were still rental car companies that said I was too young to rent a car, but The Firm was going to trust me with a live deal? I felt the beginning of a panic attack. Losing my composure, right there at my desk, in front of everyone would not bode well for my career path. Still, I couldn't get past the fact that they were sending me *alone* to meet a winner. *Why not have me perform a little surgery, too?* Were they insane? I felt like screaming into Ben's face, demanding that he come to his senses and join me, just in case. I calmed down just as Ben called me into his office to go over the deal.

He sat with me for all of thirty seconds to review the documents. The instructions boiled down to his telling me to get her to sign everything and get all the supporting documents she had. "In the end," he said, "if all else fails, FITFO!"

"What?"

"Figure It The Fuck Out!"

And with that bit of imparted wisdom, I was off. I was out the door, with a check and a binding contract—all before 6:00 P.M. Ben did not mess around when there was a deal in the air. In less than two hours, he'd gotten the staff to crank out contracts, a live check, promissory notes, and all sorts of legally binding, scary shit.

I barely remember the trip out to Richmond. I was in a daze. I was full of excitement and nerves. It seemed like every other mile I'd jump from joy to fear. I had the music, Springsteen's *The Wild, The Innocent & The E Street Shuffle,* turned up loud enough that perhaps I wouldn't hear myself overthink the deal. However, there isn't a volume dial that goes high enough to drown out the dissenting voices that travel with me in my head. I smoked 698 cigarettes; at least it felt that way in my lungs.

As I was approaching the city limits, I saw a sign for a Holiday Inn on the north side of town. I didn't know where I was in relation to Sarah's part of Richmond, but I figured I'd be up at dawn anyway to take the first of what I could only imagine would be several nervous shits before show time. North Richmond was close enough. I had to get out of the car. There were too many conflicting personalities in there. I was feeling overcrowded.

Exiting the interstate, I noticed a Krispy Kreme doughnut shop that was not only open, but flashing the most beautiful neon message, custom-tailored for this moment. The sign blinked, "HOT DOUGHNUTS NOW." I was not alone in this big universe after all. It was October 1997 and I'd never had a Krispy Kreme dough-nut. Today, that makes me sound like I grew up Amish. But in my part of the world, Krispy Kreme was just becoming a thing. I'd heard rumors about this perfect doughnut, but they were vague and confusing. I had to see for myself.

Walking in, the first thing I saw was a conveyer belt carrying dozens of hot doughnuts, each one being brushed with glaze by an actual human hand. Another woman stood farther down the line dipping the lucky ones halfway into thick chocolate. So far, so good. Everything was fine, but for one little problem—the girl at the counter. She was stunning, an absolute knockout beauty. She was the last person I wanted to give *this* order to. There's no cool way to order doughnuts, especially for an insecure fat guy, espe-cially when the girl behind the counter looks like a young Sophia Loren. Think about it. "*. . . And one apple crumble, and two chocolate-topped, and one old-fashioned—no, um, make that two.*" You want the person at the doughnut shop to be either a zitty, depressed junior-college freshman named Carl or a cute little old lady who thinks you are her grandson. Still, "HOT DOUGHNUTS NOW." I had to know. Sophia Loren or not, I was going for it.

I did my best to seem as if I had a car full of hungry family members waiting outside. "Uh, yeah, hi. A half-dozen, to go," I said, trying not to look into her eyes. "Half glazed, half chocolate-glazed. And a milk. Wait, do you have chocolate milk?" Not exactly James Bond, but what can you do? Fatty needed doughnuts.

The scene in the hotel room was straight out of Kafka. Lying in bed, I rested the doughnut box on my belly and did my best not to get chocolate on the documents. Obsessively reading the contracts over and over again, I inhaled the doughnuts and the chocolate milk in one sitting. This kind of food binge can only take place in a hotel, alone. Eating a half-dozen doughnuts and washing them down with chocolate milk is not the kind of thing you can get away with at home—at least not at my house. My wife would weigh me just for *wanting* to eat six doughnuts. A sweet orgy like this called for an anonymous hotel room in an anonymous town. I felt creepy, dirty even, as if I'd called for an escort rather than a box of fried dough. The doughnuts, however, were worth the embarrassment. I loved them so much I called my dad to tell him about them. He'd want to know, and I had to tell *someone*. They were that good. Odd as that may seem, half the phone calls we make to one another in my family have to do with food or a great restaurant. It would be rude *not* to call my dad. There are still such things as manners—even for a chubby lottery salesman off to make good on his first deal.

It was a restless, sugar- and nicotine-infused night. My mind was racing and I could not stop thinking about the meeting . . . or the doughnuts. You're not supposed to dream about baked goods, *right*? As predicted, I was up at dawn, having resigned myself to the fact that a good night's sleep was not in the cards. I'd have to rely on caffeine and adrenaline. The caffeine was across the street at Starbucks. The adrenaline had been coursing through my veins since yesterday when I took Sarah's call. Sleep or not, I'd be wired and ready to roll.

Finding Sarah's house was easy. Not only did she live on the north side of town, but her place was a stone's throw from the Krispy Kreme, something I took as a good sign. The neighborhood was fine, nothing to brag about, but in hindsight a lot better than most places I'd end up going to sign deals in the years to come. Pulling into her driveway, I tried to talk myself into calming down. Was I nervous? Yes, incredibly. I wasn't afraid of her or her son. I wasn't afraid of what could happen once inside the house. I was afraid of what might *not* happen. I was afraid of failure. I dreaded the long drive home if things didn't go my way.

Getting out of my car, I realized that my used, cherry-red 1991 Acura Integra with hard miles, dents, and dings didn't exactly convey the message of success one would want, given the fact that

I was trying to buy well over a million dollars in lottery paper from the woman inside the house. I needn't have worried. When Sarah opened the door, she looked at my car in her driveway and chuckled, "You're as broke as me, huh?"

"You have no idea," I countered.

"Do you really live with your parents?"

"If I say yes, are you going to let me in?"

Sarah paused, biting the inside of her cheek. "My boy lives with me, too. Are you trouble like him?"

"Only for my folks. Everybody else loves me."

And, with that, I was in the door. Before I'd passed through the threshold, I'd established that I was a poor, harmless mama's boy—driving a beat-up old car, just out to make an honest buck. If she had any reservations about me, they were replaced by a sense of compassion for my crappy little life. (Whatever works.) It was clear that the young man in the house whom she didn't trust was not me, but rather her sponging son, currently asleep upstairs. I checked out. I could have been anyone, as long as I wasn't kin.

The interior was not what I'd expected. Jesus, did Sarah love her fish! Aquariums and photographs of fish were everywhere. She had two huge saltwater tanks. I've killed enough fish in various aquariums over the years to know how expensive the tanks and the fish are. Plus, saltwater tanks are the cream of the crop. They're harder to maintain, and the fish themselves are extremely difficult to keep healthy, much less alive. She probably had ten grand worth of fish in her living room alone. She told me there were more upstairs. I took her word for it, as there was no way I wanted her son to wake up and have *me* be the first thing his crusty eyes saw.

So, this is what a lottery winner looks like. She didn't have wings, two heads, or special powers. She was just some middle-aged lady with a deadbeat son living upstairs. Sarah was easygoing and approachable. She poured me coffee and, I swear, put out a plate of Krispy Kreme doughnuts. Kismet! It seemed only right to tell her about last night, my first Krispy Kreme experience. She laughed and relaxed, right along with me. I pulled out the contracts, at her request, and we looked them over together. I was so amped up, I almost forgot to pull out the big gun, the live check with her name on it. When I showed her the check, she exhaled and said, "Let's do this." It was that simple. *I'd been there five minutes.* On the way down, I'd figured that if I caught a break, things might go smoothly—but not five-minutes smooth. I was about to put the contracts back into my briefcase, which I'd borrowed from my dad, and get ready to head to the notary. That's when I looked up and saw her son walking down the stairs. He was not happy to have guests. He looked at me as if I'd come to eat the fish. Little did he know.

Sarah had told me that he was thirty years old, but, as she delicately put it, "lazy like a hobo's dog." The emaciated figure walking down the stairs didn't look a day over nineteen. He was rail thin, gaunt even, with tattoos descending both arms. His chest was small but muscular. He was wearing only boxers and a pair of jeans. The jeans hung just off his ass, so baggy that they nearly dragged on the stairs as he walked toward us. He was tough and mean-looking, at least to me. However, I may not be the best judge of such things, as I'm the guy who was afraid of a doughnut girl last night.

Having no tattoos myself, his body art fascinated me. It was hard not to look as he got closer to the table. I was most taken with the one on his left bicep that simply stated, "Bros B4 Ho's." At least he was loyal to his guy friends. Were I ever to get a tattoo, I would have to consider the same phrase. My wife and daughter would, no doubt, see the irony.

He walked right up to the side of my chair, so close he was actually stepping on the shoulder strap of my briefcase, something I took as no accident. Looking straight through me, he asked his mother, "Who's this?" Sarah wanted to keep our business private, so I sat there, silently adding to the mystery of who I was. Sarah reached for a cigarette, took her sweet time lighting it, and gave what I considered to be a poorly chosen response.

"Well, he's not your daddy, is he?"

Check, *please*!

Clearly, Sarah was not scared of this guy. I was. But did she really have to bring up his father *and me* in the same sentence? It's not the way I would have gone. Also, the way she said it, looking me up and down, exhaling her cigarette smoke in his face, gave the comment the slightest hint of sexuality. Not good. The son, whose name I never got, whose foot was on my briefcase, surveyed the table for incriminating evidence, what exactly I'm not sure. Thankfully, there was only an ashtray and a glazed doughnut. His bluff being called by his mother (something to which I could definitely relate), he thought the better of making trouble in her kitchen. But, to mark his territory, he took the last Krispy Kreme, spun around on the briefcase strap, and headed back upstairs. It was all very tense.

He didn't know that I was about to buy his meal ticket from his mother. He got a bang out of stepping on my dad's briefcase. Fine. I'm too much of a pussy to say something, much less *do* something about it. But I was going to leave that house with something a lot more valuable than a briefcase. I was taking Mama's lotto money with me, so . . . enjoy the doughnut.

He was a sheep in thug's clothing—something I'd bump into a lot over the next few years. Sarah and I got out of there the second he went upstairs. Backing out of the driveway, I jokingly (at least to her) asked if he was crazy enough to follow us. Laughing, Sarah said, "Honey, he can't follow us without a car, and he ain't even got money for the city bus. You're safe. We're safe. You got the check, right?"

Just as I'd hoped, Sarah was focused on one thing: the live check in my hand for $5,000. We went to her bank to get the documents signed. Knowing the tellers, Sarah used the bank's Xerox machine to make copies of her win letter and anything else she had scrounged up for me before I'd arrived. As we were signing the contract, she asked twice if she could go ahead and cash the check. I'd promised Ben that I'd call him first to get his verbal approval before actually giving her the check. The second time Sarah asked me for the check, I playfully slapped her hand away. She gave me a look that meant I'd gone too far. Scared I'd really blown it, I slid the check toward her.

"Why don't you go ahead and deposit this?"

"Yeah?"

"Yeah. We're good."

To this day, I'm not sure who between the two of us was more relieved. I'd just signed my first lottery deal. Sarah was able to pay down some markers and come good on a few promises. The second she got her hands on the $5,000, Sarah asked the teller if she could just cash it all. She asked softly, hoping that I wouldn't hear. The teller, looking at her account balance, denied Sarah's request. Instead, she gave her $200 cash and the rest had to wait until it cleared. Here was a multimillion-dollar lottery winner, too broke to be able to take more than $200 out of her own checking account.

We parted ways right there at the bank, as she said she wanted to do some shopping. She'd get a cab home when she was done. I offered to take her to lunch, to celebrate. She declined. I was thrilled. I wanted to get on the road and start making calls to the office. I was due some congratulations. I wanted it, needed it, right away. Any ideas I might have had to play it cool instantly went out the window. I couldn't wait until I got home to tell the office folks about my deal. I could barely get out of the parking lot. As fast as I could, I hopped back onto the highway, making my way out of town.

I pressed the gas and drifted into the hammer lane. I didn't care about a ticket. Eddie did good. Surging down the interstate, singing along to any song I knew, I felt something strange, something I hadn't recognized at first. I felt proud. It had been a while. I called my mom.

6

CAN YOU HEAR ME IN THE BACK?

"These are my principles. If you don't like them, I have others."
—GROUCHO MARX

I'M ONE OF FIVE siblings—smack in the middle. I grew up surrounded by characters, fighting for air time, desperate to tell my stories before one of them cut in to change the subject. *The nerve!* The dinner table is where I learned to talk, to sell, to use my sense of humor as a tool, a shield, a cannon, a threat, insurance. That was my sales training.

Selling is communication. Selling is an art form. Nobody sets out to become a salesman. Telemarketers alone keep everyone's shelves stocked with hatred for salespeople. A career in sales just kind of happens to people. It surely just happened to me. But I realized that sales could be a creative avenue, where I could make money by talking, by telling stories. Sales isn't just some creep interrupting dinner selling credit cards. It's that, too, but it's so much more. It's politics, entertainment, talking to your family. It's why we call fish eggs "caviar." Who wants to pay $80 an ounce for fish eggs? Sales is joking your way into a girl's bed; it's getting into school despite your SAT scores; it's talking your way out of getting the baby for the fifth morning in a row. Sales is the only word. We are all in sales, like it or not.

In one way or another, I'd been selling my whole life. The only difference was the product. When it was due time for me to find a way to make a living, I figured if I could sell, if I could control rooms and moods the way I already did, and people would pay me to do it, and I wouldn't have to work outside in the heat, well, okay. Call me a salesman. So are you. It's not that I hadn't worked or earned any money in my life. To the contrary; I'd had a job, one gig or another, since I was thirteen. I'd always worked. I liked working. I liked earning my own money.

Working with lottery winners came naturally to me. I always felt a kinship with winners. I'd like to think I actually understood them. I was able to get to their truth quicker than most. In finding that truth, I found the reason for us to meet and do business. There was so much psychology to the way I sold, so many paths to take a call, so many ways to blow it, so many ways to breathe life into it. I loved the strategy that went into setting up a deal, and I loved that each deal was different—each had its tone, its characters, its twists and cliffhangers. You got to play so many roles, so many scenes, at the most bizarre locations. I used to make little symbols and notes on winners' lead sheets, reminders of things they had said on the phone or the last time we met. When I showed up at their house, I'd be in character, whoever they needed me to be. Sales is method acting for underachievers.

Some winners wanted a no-nonsense, just-the-facts professional to walk them through the lump-sum process. Others couldn't get enough of the surprisingly young, charming kid that showed up at their door. Some would want to hear all about my interests, where I went to school, anything that gave them a sense of trust in me. I'd give them a hell of a show, too. They were paying for it.

After a while, I was able to profile lottery winners with remarkable accuracy. I'd knock on a winner's door and, within seconds of meeting him—sometimes just by my gut reaction to the way his house was maintained, the clothes he wore, the time of day he wanted to meet, his reaction to me—I'd know who he wanted me to be.

There were so many clues about people in their homes, clues that I learned to use—clues that closed deals, clues that told me more about the winners than they'd ever thought to share. People's homes are their castle, their refuge, their safe place. God knows mine is. No matter how private you are, how high the walls are that you've built around yourself, I'd bet the moon that your bedroom, your bathroom, and your fridge hold as many factoids about you as mine do about me. (And, whatever you do, don't look in my nightstand drawer.)

Think about the last time you picked up your kid from a friend's house after work. You've never laid eyes on the parents, much less their home. But in an instant, in your unconscious even, what could you tell about the people that resonated with you for one reason or another—all from standing in their foyer? What did they value? What hung on their walls? Were they part of a big family? Were they clean? Did they have pets? Were they dog people? Cat people? Was the furniture from this decade? This era? Was there plastic on the sofa? Were they TV watchers, readers, artists? How did the house smell? Were they making dinner, or was dinner delivered in a pizza box? Did there seem to be two parents, or was this a divorced household? Were the parents attractive, healthy, or obese? Were they talkative, interested, or did they just want you to take your kid and go so they could eat dinner? What kind of jobs did they have? What kind of education level did they need in order to have those jobs? How much disposable income did they seem to have?

The skill isn't seeing it; it's knowing how to use what you see. And there's no need to process what you see or learn from being inside your kid's friend's house. But on a lottery deal, in a winner's home, seeing the bedrooms, the bathrooms, the kitchen, was seeing him naked. You learned a lot, if you had the stomach to look. If you can't pick up clues as to who someone is once you're inside his house, you should resist the urge to go into sales.

As much as you try to be proactive, sales is often a reactionary endeavor. A bean counter—your average COO—would like to believe that in business you can predict and prepare for anything. It's just not so in lottery sales. You can try to hang a metric on every facet of the sales process just so you understand it, but wishing won't make it so. That's why sales appeals only to a certain breed of cat. Some have the stomach for its *you-never-know* biorhythms; many don't. A saleswoman is paid well to think on her feet, to take chances, to follow through on a hunch, to take risks. Salespeople, like gamblers, are betting on the results, on *what if*. Is it any wonder we had so many sales reps making a beeline to Atlantic City on an all-too-regular basis? But, unlike a casino, salespeople bet on *themselves*, not the turn of a card—something I've always found noble about the profession. If the salespeople close deals, they make money. If they don't produce results, they don't get paid. That side of it has symmetry to me. You say you can do something, you do it, and you get paid for having done it. It's clean. It makes sense. It's downright American—before that became a bad thing.

Lottery winners are likely to shock your expectations. Still, working with them for so long taught me to ring their doorbell, put a smile on my face, and not blink—no matter who opened the door or what happened next. Nothing holds a candle to the Russian roulette of knocking on a winner's door. Sometimes, things just get downright weird.

In all my years at The Firm, through the hundreds of winners I met, no meeting ever came close to the one I had in the summer of 1998. Things seemed standard enough going in. I'd been speaking with a winner who sounded to be in her early sixties. She had won the New Jersey Lottery almost twelve years before, so there wasn't much paper left to buy. She was older and knew that it was time to sell the remaining payments.

It was a "ham and egg" deal, nothing special—get in, get the deal signed, get it funded, get it paid. This time I had another salesman, David, with me. I may have been training him, but it was my show. His job was to watch and listen as I sold the deal. Pulling into the lottery winner's driveway, I gave David one last bit of instruction: "Talk less. Listen more. If they ask you a question, you don't speak English." Just as we knocked on the door, it creaked open. It seems Ms. Miller was expecting us.

She looked about sixty-five or so. She was the spitting image of Bette Davis on the back nine. Even the house screamed *Now, Voyager.* She had the bee-hive hair, the big glasses she'd been wearing since Nixon left office, and a cigarette hanging out of her mouth. If I chose one word to describe the place, it would be *yesterday.*

The living room was lit like Brando's study in *The Godfather.* It was both creepy and beautiful. The shades were partially drawn, with afternoon sunlight filtering through white lace patterns embroidered onto the curtains. The smoke from the woman's cigarette was sliced into dozens of sections by the rays of sunlight poking through the holes in the lace. The sunbeams seemed to dance as the wind outside blew leaves from a dogwood tree in and out of the sun's rays.

Ms. Miller took a final drag of her smoke, tapped it out into one of the many ashtrays within reach, and motioned toward the basement. "He's down there, at the piano. He's expecting you."

"Ummm . . . okay, right. Thanks." I thought she was a widow. *Who exactly was down there?* Why was he expecting us? What was he going to do with us? Was he alive? I didn't want to trot down there to find some stuffed husband puppet watching the news or an ash-filled urn "having lunch" next to a prayer candle and a chicken salad sandwich Ms. Miller had whipped up in the loony-bin kitchen upstairs. *Winning the lottery doesn't make you any less crazy than you were before you won.*

Years ago, I did a small deal with a nice old lady who had one particularly creepy habit. She would refer to her dead husband in the present tense. It's one thing if she does it to you at the grocery store; it's downright macabre when she's doing it in her living room. She talked about him the entire time I was there—"Nestor never cleans *this*," or "Nestor always brings me the wrong *that*." It really made me sad.

Fighting off the urge to push David down the stairs and hightail it out of there, I walked toward the staircase, pretending to know who I was going to see and why he was in the basement. I did, however, make sure David was right behind me, just in case.

The basement felt claustrophobic, as if fresh air was being pumped out to protect the musty conditions inside. The ceiling sat just inches above my head. It being a basement, there wasn't a lot of light in the first place. Stacks of books, *National Geographics*, and newspapers were piled everywhere, blocking what little light it had. An older man we desperately hoped was Mr. Miller sat eerily on a piano bench. A metronome clicked in time. Tic-tock-tick-tock-tick-tock. It was the perfect soundtrack to the scene unfolding before us. *(Music to be killed by.)*

This being New Jersey and not *Creep Show,* the man at the piano was indeed alive. He was not, however, totally well. Mr. Miller suffered from some sort of throat ailment. I didn't ask what it was but with the smoking scene upstairs, my money was on cancer. The thick scar that covered the length of his throat was indication enough that, cancer or not, the man had serious health issues. Mr. Miller used a voice box, the little device about the size of a mini-cassette recorder that allowed him to talk. (I feel the need to remind you that David and I are both nice guys and that, at the time, we were both smokers, so while we were absolutely terrified of him, we also felt terrible for his situation.)

I say this with all the respect and sympathy in the world—people who talk with a voice box make me incredibly uncomfortable. In the rare instances when I find myself face to face with a voice box, I get goose bumps. I never quite know how to treat the person nor my morbid fascination with the little hole he has in his throat—not to mention the bad robotic tone of the user's voice.

Mr. Miller was far and away the most comfortable person in that basement. To his credit, and to our great relief, he was as natural and friendly as he could have been. He seemed happy to have company. Using the voice box, Mr. Miller jumped right into his list of questions regarding selling their annuity. I've never been so mesmerized by the words "discount rate," "taxes," and "funding date." It was like a job interview with E.T. I kept waiting for his finger to light up. Once he'd rattled off his questions, things got distinctly more freakish.

Unsolicited, Mr. Miller decided to shed some light on the hole in his throat. Despite our morbid curiosity, David and I would just as happily have jumped past the story altogether and gotten back upstairs. Yes, he was a nice man, but we were not *that* nice, and time was ticking away from what we really wanted—to get back to the car and make nervous jokes about the entire scene for the remainder of the evening.

The voice box made Mr. Miller difficult to understand. As a result, David and I found ourselves awkwardly inching toward him, like nervous kids who'd been dared to pet a tarantula. In order to fully understand the details of his speaking troubles, we had to get over our fears and stand right on top of him just to decipher what he was saying.

"I can't talk at all without this machine."

"Right."

"I hate using it."

"Sure. But you use it quite well." (What else could I say?)

"I'll never be able to talk to my wife without this box shoved up against my throat."

"Some would say that's a good thing, Mr. Miller." (When I'm nervous, I joke, making me a loaded gun at funerals.)

Out of nowhere, I then witnessed the most baffling thing I've ever seen. Mr. Miller put down the voice box, started banging the keys on the piano, and then . . . he sang—beautifully. Yes, he *sang* . . . in a deep, booming, perfect baritone voice.

"BUT, I CAN STILL SING LIKE I ALWAYS DID! I CAN-NOT TALK, BUT I CAN STILL SING! DO YOU HEAR MY VOICE!? WHEN I SING, MY VOCAL CORDS WORK JUST FINE!" He delivered this message to the tune of "Oklahoma!" "*AND YOU KNOW WE BELONG TO THE LAND, AND THE LAND WE BELONG TO IS GRAND!*"

Stunned silence. There are no words.

We'd have been less surprised if he pulled out his own liver and started eating it. And how, may I ask, is one supposed to respond to that? I had nothing. I looked at David for help. He looked panicked. He was worthless.

Thankfully, Mr. Miller just kept on singing. Once the cat was out of the bag, there was no stopping him. We didn't need to respond, just clap along and smile. Things might not have been so bizarre if he'd sung only a verse or two. No such luck. Mr. Miller wasn't interested in show tunes, nor the Golden Oldies; the only way for him to communicate with his own voice was to sing—loudly.

The rest of the meeting felt like a scene from *The Cuckoo's Nest: The Musical*. Mr. Miller sang about relatives wanting their lottery money and which competitors he'd spoken to in the past. David and I stood suspiciously close to one another, slowly inching our way toward the stairs. We were desperate to make our way to the notary, anything but stay in the basement for one more minute.

"WOULD YOU BOYS LIKE A CUP OF JOE, BEFORE WE GO!?" The rhyme was no accident. He was showing off.

Us, in unison, the chorus, if you will: "NO!"

"*WHEN* WILL WE GET THE *MONEY*!?" The piano

keys emphasizing the first and last words, like an opera gone wrong.

"Should be about two months."

"DID YOU BRING THE ADVANCE CHECK!?"

"Yes sir. It's in with the contracts."

"SOUNDS GOOD!"

7

SALLY STONE

I GET A PIT in my stomach every time I think of Sally Stone.

I'd been selling at The Firm for just over six months. Well past my ninety-day probationary period, I was finally keeping my commissions rather than kicking them up to Ben. In my first three months, I'd made Ben close to $30,000 in commissions. It's not as if I really needed it or anything. If I'd gotten the $30,000, I'd have gone ahead and spent it on things like my own place, paying off my credit card debt, silly stuff like that. Knowing that the money went to a better home where it could be pissed away on twenty-five-year-old Scotch and Rolex watches made me feel better.

Over the past three months, I'd developed a nice pipeline of deals. The Firm was beginning to feel like home. Money had started trickling in, a few grand here or there, but to date there had been no major payday.

One evening, the lead of a lifetime landed in my lap. When it was all said and done, that piece of paper changed my life, for good, for bad, and forever. Everyone in The Firm would have killed to get their hands on this lead. But, as the saying goes, nothing's free in this world. For all the money I made, for all the attention it brought me in the office, for all the freedom that this commission allowed me—if I could do it all again, I'd have whispered one thing into the phone when Sally first called that February day so many years ago: "Hang up, and never call here again."

Whenever someone felt like reliving the good old days in the lump-sum business, they'd talk about the Sally Stone deal. People would make bad jokes about all of her deals in order to relate to me—or as a sign of respect when I was running sales for the company. Ethan would bring her up as if fondly remembering a bear he shot long ago. Of course Ethan loved to remember her deal. He'd never met her. He just got paid when it was all said and done.

The final deal we did with Sally was one of the biggest the industry had ever produced. I got out of debt. I was the toast of the office. It made me a lock for a promotion. I moved into a rented penthouse condo. I bought a new 4Runner. I had a savings account. I made investments. I furnished my new place in a day, spending $20,000 on fancy end tables and sofas at Crate and Barrel. I had a fish tank full of exotic specimens (all of which I killed on an ill-timed trip to Manhattan).

Years ago, when I was in my early teens, my grandfather gave me a framed picture with a line on it that reads, "*A good life has a number of days, but a good name continues forever.*" I made the mistake of hanging that quote up in my bathroom, on the wall behind the toilet. Ever since Sally Stone came into my life (and we're talking about the better part of a decade), I can't take a piss without thinking of her. I wish things had been different. You could say that she should have known better, caveat emptor and all that jazz. You'd be right. You'd be a heartless, cut-throat bastard, but you'd be right. And you'd be perfect for sales.

A lot of the commission money went to the casinos. I wasted the money she'd lost to me. Ugly, dumb circle. The day the big deal funded, I went to Atlantic City with the usual gang from work. Ironically, that was the day I decided to open a line of credit at Caesar's. The guy in charge of the credit department gave me the eye when I asked for a $5,000 line. He looked at me as if I'd just gotten off a shift at the fish market. I imagine there weren't a lot of guys in their mid-twenties able to set up that kind of line, or dumb enough to want one. Luckily for Caesar's, I happened to be both. The credit guy made a big deal about pulling up my bank records right there in the casino to verify the balance. Obviously, he thought I'd be ineligible for the line once he opened my account. When he went in and looked at the balance, there was a mountain of cash available. Honestly, I was as impressed as he was. All of a sudden I was "*Mr. U.*" At least the casinos don't pretend to be anything other than what they are. I respect that about them. You've got no money for us to grind out of you? Piss off. You've got money, or at least access to cash on your credit cards, never mind the 23 percent interest rate? Well . . . hello, "*Mr. U.*" Care for a cocktail?

I've still got the line of credit at Caesar's. These days it's got some dust on it, but it's there. Over the years, it's cost me thousands. Every time I lose, which is more or less every time I go to Caesar's, I think of the line and how I got it. Sometimes I wonder if the losses aren't a reparation of sorts, the universe keeping and settling scores. If so, I can see how that's fair. I accept it. It's the right thing.

Ben gave me the lead in the first place. He could have given the call-in to anyone, but I'd earned it. I'd made him a bunch of cash. He'd seen what I was doing on the phone and on the road. Ben always had a freakish nose for a deal. He knew well before I did not what the lead was, but what it could become. When he handed it to me, late one evening in February 1998, all he said was, "Get on a plane to Dallas. Thank me later."

By now, Ben and I had become friends. I'd logged enough hours on various bar stools around town with the guy to curry some favor on a hot lead. It's not that I was using him; we were just convenient friends for each other at a time in our lives when we both needed a sure thing. Sometimes, you just need someone to keep you company while you figure yourself out.

With the two of us working a deal, it was like 1 plus 1 equals 6. Also, my sales skill allowed Ben to focus his energy on strategic growth, marketing, and other business development issues while I kept the sales numbers surging. Ben was a brilliant marketer. He could *always* make the phones ring. It was uncanny.

Ethan made Ben vice president of sales, and then chief operating officer, giving Ben the power to match his skills, and the title to throw around for good measure. Ben had a choke hold on the company. Ethan loved it. Ethan finally had someone to run the business. Soon enough, Ben signed off on all personnel moves, as well as major strategic decisions. Ethan owned the place, but it was Ben's company.

Ben had the power; I had the people. Almost everybody in the growing company liked and respected me. Each deal I signed, each joke I told, each time I helped someone close a deal, my stature in the place grew. For a while there, I was the new *it* kid around the office. The sales assistants and research group practically did the wave when I came into work. While the fan club did a lot for my ego, Ben wasn't exactly helping out with their newsletter. Still, I was never a threat to Ben, and Ben never felt threatened by me. In fact, he loved me. He really did. He grew to rely on me, as well he should have. He did, however, resent the fact that everyone liked me.

Ethan was happy to see Ben take over the day-to-day operations. Ben was equally happy to have me win over the masses, his masses. If I could run the floor, all Ben had to do was run me. All Ethan needed to do was manage Ben, while Ben managed me. Just like in a casino, everyone kept an eye on the people around them.

Who was I watching? I was watching Ben—watching what he did right, what he did wrong, studying him, learning from him, stealing his best stuff. I watched Ben the salesman and I watched Ben the manager. I watched him handle all kinds of pressure. I watched him on the phone with winners. I listened to the way he quietly led the conversation, the way he used humor as a tool, the way he could tell what people were thinking, what they wanted, what they needed to hear.

I watched Ben run sales meetings. The guy could carry a room. He'd blow through those doors like Sinatra after a set at The Sands. I half expected the new guys to ask for his autograph. Running a good sales meeting is like doing live comedy. You're up there doing your thing, riffing, getting a few good lines in, and all the crowd sees is a pro in action. But, like watching a duck swimming on a lake, they don't see the poor bastard furiously paddling away beneath the surface. When you're running a sales meeting, you've got six things in your head, trying desperately to keep the audience on your side, entertained, impressed. Inherently, you're going to say something stupid. The odds are stacked against you. I'd watch Ben mess up in a meeting and look at the sales group like Carson when the *Tonight Show* audience didn't laugh at one of his jokes. Ben could take a punch.

I'd watch him price transactions with imagination, with guts, with an outright ardor for cutting deals. He sometimes had horns coming out of his head. He sometimes had that sparkle in his eye—one part madman, one part genius, one part little kid playing with an adult chemistry set, mixing and experimenting without fear. That was always his thing, right or wrong—never any fear. That stunned me. That inspired me. That scared me.

At times, Ben was twenty feet tall.

Sally had called in that morning after seeing our commercial on TV. The notes said she was looking for $200,000. I was happy to have the lead. Still, I didn't understand why Ben had made such a fuss over a winner who was only looking for a few hundred grand. Two hundred thousand was small potatoes in the lump-sum game, especially back then. How big a fee could we really put into the deal? By my math, I'd be lucky to tack on $50,000, making my commission somewhere in the neighborhood of two or three thousand. God knows I had plenty of places to put the money, but I needed a bigger hit.

I stopped into Ben's office to tell him that the lead was smaller than he'd thought. He listened to me while I tried to sound like I knew what I was talking about. Finally, he cut me off.

"Do you know what you have in your hands?"

"A mini-commission. A nosh?" I said. Ben wasn't in the mood. I doubt he knew what a nosh was.

"You've got a monster. She thinks she wants $200,000. Your job is to convince her otherwise. Does she want the money gross or net?"

"I think net."

"You *think?* Then she needs a lot more than $200,000. Right?"

"Right," I said, hating the lecture I'd walked into. I hated more so that he was correct and that I hadn't even thought to go through the basic sales process that I'd been taught *by him* in training. I was, perhaps, listening to that "rising star" crap a little more than I should. There were still glaring differences in our skills, more than I wanted to admit. Ben was my boss for a reason. I'd been telling myself that he and I were basically equals. Not so. He was better at this than I was. Much better.

He saw things I still did not see. He knew how to move a deal just by asking one perfect question. *One question;* I saw it dozens of times. He knew that a lottery winner will often do what you tell her to do, regardless of what she thinks she wants. He knew that what the winner wanted was often at odds with The Firm's interests. It was our job to find a middle ground. To do what he did, I had to see what he saw. Until then, I was to follow his lead.

"Does she have any other debts to pay? A mortgage? Credit cards?"

"I didn't ask."

"What's she using the money for?"

"I don't know."

"How soon does she need the cash?"

"I don't know."

"What *do* you know?"

"I know I feel like a schmuck right now."

"Good. You *are* a schmuck. Now what?"

"Call her back and start over?"

"Bingo. One last thing. Who's your daddy?"

"Apparently, you are."

"Come back when you can sell like me."

I bowed out of his office.

"You've got five minutes to turn her around. If not, I'm on it," he said. He wasn't kidding.

I walked back to my grade-school-sized desk, leaving Ben alone in his sunny, well-furnished office. He was being a prick, but a prick with a point. The worst kind. I hated that he was right. I hated that he was better than I was at this. I muttered something under my breath about his height, making sure no one heard, especially him.

Sally answered the phone just as it rang, like someone waiting for news regarding a sick loved one. Before I could say boo, she asked, "Can you get me the money I want?"

"Sally, I can get you any money," I assured her. "But the question isn't what you want. The question is, what do you *need*?"

"I told you what I need. I *need* $200,000!" She wasn't loving me yet.

"You didn't tell me if you were looking for $200,000 net or gross. It makes a big difference," I added authoritatively. "The pricing manager asked me, and I didn't know what to tell him."

"What does net or gross mean?" she asked suspiciously.

This is why Ben is a genius. Her suspicions aside, I was about to move this spread up. If not for Ben, I'd be pitching her pricing on a $200,000 lump. In my mind, I took back the comment about his height.

"Gross means *before* taxes. Net means *after* taxes."

"Taxes!? You didn't say nothing about paying taxes."

Panic. (Me, not her.)

"Sally, do you really think Uncle Sam is going to let me give you $200,000 without taking his piece? Honestly, have you met this guy?"

If Jesus worked for the IRS, would people still love him? It's hard to make paying taxes seem like a good thing, no matter who you are. I found the best way to handle the entire tax issue was to simply acknowledge the truth. Taxes stink. *Yes.* Uncle Sam is a no-good meanie. *Yes . . . a very bad guy—very bad.* Better to blame him than me. Plus, if a winner really wants the money, if she's committed to a deal, she'll find a way to get over the tax hit that comes with a lump sum. What choice does she have?

Sally hummed, "Mmhh huh," like a woman responding to a preacher during his Sunday sermon. I'd hit the right nerve. I all but got an "Amen!" People love being right about their feelings toward the tax man. Validating that frustration only helped me close deals. What was I going to do anyway, take sides with the IRS? And, when a winner called out of need or conviction, not just to claim a $100 U.S. Savings Bond or whatever incentive we were pitching that week, when she was hurting—without you even twisting the knife a little yourself—that was when you could tell her what to want, what to need, what to do.

"So, how much do I give up to taxes?" Sally asked, seeing I was on her side, commiserating with the question, not to mention the answer.

You just knew she dreaded the answer, which was okay because I wasn't about to give her one. I'd answer a million other questions. I'd ask her questions until she hung up on me. But there was no way I'd sit there and tell a winner how many tens of thousands of dollars, or hundreds of thousands—even millions—she'd have to pay the IRS. I didn't know. I didn't want to know. That was between Sally and her accountant.

"Sally, I'm not an accountant. I can barely count to ten."

"But the taxes are . . ."

"The taxes are what they are."

"Then YOU pay 'em."

Touché.

If winners wanted to know the tax implications of their deal, they'd have to find out on their own. They'd have to make calls, find documents and receipts, set up appointments, and face people who would have to look into the winner's spending habits.

Often, winners would pull in the right people—accountants, attorneys, financial planners. (*Can you say plummeting spreads?*) But just as often, they would convince themselves that paying a bunch of expensive white-collar advisors was unnecessary. When winners really needed money, they found a way to get themselves over the tax hit, with or without advisors. Most times, you'd just sit there and watch it happen. Winners talk themselves into more deals than any sales rep ever could. Sometimes, the smartest thing to say is nothing. If the winner is convincing herself that selling her annuity is the right thing, pretend there is a big grizzly bear in the room. Stand very still, and shut up.

I had no idea what Sally's tax hit would be. And, if I didn't know what her tax hit would be, she sure as hell didn't know. It didn't matter. I knew Sally wasn't going to slow this money train down in order to get a bunch of bankers involved.

"You mean to tell me that you've got no idea what I'll owe?"

"That's exactly what I'm telling you. I imagine you're up there when it comes to paying Uncle Sam, but I just don't know."

In sales, you try to beat bad news home. If you know there's a problem with a deal, and you *know* the winner will become aware of it, you do your best to tell her before she tells you. If nothing else, you get points for candor—more than you'd think. There's power in being able to point to some issue delaying a winner's deal from funding and being able to say, "Hey, I pointed that out to you in the first place." It isn't much, but sometimes when a deal turns sideways, *not much* is all you need. To a skilled salesman, *not much* is like giving MacGyver a pack of matches and some duct tape.

I don't care what you sell. If you sell for a living (and by the way, you *do* sell for a living, you just may not know it or like to look at it that way), always, *always* call a client when you have bad news, *before the client calls you.* That's the hardest sales call to make. Sometimes, a winner has to wait for her money a lot longer than she had been promised. When bad news comes again and again, that's when the phone feels like it weighs eighty pounds. Calling winners with bad news about their deal is akin to being asked to kick yourself in the groin.

What's worse than making a tough call to a frustrated winner who lost faith in you weeks, even months, ago? Not calling at all. I've made the mistake of avoiding hard calls to people for whom I had only bad news. Invariably, when you're avoiding a winner, the winner finds you. You answer your phone without looking at the caller-ID and there you are, on the line with her anyway. When you say, "Listen, I was about to call you. I've got bad news," she's ready to skin you. It's ten times worse.

"You're worried about the wrong thing with the whole tax issue, anyway," I baited Sally.

"Why?"

I dropped my voice to a whisper, implying that she was hearing things I wasn't supposed to share. "Do you even realize you'll end up paying more in taxes over time than you would if you sold your whole prize for a lump sum?"

"Why?"

I explained that winners paid more in taxes over time than if they'd paid all their taxes at once during a lump-sum transaction. (You take the number of payments the winner has left and multiply that by the amount of taxes she pays each year. If the winner pays $100,000 in taxes every year and has twelve years left, you calculate that she would be paying $1,200,000 in taxes over the next twelve years. Then, you compare that with whatever the winner predicts her tax percentage would be on the lump sum—let's say, 50 percent. If the winner was going to get $2,000,000 from The Firm in a lump sum, you'd multiply the $2,000,000 by the suggested tax rate. In this example, $2,000,000 x .50 equals $1,000,000.)

Using the above example, you'd amplify the fact that the winner would have to pay less in taxes from a lump sum ($1,000,000) versus the long-term annuity ($1,200,000). You'd explain that she would pay $200,000 less in taxes by lumping out to The Firm. Was it true? Yes, but for the fact that you'd neglected to mention that the lump sum is discounted, so the $1,000,000 she is paying is coming off a smaller amount of money than if she waited for the cash to come in over the lifetime of her annuity. Was it incorrect? No. Was it a lie? No. The flat math was *correct,* but only in a vacuum. Once you add in all the facts—the time value of money, what a discount rate means to the winner's lump sum amount, and on and on—that math isn't all that it's cracked up to be.

Then, like clockwork, Sally asked the question I'd hoped to hear. "Maybe I should get more money from you, you know—so *I* save in taxes?" If this were a movie, this is the point where I'd look into the camera and wink. Could it be so easy? Was Ben's advice so good that I just nailed the pitch? Who cares. She was suddenly open to getting more money.

"We can do that. But let's slow down. Let's get you the *right* amount of money, not just the *most* money you can get. That's not the way to do this. Let's do what's best for you, not what's best for my investors."

"Edward. Let me get some *more* money." She meant it. She said it as if it dawned on her that doing otherwise would be downright irresponsible. Suddenly, I was the one telling *her* not to get more money and she was telling *me* to be more aggressive. Selling—I was born to do this.

"Let's go one step at a time. You can do another deal once this first one is over—if you're happy with the first deal."

Sally wasn't listening. She'd already decided. "How much do *you* think I should get?" She was asking *me* to tell her? Talk about hiring the fox to guard the hen house.

"I'd get at least enough to pay taxes and still be sitting on plenty of money. But I wouldn't go overboard."

If I'd tried to buy her entire prize right there, or gone for a much larger partial purchase, I could have missed my shot at writing any deal. With luck, over time, she'd get the itch to go ahead and sell the entire prize to us. In the meantime, I was just as happy doing a few smaller deals with her. If I could be patient, and if I could keep Ben and Ethan patient, this might be one for the ages.

Twelve hours later, the wheels of my plane touched down at Dallas–Fort Worth Airport. I was nervous. Had I known what would transpire between Sally and me over the next year or so— that I'd eventually do several deals with her, that the last deal would be, to my knowledge, the single biggest in the history of the lump-sum industry—I could have been a lot more relaxed on the plane. Instead, I was a mess.

Getting my ass handed to me by Ben had really taken the wind out of me. I was embarrassed, and deservedly so. As the plane crept to the gate, I was still thinking about the dressing-down I'd gotten in his office. Based on how I'd started this deal, I wanted to close it quick and easy—drama free. The best way for me to get Ben to forget my weak phone call was to bring home a signed deal. Feed the angry man.

At the time, I'd never traveled on a deal and not signed it. I thought that was a pretty remarkable statistic until I bragged about it to Ben. He cleared that up for me rather succinctly. He said that closing a call-in from a cash-strapped winner was akin to a kid successfully filling a small order of fries at McDonald's. Big deal. What turned a salesperson into a closer? Being able to take that same customer and convince her that she didn't want just fries; she was much too hungry for that. In fact, she had no idea just how hungry she was. When you got done with her, she would need two trays to carry all the food she'd bought. If you did it right, she'd even thank you for saving her from starving to death. That's a closer, and they're worth their weight in gold. Still, I wasn't looking for this deal to "finally" be the one I didn't close. Mixed messages aside, I wanted to close this one—bad.

While the flight attendant was reminding us not to unbuckle our seatbelts, I started my pre-deal ritual, which always calmed me down and pumped me up. It got my blood flowing and my nerves soothed, or at least in check. Before every meeting, just prior to show time, I'd repeat the same line to myself, over and over again.

"I *am* King Kong."

"I am *King* Kong."

"I am King *Kong*."

"I am King Kong."

Why King Kong? No idea. I'm not even a fan. Honestly, I've never seen any of the movies.

It took forever for the rows ahead of mine to deplane. Additionally, the captain had turned off the air, so it was hot as hell as I waited to get out. By the time it was my turn, the high from the King Kong pump-up session had come and gone. I was me again. But, like it or not, it was show time. Sally was supposed to be waiting for me at the airport. Whoever I was, King Kong or Elmer Fudd, it was time to go. So, with little choice in the matter, there I went—a neurotic, anxious, Jewish King Kong walking off the plane. Where's Fay Wray when you need her?

Sally and her fiancé, Evan, had gone to great lengths to make the deal easy on me. They were not only going to meet me at the airport, they were waiting at the gate. Moreover, Sally had located a notary in the airport. It was perfect. So perfect that I thought it was too good to be true. Everything was set up too well; it was too easy. I was sure that something would go wrong. King Kong did his best to keep Elmer Fudd quiet. I could do this. I *had* to do it. It was all set. I was King *fucking* KONG, man!

Sally, a big, beautiful black woman, was there as promised. She threw her arms around me, like an old friend. This massive teddy bear, wrapping her plump arms around me, smelled of Texas heat and deodorant. She was nervous. She could hardly see my gorilla suite.

"Hi, Edward," she said, friendly as hell, squeezing the juices out of me. She was holding on for dear life. What the hell was this? Was she actually this nice? Oh God, don't tell me she's this nice a person. I don't want her to be *too* nice. It's best when you can keep winners an anonymous, faceless mass, sitting on top of a big pile of found money, there for the taking, guilt free.

Deal One

She was mine from the start.

The first deal was easy. I didn't even have to leave the airport. As promised, Sally had found a notary in the main concourse. She and Evan had brought all of their documents—their win letter, W2-G, they had even made copies of her driver's license. In hindsight, it makes complete sense. While I was on the plane convincing myself that I was a big, tough monkey, they were driving to the airport, doing everything they could think of to make sure that *I* didn't pull out of the deal on *them*.

That's the irony of this business. For weeks at a time, you get nothing but angry, disinterested winners, avoiding your calls and blowing you off. Then, out of nowhere, you find a winner in need and suddenly she's more into the deal than *you*. The trick was to see it and recognize it for what it was—before you thought yourself right out of an easy deal. If you've been getting turned down left and right, it's hard to realize when someone is actually interested. Even "yes" sounds a lot like "no." Sometimes in sales, you can't get out of your own way. During a bad stretch on the phones, it was hard to turn on the "I've got the money and you don't" persona. But that's exactly what I had on my hands—a winner who needed me even more than I thought I needed her.

All the worry, all the nerves I had during the flight, and all the confidence that Ben had sucked out of me in his office the day before was much ado about nothing. This deal could have been done through the mail. It would have gotten signed had I sent it via carrier pigeon.

What I'd have missed by not coming down on my own was the chance to build some rapport, some trust, to establish a face to go along with my name, to give some personality to The Firm. After all, this was a big winner. She was selling us only a tiny slice of her annuity. There was a lot more to buy—a *lot* more. While this was a nice deal, the potential add-on deals could be massive. And the key to doing more than one deal with a winner, a *partial*, is to knock the trust issue right out of the equation. If the person likes you and trusts you, there's less reason for her to shop around when it's time to do the *next* deal. And, as you know by now, at some point, it *will* be time to do another deal. You can all but set your watch to it.

Sometimes, we'd do a skinny deal with a big winner, making only a small fee. Regardless of the size of the first deal, having it in the books was key. Odds were, when the winner needed money again, they'd call us rather than a competitor. When they did, follow up deals were a lot easier than the first ones. Once you signed a partial deal with a winner, you'd be wise to stay in excellent contact. Our best salespeople talked to their partial winners more than they did their own families.

If we did it well, and got a little lucky, the winner wouldn't shop the next deal and wouldn't call in private advisors. He'd look at The Firm as his own ATM. We could get him cash in a matter of hours. And we could often do so without any of his extended family and friends knowing, protecting the winner from the shame of admitting to anyone except us his dirty little secret, that he was in need of a little walking-around money, strapped, or just plain broke.

The people in the winners' lives, who saw them only as lucky, blessed millionaires, would never believe, much less understand, how they could *possibly* need money from a company like The Firm. But we understood. We didn't judge, at least not in front of them. And we could help—quickly and quietly. The quieter the better, for both sides. That's all they knew about us, that we came through in a pinch. And when we did it right, that's all they needed to know. When you have no competition bidding against you, when you have no issues of trust to get past, when the winner believes what you are saying is fact, this business can be quite lucrative.

Signing deal one was a breeze. We were together for less than an hour, but it was some hour. Sally and Evan treated me like I was a loan officer, as if they had to earn my approval, *my blessing*, to get the deal done. We walked from my gate to a private row of bucket seats near the main shopping area in the terminal. They laid out their documents as if to make a case for approving their deal. I remember Sally's hand shaking from nerves. Always one for drama, I took Sally's hand in mine, patted it as if she were my anxious child, and said, "We'll make this work. You need to relax, and trust me. I'm here and I'm not leaving until we get you set. Okay?"

"Okay. I'm sorry, Edward. I just want everything to work. It's all gonna be okay?"

"If not, I'm moving in with you till it is."

"Be my guest." She was talking to me but looking right through her fiancé. Whatever she was saying was meant for him as much as me. "Soon as *everybody else* gets out."

Interesting. Do tell! Who was "everybody else"?

"Who's there? Family?" I asked innocently.

"Uh huh." She shook her head at Evan.

"Let me guess, they've been there since you won?"

"Half of them are *his*." She pointed at Evan, as if identifying him in court. He didn't fight the accusation. He simply nodded along in agreement.

"I'll tell you what. With all respect to your family, they aren't leaving until you sell your prize. Why would they? Hell, if I was your kin, I'd move in, too." (*Kin* . . . I couldn't help myself.)

"You'd be more welcome than they are."

I quickly followed, knowing just where we were going. "So, why let them stay?" (Talk about your leading questions. What was she supposed to say?)

"I keep telling Evan!"

Evan knew enough to sit there and keep quiet. Still, I thought it was time to throw him a bone, knowing that he'd be a strong ally for me in the future.

"It's not *just* Evan. It's both of you. I see this all the time. Your families are locked in on that lottery money. They aren't going anywhere. I wouldn't either."

Whether they knew it yet, we were already talking about a second deal, even though we hadn't yet signed the first one. "I'll tell you what. Let's do this. Let's get the paperwork done on *this* deal and I'll go back to the office and talk to my boss about what's going on at your house. Maybe we can solve this whole problem."

"How?"

"Make the money go away and the family goes, too." I felt like Professor Hill from *The Music Man,* blaming the world's problems on a pool table. "What happens when a party runs out of beer? The party dies. What you folks need to do is run out of beer—fast—because they aren't leaving till the keg's dry."

"How much money would I get if I did it that way?"

"Which way?" (It was too easy, feigning ignorance, but I couldn't help it. I wanted to hear her say the words, so I knew I wasn't just making it up in my head.)

"Selling everything."

"A FULL BUYOUT?" (*Well, we got trouble, right here in River City, with a capital T and that rhymes with P and that stands for POOL!*)

I acted as surprised as I could. "I have no idea, but I can find out tomorrow when I get back to the office." Then, a little soft-shoe. "You think about it, and if you want me to run some numbers, you let me know. I won't do anything until I hear back from you."

And three, two, one ... "No, Edward, go ahead and find out."

What the hell just happened? Did we just move into a full-buyout discussion right here in the DFW airport? Didn't I at least have to rent a car or stay in a crappy hotel for a few days? Didn't I have to earn it in some way? Was this thing just going to land in my lap?

"You know what's really good, Sally? If we *did* do a full buyout, the investor would likely give you a better rate since you'd already be a customer. They'd know who you are, and the deal would probably fund pretty fast."

"So, it won't hurt us to do this deal here?"

Oh, shit. I'd gone too far.

"NO! It helps," I gulped.

I decided to quit while I was ahead. I'd planted the seed. Anything more was overkill. "Let's go ahead and fund this *first* deal and we'll worry about getting everyone out of your house after that, okay?"

It was okay.

I took the copies of Sally's social security card, her congratulatory award letter from the lottery, her W2-G, even the last monthly statement from her bank. I acted very official and interested in each and every document, as if I might find something that would kill the deal. She could have handed me her dirty socks and we'd have still had a deal. I examined her award letter, pretending to verify its authenticity by carefully reading the winning numbers. The two of them sat there, staring at me like a couple nervously waiting while the adoption agency reviews their file. They figured that I needed to approve the documents. Shocking as it may seem . . . the documents checked out.

When I have a winner sign her documents, I do my best to make it seem like it's no big deal—as if signing the documents is the natural conclusion to a well-thought-out decision, made by the winner. You don't want a drum roll when you pull out your pen. The last thing you want to do is make signing the docs seem any more torturous or mysterious than necessary. These are financial documents that determine the allocation of millions of dollars. There are legal complexities and security measures piled on top of one another, paragraph after paragraph, page after page. To the layman, the docs read like a maze of traps, caveats, and loopholes. I can't imagine why. . .

Winners can read every single word, line by line, before they sign anything. Moreover, they can, and often do, have their own counsel read the docs, too. Actually inking the deal is a delicate balance between doing right by the winner and keeping her from losing her nerve once she sees thirty pages of legal Sanskrit—most of which I don't fully comprehend, much less your average winner.

From day one, I'd dealt with the issue of signing documents the same way. Knowing my own ignorance regarding the legal nuances of the contracts, the last thing I wanted to do was to sit there and glad-hand a winner about some legal term when the stakes were this high. Not to mention, it wasn't kosher for me, or any salesman, to put on a legal hat anyway. To avoid the issue all together, I'd open the contracts to the Terms Rider page. The

Terms Rider is the "brains" of the contracts. In other words, if the Terms Rider page is correct, everything else in the contract should be correct, too.

The Terms Rider spells out the black-and-white data of a deal. It lists the winner's full name, social security number, address, win amount, win date, win state, and annual payment date; the total number of payments the lottery winner is due to receive; the number of payments the winner has remaining; the number of payments being sold; the amount of each payment being sold, and the lump-sum amount the winner will receive from us.

Certain states require that the Terms Rider page include the discount rate, something we would obviously prefer not to have to provide. It's a lot harder to cut a deal buying a winner's payments at *any* discount rate when it states the number right there on the Terms Rider page. Very few people understand what discount rates actually represent. Even deals that have extremely favorable terms for the winner are misunderstood by winners who view *any* discount rate as something to fear or distrust. Even a schnook's eye tends to be drawn to that number. Still, believe it or not, a lot of winners never even ask what the rate on their deal is. Some don't know to ask. Others don't want to know.

Sally sat, pen in hand, while I pulled the docs out of my briefcase. She was proving to be an easy close, but the contracts have a way of knocking the smile off a lot of winners' faces. Things get very real, very fast. So despite her excitement, I was cautious.

Pulling contracts out at the right time is an art form in and of itself. Do it too early and you can come off as presumptuous; do it too late and you may have missed your window of opportunity. Pulling out a contract too early is like showing up on a date wearing a condom. Even if the date is a sure thing, you still look like a moron. So you slow it down. Let the winner think it's her idea to open the docs. Sell it a little. The drool sliding down Sally's cheek was sign enough. It was time for the docs.

I opened the contracts to the Terms Rider page and started my canned spiel. By now, I'd done my signing monologue so many times, I felt like Laurence Olivier getting ready for his 576th performance of *Richard III*—very businesslike, very focused, very natural.

"Sally, we can go over this contract line by line. That's why I'm here. I'm in no hurry. I can answer any questions you have. Plus, if you want, you can hold onto the docs and take them to your attorney to review. If there are any issues, we can deal with them and then sign the docs sometime next week, when I can clear my schedule to come back down." I paused to take a sip of water from the bottle I'd taken off the plane. I took a slow, calculated swig of the water, giving Sally enough time to do the math on her own. "This is the 'Terms Rider' page. It's the brains of the contract. If everything on this page is correct, then the deal is correct. Everything else is basically boilerplate legal stuff. Normally, I verify that all the data on the Terms Rider page is accurate and if so, we go over the rest—if you want to. Some people do, some don't. It's your call."

"I don't need to go over it all," she said the second my lips stopped moving. "There's nothing in there you wouldn't have your mom sign?" she added.

Jesus. *That* came out of nowhere. Why'd she have to bring my mom into this? Talk about your low blows. Bringing up my mother in the middle of a lottery deal was just one step above talking about her during sex. This was no place for my mother. This was no place for *anyone's* mother.

I could sit here and say that I wrestled with the question, that I ruminated it, debating the pros and cons of dragging my mom into the inelegant world of lottery deals. But that would just be me trying to look like a better person than I really am. If necessary, I'd have flown my mom to Dallas so she could personally endorse the contract. "I wouldn't treat you any differently than my mom. I always tell my mother that she should take a lump sum if she ever wins the lottery." That *was* true. There's no question that a lump-sum payment is the way to get your lottery prize. Still, I wouldn't let my mom in the same room as me, much less anyone from The Firm, if she'd won the lottery. I'd make sure that she got a lump sum, but I'd steer her clear of the likes of The Firm altogether.

Once I put Sally and my mom on the same pedestal, she was good to go. I think she'd have signed the docs either way. She had one or two cursory questions as she signed here, here, and here. I sensed that she was asking questions just to look interested. I can relate.

There are a handful of pages in the contract that need to be signed in front of a notary, another major headache. Why? Because you're bringing a third party into the mix, at the most pivotal point in the deal. Whatever the scene, whatever the mood or the connection between the winner and yourself at the time, whether rock solid or as awkward as a first date, the notary can turn your deal upside down.

The notary enters the scene at the last minute when you are mere moments from saying good-bye, getting into your rental car, lighting up the smoke that you've wanted for hours, and throwing this deal on the growing pile you're accumulating back in the office. If I had my druthers, all notaries would be mutes. Remember, lottery winners have some notoriety. Often, especially in a small town, they are well known, almost celebrities. So when the local big-shot winner comes into the bank, or the Kinko's, or wherever the notary is, with a contract that says *lottery* all over it, it's bound to catch a few eyes.

"Lottery" is just one of those words. It has its own power, like "Elvis" or "nude." People have to take a second look. People, especially notaries, can't seem to help themselves. Add to the mix that most winners are private people, and desperate to remain so, and you can see how a simple trip to the notary can turn into an adventure. Thankfully, the airport notary, tucked behind bulletproof glass, was more interested in her tuna sandwich than our documents. I could have been notarizing a deal with The Unabomber as long as his signature matched the one on his driver's license. The notary did her thing—stamped, sealed, and signed each page along with Sally. It was over in five minutes.

And that was that. Deal one was signed. I hadn't even breathed in any fresh Texas air, for God's sake. All in all, it was a good day.

Dying to get some time to myself, I told Sally and Evan that there was an early flight back home that left in an hour. I wanted to celebrate. I wanted to call Ben. I wanted a cigarette. And, even though I'm not a big drinker, especially at 3:45 P.M., a cold beer seemed appropriate for the occasion. But I couldn't do any of these things without first making a quick but inconspicuous departure from Sally and Evan. After all the hard work, it would be a disaster for me to leave the two of them with a bad taste in their mouth because I made a beeline for the door the second I got the docs signed.

They bought the early-flight story. We *were* in the airport, after all. We wished each other well, gave the second round of hugs for the day, and I made my way to the security area to pretend to board a make-believe flight. Once they were out of sight, I doubled back and made a dash for the exit. I went downstairs to Departures to make sure they wouldn't see me. As the sliding glass doors opened, I felt the warm, humid Texas air on my face. I reached into my briefcase, now with a signed contract—far more valuable than ten minutes prior—and grabbed a smoke. I lit up and took a drag. I hadn't had a cigarette all day. I felt high. I finished the smoke and headed inside to have a beer and call Ben. Somehow, the deal didn't seem real until he knew about it.

While we waited for deal one to fund, Ben and I played around with numbers for a full buyout on the rest of Sally's payments. Ben pointed out that I shouldn't have said it would be easy to sell the entire annuity. I thought I'd come home to a hero's welcome having not only signed the deal, but also set up the winner to think seriously about a full buyout. Ben's point, and rightfully so, was that I could have taken the opportunity to lower her expectations as to the amount of money we'd give her for the full buyout.

I should have made her think she'd be lucky to get a few million dollars. Instead, I'd done just the opposite, telling her that she'd do quite well as our investor would be happy to do another deal with her. Consequently, I spent the next few months both babysitting her nerves, since deal one took a while to fund, and resetting her expectations as to the amount of money she could get from a full buyout.

The Full Buyout

Sometimes, things are not what they seem.

My relationship with Sally strained, as the funding process on her first deal took an eternity. It wasn't anyone's fault. There were so many legal knots to untie, so many people who had to bless the deal, so many hoops to jump through, we were lucky it got done at all. I was babysitting this deal for months. It was not pleasant. Once seen as the solution, I was now becoming persona non grata, just another in a growing line of people in Sally's life who said one thing and did another. I was losing credibility by the day.

When I left her at the airport—now months ago—I'd given her the impression that the money was as good as in her bank account. In the heat of the moment, while in deal mode, God only knows what I actually said regarding how long the deal would take to fund. You learn early on not to overpromise. I should have remembered that. I didn't. It was just too easy to promise a winner the moon when you were trying to get a deal done. Most new sales reps went through the same hard learning process. You were so hell-bent on closing the deal that you'd leave yourself quite a mess to manage once the deal made its way to the back of the house for processing. I should have known better. I was no longer the new guy.

Sally called me seven days a week. I'd made the mistake of giving her my cell number, and she used it at will. For the last two months, I'd dreaded the sound of a ringing phone. Still, the delay created a great selling opportunity. Sally was broke. She'd been broke when I went to Dallas a few months back, so, suffice it to say, she was even worse off now. What could I do? I had no power to expedite the processing of her first deal. The processing group wanted it funded just as badly as I did. They weren't due a commission, but funding the deal would get *me* off their backs, and that, I can only imagine, was payment enough.

The delay meant I spent hours on the phone keeping the deal together. All that time babysitting the first deal made us that much closer. The phone calls became more conversational. We had things to talk about—the weekend, vacations, the weather. The more you talk to anyone the easier it gets. It makes deals and selling part of the conversation—not the reason you called.

When Ben first brought up the idea of pitching her a second deal before her first deal had even funded, I thought he had a screw loose. That was the difference between the two of us. He had the moxie to not only think up the idea, but to make it happen. I was a great closer, but I had yet to develop that big-picture, nothing-ventured, nothing-gained mind-set.

When Sally's first deal finally funded, we had already signed her into a second, identical transaction. Better still, she'd had ample time to spend the money we had yet to give her. Once deal one hit her bank account, the money was as good as gone. Another benefit of doing a partial deal was that the winner had fewer dollars scheduled to come in via her annual check from the lottery. Every time she sold us another chunk of her prize, the winner would be that much closer to doing another deal because she was eating up her annual check.

Inevitably, winners would spend the lump sums that we gave them. No one ever did a deal *not* to spend the money. When the reduced annuity check arrived, it was often too small to live off for the year. In order to make ends meet, the winner would sell off another slice of her ever-shrinking annuity. It's like using your credit card to pay off your credit-card bill. It's a vicious circle. Once you see it and, moreover, once your sales staff understands it, you'd do very well signing partial deals while the winner's financial position evolved from bad to worse. We'd do deal after deal with a winner. We'd colonize her annuity, eating it piece by piece, feeding the winner her own discounted cash which she'd always spend, until there was nothing left. Once the winner's payment stream dried up, everything changed. It didn't matter if we bought the prize all at once or over several deals. When there was nothing left to buy, the calls would stop. The mail would stop. Suddenly, the winner wasn't so popular. That was the one absolute way to get off the lump sum industry's radar—sell your prize.

Sally still showed enough interest in selling what remained of her prize for me to run some pricing and see what a full buyout would look like. Ben would have final say on the pricing. Still, I wanted to price it and see how I did in comparison to him. Anyone with a high-school education and a half hour to kill can learn the formula the industry uses to determine the present value of a lottery annuity. You can buy the software at Staples. It's not a secret. Yet the formula has nothing to do with skillfully pricing a deal. The formula just tells you what you've got to work with, how much cash there is to whack up—some for them, some for us. Knowing how to add doesn't make you an economist, and knowing the formula doesn't qualify you to know how to price a lottery deal.

I ran the numbers on a full buyout. I was stunned to see that with some heavy selling, and a little luck, I could build a major fee into the deal. I all but flew into Ben's office to show him. I mean, that much money, on *one* deal? It was unheard of. But, even after your fee, there was more money for Sally than she had ever seen. That seemed fair. I really thought I could sell the deal. I knew it was aggressive, but . . . well, I knew I could do it.

Ben looked at my pricing printout, did some quick math in his head, and then crumpled the paper, tossing the wadded ball into the trash.

"What was that?" I demanded. I was not pleased.

"You tell me. Is that how you'd price the full buyout?"

"It's too aggressive, so it's trash?!"

"It's *not* too aggressive. It's weak-assed, nervous pricing. And, that's why *I* price the big ones, not you." Ever the charmer, this guy. . .

"What's *nervous* about a fee that big?" I was indignant.

"Big?" The word hung out there like a cartoon coming from his mouth. "I want more." He said it as if he were telling me the time of day. As if he were ordering a plate of eggs.

I'm unsure about everything in life, but Ben was clear in his belief that I could sell a deal with that big a fee in it, just like that. I didn't know whether to hug him or punch him. This guy was too much. Who did he think he was? Who did he think *I* was? Who did he think *Sally* was? I wanted to make a fat buck too. But to put that much money into the deal? Wasn't there a line? Wasn't there a point where enough was enough? For me there was. But, as Ben pointed out, that's why he priced the big deals, not me.

What was I going to do, run to Ethan and tell him that Ben was trying to make The Firm too much money? That would have gone over like a lead balloon. Whatever I thought of his idea, there was little to do but nod along.

Unnerved, I meekly sat there as he banged out a few numbers on his keyboard and printed out *his* pricing for Sally's full buyout. He snatched the page off his private printer like it was fresh copy for the evening edition of *The Post*. Handing it to me, he pulled the paper back at the last minute, leaving my arm extended awkwardly across his desk. "You can't sell this unless you believe in the deal," he said.

"I know," I whispered. I was so intimidated. It still haunts me.

"Do you believe?" He was having a ball, like a big brother infuriatingly in control of a sibling.

"I believe." What a lemming! I was mad at him, but I hated me.

I felt sad, for Sally and for myself. All ego and flexing aside, this wasn't what I'd signed up for. He wanted to price the deal like this just to prove that he could—to me, to Ethan, to himself. He didn't have to prove anything to me. I knew who he was. He made the calls, not me. I was there to listen. I was the new wonder boy. I needed to be seen as tough, hard-nosed, and ruthless. Fighting his pricing would have set me back years in my career.

"No." He wasn't letting me off the hook that easily. "Do you be-LIEVE!" Suddenly he was Louis Gossett Jr. in *An Officer and a Gentleman*.

Like a trained dog, I gave him what he wanted. "I BE-LIEVE!!!!"

That was a real moment for me, one I'll never forget. That's when I knew I'd changed. I was a man; my driver's license said as much. But I didn't feel like a man, and certainly not a *mensch*. A few years earlier, I never would have done that. Had my dad been in the room, I'd have died. I'd have just died.

This was too much. I was excited at the prospect of making more money in a day than I'd ever earned in my life. Still, part of me wanted to throw the deal. Part of me wanted to warn Sally not to sign. But it was a small part.

I filled out the travel paperwork and gave it to Shannon so she could book me on a morning flight to Dallas. Like it or not, there was a fat deal in play. And, while I was troubled at the excess of the fee, I wasn't about to give up a shot at all that money. Not me. Not back then. Now? Thankfully, I don't have to contemplate that. Still, I'd like to think it would be different. But I wouldn't make any promises.

I flew into DFW the following morning. With the time change, I landed just before noon. I got my rental car without incident and made my way toward Dallas. I had almost two hours until our meeting. Since the last time we'd met, Sally had gone out and bought a new house. I'd advised her against it, but I knew that Sally's new house put us that much closer to our next deal. The good news was that the family didn't move into the new place with Sally and Evan. The bad news, Sally had left them in the old house rather than selling it. So now she had *two* homes and *two* mortgages. For me, for the deal, for The Firm, the second mortgage was manna from heaven. For Sally, it was like finally admitting that you were an alcoholic and, to remedy the situation, picking up cocaine as a side hobby. She'd gone and made matters worse, a lot worse. What could be worse than your family living with you in your own house, sponging off your lottery win? How about that same family living in one house, on your nickel, while you're down the street spending more money on another place? I'd told her to solve the family problem by getting them out of her house. Instead, she's taken a less combative path and bought herself another home. *The mind of a lottery winner in all its glory.*

Even though I had a few hours to kill, I drove right to her new neighborhood to make sure I could find it and to get a sense of the community. You can tell a lot about a winner from where she decides to live. Did she go out and buy her dream house, or was she smarter than that? Are there a handful of shiny new cars in the driveway? Is it a gated community? Is she still living in the same double-wide trailer she had before she won? Either way, mansion or shack, you learn a lot just by knowing what to look for. I was not surprised to see that she lived in a gated community.

Yet compared to other winners' homes I'd seen of late, hers was not nearly as over-the-top as it could have been. But there were two brand-new cars in the driveway—a Mercedes E-Class sedan and a Cadillac Escalade. Typical. I could have called that—even down to the color.

Not so typical were the two sickly horses corralled in the front yard. Yes, there were *live horses* in Sally's yard. Don't kid yourself; the fact that this was Texas didn't make the scene any less bizarre. This wasn't *Texas,* this was *Dallas,* and horses on the front lawn were as welcome in this upscale neighborhood as they'd be in your next-door neighbor's yard. I'm stunned it was even legal. Who knows? Anyway, Sally wasn't a real horse-riding kind of gal. Even more disturbing was how thin, gaunt even, the horses looked. They were obviously thirsty. They looked like they hadn't eaten in weeks. They actually looked *malnourished.* I was no cowboy, but from an equine perspective, things were not good. I'd later learn that the horses came with the house. I can just see the realtor negotiating the deal. She probably threw in the horses to sweeten the deal and get it closed, something I'd have used in a second if the opportunity ever presented itself.

I drove out of the neighborhood, away from Rancho Bizarro, and set out to find my traditional pre-deal meal—a three-piece spicy white meat from Popeye's. If it's humanly possible, I like to eat Popeye's before I meet with a winner. It's my good-luck charm. Back when I traveled a lot, it got to be quite an obsession. Once, I drove twenty miles out of my way just to get some chicken. Why? Because I'm a superstitious freak. And Popeye's makes me happy. It's familiar to me and when I'm on the road, in a strange town, waiting to meet what will invariably be an odd lottery winner, a little comfort from home (or New Orleans) is just the ticket to soothe my nerves. Plus, I'm a fat guy and we tend to like fried stuff. Luckily, I found a Popeye's just a few miles down the main road from Sally's house.

The meal itself is so greasy that it's hard to hold a pen. Washing your hands only helps so much. It's like trying to get the smell of Old Bay off your hands after a crab feast. You can wash and wash like Lady Macbeth but you still go home smelling like dinner. Sitting there, picking at my chicken, I grew increasingly worried about the deal. I read over the contracts for the fifth time. I was nervous and my palms were sweating. The sweat mixed with the grease from the chicken, forming a super-paste. I was a mess. I laughed nervously at the thought of these huge contracts surrounded by bones, honey wrappers, and the perspiration rings from the Diet Coke I had sitting precariously close to the docs. The notion of spilling the drink on the contract suddenly overwhelmed me. I had to get out of there. I stopped into the bathroom and compulsively washed my hands, soap and water, soap and water, soap and water, trying to get rid of the grease.

"I *am* King Kong."

Scrub, rinse.

"I am *King* Kong."

Soap, scrub, rinse.

"I am King *Kong*."

Well, you know the rest.

I had to get to Sally's. If nothing else, I had to be strong for the horses. I was distressingly worried about the horses.

Normally, I wouldn't smoke before a meeting. I hate smelling like cigarettes. It's also completely unprofessional, even in the lottery business. But today, two things were different. First, Sally knew I smoked. Second, my heart was jumping out of my shirt. I needed to calm down. I wanted a smoke to relax, and I was in no position to argue with myself. Instead, I chain-smoked all the way from Popeye's to Sally's. Pulling into the driveway, I was no longer nervous. I was too stoned from the double shot of nicotine I'd just inhaled to feel much of anything except dizzy.

I parked my car next to the fence separating the horses from the free world. To hide the smoke, I threw in a Tic-Tac but suddenly found myself gagging on it. I had managed to toss the mint directly into the back of my throat, hitting what can only be described as my tonsils. Perfect. Somehow, the gagging caused the Tic-Tac to lodge itself inside my nasal cavity. It felt like the mint was almost up my nose. There I was, with a major deal in my briefcase, gagging on a mint, contemplating the best way to get it out—all the while praying that Sally wasn't watching the scene unfolding in her driveway. Convinced I was about to die, out of the corner of my eye, I saw the two horses. They'd walked over when I pulled up and, as it turns out, their heads were now no more than a foot away from my windshield. We were quite a threesome: two emaciated, befuddled horses stuck in a lottery winner's front yard and me, a tin-man about to be the first person ever to literally *choke* while trying to close a deal.

I could only imagine Ben telling the staff how I died. He'd have a field day with it.

As I saw it, I had three choices. First, I could simply blow my nose and hope that the mint would shoot out my nostril. I'd had a kidney stone in college and survived the delicate physics of a calcium pea making its way through my penis. If I could do that, I figured, I could stand a Tic-Tac shooting through my nostril. (Still, I was not thrilled with this option.) Second, I could plug my nostrils and quickly inhale, hoping to suck the capsule back into my mouth. Or, third, I could leave it there for the duration of the meeting (the path of least resistance). It wasn't hurting anyone, stuck back there. Still, I had enough on my plate and I didn't want the Tic-Tac distracting me the whole meeting—which I knew it would. Plus, I might be tempted to deal with it while sitting with Sally and Evan. I could imagine the coughing, snorting, and gagging noises I'd make, eyes watering all over the place, as I tried to clear out the Tic-Tac. Not exactly the perfect ambience for closing a deal.

To get some cover, I leaned down toward the floor on the passenger's side, as if to collect my things for the meeting. If I was going to shoot a Tic-Tac through my nose, I didn't want witnesses. But just as I was about to blow it out, increasingly the most terrifying but pragmatic option, the mint simply dislodged and rolled down the back of my throat. Gagging a bit, I swallowed it. And that was that. Not exactly the smoothest entrance onto the scene, but a tragedy narrowly averted. I decided to assume that Sally and Evan hadn't seen "Mintgate" and pretended it had never happened.

As I hopped out of the rental car, collecting myself from the Tic-Tac panic, the mare looked at me and seemed to wink. I couldn't tell if she was somehow acknowledging the fact that I had survived the Tic-Tac incident or if her crusty eyes were begging me to take her with me when I left. Either way, we had a moment. Not that I'm special. I'm sure anyone who came up that driveway represented the next best hope the horses had. I was no horse-whisperer; I was simply there.

Sally met me at the door, answering before I knocked—adding to my suspicions that she'd seen me choking out front. If so, perhaps it would make me look more vulnerable? Maybe it was like showing up wearing a cast around your arm or using crutches? (*Note to self: Consider crutches or a severe limp at next winner meeting.*)

Sally and Evan were smooth and completely at ease with me, a far cry from that first day at the airport last year. She was all hugs. She couldn't wait to show me the new house. It was modern and well furnished. There was art on the walls—all of it looked like stuff you'd get at Ikea or Pier One Imports. As is often the case with winners, everything looked new. There wasn't an heirloom in sight. It was as if the entire place had been furnished in one day, at The Lottery Winner's Store. The decorating motif: the bigger the better. Everything was big and everything was gold. Gold trim on the sofa. Gold end tables. Gold candle holders. Gold drapes. Gold bowls. Gold carpets. It was par for the course. By now I'd learned that gold was the official color of lottery winners everywhere. Sally's place, like those of so many other winners, looked as if it had been furnished by Donald Trump . . . you know, *classy*—like him.

After the tour, we settled into the living room (Liberace, eat your heart out). By the looks of it, things were off to a good start. My gut told me the deal was set. I played it cool. The biggest deal in the company's history sat in my briefcase. A commission the size of Montana was close enough to taste. I was relaxed. I was actually calm. It was good to see them. I liked them. I honestly did. I could feel myself *meaning it* when I asked them about family, the houses, life. I cared. I couldn't believe it, but I cared.

We chatted for ten minutes. Soon enough, they shifted the conversation into deal mode, just like clockwork. If you wait long enough, winners will bring up the deal *for* you. Believe it or not, they get tired of waiting, even more than you.

They were doing my job for me. *They* were ready to talk business, not me. I was going to get this deal done and not have to lift a finger. The deal was falling in my lap. My cup runneth over with good fortune. I could just feel it on the tip of Sally's tongue. Any second now. . .

"Edward. Let's talk about the full buyout."

Here we go. My blood—flowing. My heart—pumping. Adrenaline taking over . . . deal time. I thought about buying my own house, or maybe a Rolex.

"Okay." I did my best to look nonchalant about the whole topic, as if she'd just brought up the price of milk, or the weather. I remember thinking that it was a shame no one from my office could actually watch this grand slam go off without my having to give the deal a hard close. Where was the webcam back in the nineties, when you really needed it? My confidence was about to crack the windows. Inside, I was doing the moonwalk. "What do you think?"

"We're not gonna do it, Edward."

Silence. What do you say after being kicked in the stomach? Once again, the air left the room. I couldn't come up with anything to say. The only thing I was able to think was, "Holy shit, oh no!" I just kept repeating that line to myself. I couldn't recover from the impact of her words. I didn't breathe. I *couldn't* breathe. I was stunned—and it was showing. I was expecting a nice, long kiss and I got punched in the mouth just as I'd leaned in to get it.

All I could think about was how Sally always called me "Edward" rather than "Ed." The only people who called me Edward were my mom, my nana, and my soon-to-be wife, Brooke. To everyone else, I'm Ed. Why was she always calling me Edward? That was all I could think once she'd pulled the rug out from under the deal. Why Edward?

Then, it just happened. Manic words started flying out of my mouth. All I could do was watch myself and hope that I knew what I was doing. I was hardly convinced. It was like watching someone else take over your deal and start thrashing it about with a sledgehammer. It was crazy. *I* was crazy. I guess I just went crazy. It was long overdue.

I have no idea why I did it or where it came from. I hadn't planned it. This wasn't some "in case of emergency" technique that Ben had fed me in training. Come to think of it, it went against every tenet of sales and closing altogether. At this point, I was just along for the ride. I couldn't think of anything else to do. I didn't think of the consequences if this failed. The deal was tanking anyway. There was little to lose. Still, the decision to try and close the deal this way would either work in the next five minutes or kill it forever.

"Sally. I'm just going to say this once." I really sounded like I'd had enough of them. To sell this, I couldn't simply jump off the cliff. I had to lunge off, way off, as far as I could go. Doing it halfway, leaving outs, hedging, guarding my words would have guaranteed failure. "I want you to listen to me very closely." I was pointing right at her, hardly my typical sales style. "I came down here because *you* asked me to. Now, I love seeing you and I surely don't mind coming down. It's my job. But, the deal I was able to get for you is a one-time thing." Not true, but that's what I said. "I pulled some strings to get you this deal." I wanted to pass her a note telling her not to listen to me and to run as fast as she could out of the house. Perhaps she could ride one of the horses into the sunset? "I've got a contract in my briefcase to buy the rest of your payments. Now, if I leave here today without the deal getting signed, I promise you, you'll never see this kind of money again."

If nothing else, I'd captured their attention. They hadn't stood up and pointed to the door. At least I had that going for me. I wasn't sure where I was going with the whole speech. I didn't want them to tire of the drama, either, so I went into high gear. I'd be exaggerating if I said that I started yelling, but I was just under that level. I was definitely raising my voice. All or nothing—that's the only thing I kept thinking to myself, all or nothing.

"I don't give a damn if you sign it or not. It's *your* money, and all *I'm* trying to do is help you. But I can't help you if you don't want to be helped." They were nodding along. If nothing else, they were going to hear me out.

"Here's the deal—you two are getting eaten alive by your families. You're out there spending all this money on houses and cars. It's not going to last. I've seen it a dozen times *this month*. I see what you're doing. You don't, because you're too close to it. So, let me make this clear for you. I'm trying to help you. If you don't sign the contracts today, God bless you, but I'm done with you. I take no responsibility for your financial life. I'm done helping. I'm done caring. I'm not just going to sit here and watch the two of you piss all this money away doing one small deal after another. I've told you to sell it all, get rid of the hangers-on, and put the money away. I've begged you to do it. I can't *make* you do it. You're not my kin and I'm not in charge of you. I'm sorry to get upset, but I can't take this offer home and put it on ice for you. It's today or nothing."

And, finally, the big finish. I needed a way out of the soliloquy. I needed a call to action for them to follow. "Now, I'm going to go outside and smoke a cigarette, *one* cigarette. When I'm done, the three of us are either going to the notary or I'm driving to the airport and going home. You've got until I'm done smoking."

And with that, I grabbed my smokes and walked out the door. It was either brilliant or the dumbest thing I'd ever done. I'd know soon enough. I don't know who was more stunned, them or me. I know they weren't expecting *that*. Neither was I. I quickly reviewed what I had just done, looking for possible ways to backtrack. Nothing. Either way, win or lose, I'd done it and there was no turning back. I was dying to spin around and talk my way out of it, to convince them that I was just kidding, to throw myself at their feet and beg for mercy, to call Ben and have him talk to Sally for me. Anything to fix what I just did.

I regretted my decision the instant the door shut behind me.

Closing the front door, the horses looked at me as if I'd just laid an egg. They seemed to shake their heads in unison. With trembling, unsteady hands, I opened my cigarettes and pulled one out. I took my time lighting it, as I'd given them only the duration of the smoke to make the biggest financial decision of their lives. With little hope and acres of second thoughts, I took a drag on the cigarette.

I've smoked a few memorable cigarettes in my life. There was the Marlboro Ultra Light I snuck in at 5:00 A.M. just hours after my daughter was born. There was the Camel Light I sucked down the day my wife's stepfather died in a car wreck just months after we got married. There was the Winston I had, sitting on home plate, still in uniform, watching the sun set the day I played my last game of baseball in high school. There was the smoke I had in the garage, just after I was terminated from The Firm. I remember each of those cigarettes, drag by drag. I remember how I felt, why I needed the smoke, who was there, how it tasted. Still, there was never a smoke that compared to the one I had sitting in Sally's front yard, petting the dying horses, contemplating God and what in His name I'd just done to the biggest deal I'd ever seen. That was some smoke. The Marlboro Man himself has never had a smoke like that. It was one for the ages.

The cigarette had burned well past the tobacco. I'd smoked it as slowly as possible, but now I was inhaling nothing but filter. Still, I was dragging away, as I'd promised myself that I wouldn't turn toward the front door until Sally called me. I didn't want her to see me stalling. I'm historically poor at being patient, but I stayed focused on the horses—talking to them, petting their manes, promising them a sandwich if we all got through this in one piece.

Just as I gave up on the burnt filter, and likely the deal, I heard the most beautiful sound. It was Sally, still sitting in her La-Z-Boy chair, bellowing from the gilded living room, calling out to her trusted lump-sum salesman who was about to throw up on a stallion.

"E-D-W-A-R-D!" My name had never sounded more sweet. "You better come in here before your head pops off." She laughed. I did my best not to sprint into the house and jump into her arms.

Doing my John Wayne walk, I sauntered inside. Turning the corner into the living room, Sally was all smiles. "You mad at me?" she asked. She was serious, too. She was worried about upsetting *me*. Even then, with the deal still very much up in air, I felt bad about that. She had no reason to feel anything for me. I wasn't worth it. I wasn't the kind of guy you should feel sorry for. I was a hustler. I was the worst kind of shark. I looked just like an adorable dolphin . . . until you saw my teeth, and then it was too late.

"Okay, Edward. Let's go."

"Go where?" I played possum, wanting to make sure I heard her say it.

"To the notary." She knew I understood what she meant and didn't entirely enjoy being forced to spell it out.

"You selling the prize?" I pushed.

"You worried I wouldn't?" She returned the volley.

"Very worried—for you, not for me." I was a creep.

"Ummm-huuum." She let that one go, which was probably for the best. "You followin' us or you want to come in the Escalade?"

"I'll follow you." I probably should have gone in the same car to make sure they didn't get cold feet, but I was already thinking about how quickly I could get back to the airport, get home, and put the contracts in Ben's hands.

Backing out of the driveway, I saw the horses. They'd given up hope that I was there to help them in any way. They were right. I wasn't the one they were looking for. Both were on the far side of the yard. I thought they might be ignoring me—giving me the silent treatment. It was quite rude to do so after we'd shared such an intense moment just a few minutes ago. Perhaps in a way too complicated for me to understand, the horses had known about me all along. Perhaps they walked away out of protest, or disgust. Perhaps, out of everyone there that day, the horses were the only ones with their heads on straight.

I never saw the horses again. In fact, I never saw Sally again, either. Once we'd signed the docs and gotten the notary pages done, there was nothing left to do that I couldn't handle from the office.

Sally's full buyout funded a few months later, just as I'd promised. Because we bought everything she had to sell us, we were done with her, and she with us. She'd no longer get calls from The Firm. Instantly, she was off The Firm's mailing list. Now she's a trivia question, a tale about the good old days, a deal file locked away in storage, a commission long since spent.

Once we were done with the last deal, calls from Sally, once a daily, even hourly occurrence, tapered off as well. I think I was too embarrassed and too afraid to know how she was doing. Odds are that she's spent most of the money we gave her. Odds are she's broke, or more strapped than a lottery winner should ever be. Odds are she works at a job she hates in order to make ends meet. I just can't bear to know the truth about Sally, so I've never tried to find out. Wherever she is, whatever she's doing, she deserves a lot better than she got from me.

8

WHAT IS THE SOUND OF NO HANDS CLAPPING?

AS A SALESMAN FOR The Firm, I got a crash course in the reality of what winning the lottery actually meant. Within a matter of days after my arrival, the myth of the lottery had been replaced with the surprising truth. Winning was, for a majority of winners, a tricky, overwhelming mess with obvious benefits and a multitude of hidden dangers. Still, as a salesman, my perspective and understanding of the lump-sum industry was limited to the deals that I worked on personally; the bigger picture was cloudy at best. Only after I became a manager did I appreciate the extent to which winners were pursued by both my industry and anyone else who could figure out a way to leech onto them—friends and family included.

A salesperson's world is limited to his database, typically filled with five or six hundred leads. In truth, most salespeople are not concerned with the overall health of their company. They are not paid to care about their division's monthly, quarterly, or annual sales figures. Reps will always clap along during a company meeting, but their minds are focused on one thing—their own deals. Salespeople are paid on individual achievements. The business could be falling apart all around them, but as long as *his* deals are safe, a salesman is insulated from most of the stress and pressure that comes with a fluid business environment. The same cannot be said for a sales manager, especially at The Firm.

It's a sales manager's job to worry about all the deals, all the reps, all the marketing, all the competition, all the hiring, all the angles, *all the time*. Having exposure to that much data, keeping track of hundreds of deals at a time rather than only a handful, was eye-opening. As a salesman, I was only rarely uncomfortable with the way we pitched lottery winners into selling us their prizes. As a manager, all the gray left the equation. Now I was exposed to a plethora of new bullshit, and it was my job to convince the staff that what they smelled was opportunity. As for me, I was too interested in the money to consider leaving, even once I knew how aggressive our sales and marketing methods were. My gambling habit eroded any moral objections I might have had.

Getting my first management promotion was a big deal. At the time, it never occurred to me that I'd spend the next six years of my life as the face of this growing sales giant. And the bigger we grew, the better the sales numbers, the higher the expectations and demands were on me. The Firm was like a shark with an insatiable appetite for deals. The more deals we brought in, the more we were expected to do the next month. The pressure and stress were immense. Were it not for the paychecks that came every two weeks, *everyone* would have sprinted for the door. But the checks kept coming, and we continued to feed the monster.

Becoming a manager meant exposure to things that I'd never seen before. Sometimes, you have no idea how nice it is to be out of the loop. Coming into The Firm, I wanted to be one of the folks tucked into Ethan's office or slipping away for an important lunch meeting. I hated not being in the *wink, wink,* "off the record" crew. Had I only known.

I spent my last four years envying the middle-of-the-road staff at The Firm. I resented their innocence. I begrudged them their tuna sandwiches and the bowls of leftover Halloween candy on their desks. These lucky bastards could still come to the office and just work. They all had only a job at The Firm. I didn't have a job there; I had the weight of the world resting squarely upon my slouching shoulders. The staff could get through their day like it was nothing, whistling Dixie, like we sold paper goods, as if they didn't even see the bullets and arrows flying past, coming from both sides, blissfully unaware of the fury, the tension, the politics going on all around them.

One of the worst parts about managing was having few, if any, real peers. After each promotion, I found myself increasingly isolated. I reported to the top of the food chain, and everyone else basically—directly or indirectly—reported to me. That left little in the way of contemporaries. Although the company was full of employees, it was a very lonely place for me.

My first management title was sales supervisor. Because of my age (twenty-seven) and my friendship with Ben, the sales staff looked at my promotion as proof that the sky was falling. Soon enough, however, I was promoted again—this time managing the rest of the sales managers, too. You *can* have meaningful friendships with direct reports, but there's always the unspoken understanding that you're the boss. You can feel it in the air—over beers, at lunch, everywhere. As good a boss as I may have been, as inclusive a management style as I had, as much authority as I gave the managers who reported to me, I was never their equal, nor they mine.

My promotion at The Firm was met with the same enthusiasm as the Germans' arrival in Paris. The staff was underwhelmed, and Ethan was openly against the move. His doubts came from a place very dear to him—his wallet. Ethan had seen his share of sales managers come and go. He didn't value managers in the way he did a quality salesman. *(Cue foreshadowing music. . . .)* He saw the promotion of a closer into the management bird's nest not for what it might bring, but rather for what he assumed he'd lose as a consequence—deals. Ethan had had the same concern when he begrudgingly promoted Ben so many months earlier.

Ethan knew I could sell, but the jury was still out on the management thing. Moving both Ben and me into management meant that neither of his two best closers would be signing his own deals. He had a point.

Ethan believed that I, like Ben, was too talented a salesman to waste in management. Top producers were hard enough to find, much less replace. Despite Ethan's reluctance, Ben pushed my promotion through. Why? Scalability. Entering a major growth phase, The Firm wanted to triple the size of the sales force over the next year. Ethan didn't have a choice. He had to promote *someone*. Scores of sales reps were on their way. They needed to be hired, trained, and managed. Ben thought that I could train salespeople to sell, close, and think the way he and I did. His challenge was to convince Ethan that, with our mentoring and assistance, he could have a floor full of Mini Eds and Bens (a petrifying but entirely lucrative image).

It's a classic problem for an entrepreneur whose business is shedding its mom-and-pop roots and evolving into a more substantial company. Ethan had to come to terms with the difference between being an entrepreneur and running a growing corporation. Taking another big gun away from sales was painful medicine for him. And when Ethan took medicine, everybody got a bad taste in his mouth.

To the sales group, I got the bump only because I was Ben's mutt. No one could say that I didn't have the sales chops, that I hadn't proven myself to be a solid closer and deal strategist. Still, my position on the sales board notwithstanding, the reaction to my promotion was nothing short of a Bronx cheer. Making matters worse, everyone who didn't get the promotion now directly or indirectly reported to me.

It's quite a day walking into work after becoming your friends' boss. I've been to interventions that were less awkward. On Monday, you're one of the guys. On Tuesday, you're *telling* the guys to get to work. By Wednesday, everyone hates you. By Thursday, you think they have a point. Once you become part of management, you lose your "one of the guys" membership credentials. I had to re-earn the floor's respect, not to mention their loyalty.

Early on, it was a challenge managing people who, on one level or another, didn't want you to be their boss. In a day, I went from being *the man* to being THE MAN. I was still the same old insecure me, but I'd been given a badge and gun. The new job title didn't change who I was, just how I was perceived. But, being young, I was entirely too concerned with everyone liking me. Down the road, my reputation as a manager was hinged upon the sales group liking me, laughing at my jokes, *wanting* to work for me, dying to make me proud. Early on, I should have cared a lot less about who liked me. But back then, much like today, I was too neurotic not to care.

Something fascinating happens when you put live crabs into a steamer. The crabs, collectively dumber than a bag of rocks, have a biological instinct that is painfully analogous to my first weeks as a sales manager. If a crab resting near the rim of the pot tries to escape, the other doomed crabs hold it back, gripping the deserter with their claws, insuring the fleeing crab's demise. Their brains are too small to suggest that the crabs know, on a conscious level, what they're doing. Still, it's riveting to watch, and it begs comparison to my promotion.

Like the doomed crabs, bitter salespeople would just as soon keep you miserable, too, rather than watch you crawl your way out of the pot. Salespeople are not known for their selfless acts, at least not at work. Thus, my first few weeks as a manager were spent gently, politically, prying the claws and pincers of my former peers off my ass. In the meantime, I was doing everything I could to teach them to trust me, to think like me, to sell like me. It was like trying to cuddle with a rattlesnake.

Sales management is entirely different from other management gigs. Salespeople are crazy, *especially* the good ones. You have to know crazy intimately to manage salespeople. For me, that was never an issue. If it was crazy they needed, I was their man.

We ended up interviewing all kinds of folks for a sales position.

At 10:00 A.M. we'd interview a green college grad who'd spent the last two summers making 150 cold calls a day selling time shares. At 10:30 we'd interview an MBA with ten years' experience at an investment house. What made our situation unique? Ninety percent of the time, the hungry kid was a better fit for lottery sales than the MBA.

We tried to hire salespeople who were street smart and savvy. Still, our sales staff, myself included, would not be on the short list of people you'd ask to take your SAT. We're talking wholly different skill sets. Many of our sales hires were so slick that I'd check to make sure my wallet was there every time I left an interview. What we looked for was a blend of guts, business sense, coachability, and people skills. If I had to choose just one trait out of the bunch, it would be coachability. If someone came to our sales floor believing that he knew everything there was to know about selling, he was doomed. You could set your watch to his imminent departure. Conversely, someone who was willing to learn, to listen, to take advantage of our experience and understanding of *this* sale, was a rare pleasure to hire and train.

I imagine the folks who sell Lear jets make more money than a lump-sum salesman. Still, a sales job at The Firm was the top of the food chain. Salespeople have always been interested in working for The Firm. Finding people who *wanted* the job was the easy part. Separating legitimate talent from a minefield of nobodies and professional interviewees was the trick. Regardless of their education or work experience, most applicants realized that ours was no ordinary sales position. A lot of our salespeople made six-figure incomes. A smaller but consistent batch made multiple six-figures every year. We made sure potential hires knew what kind of money was being made on the floor. As a result, everyone was interested in getting on board.

Unfortunately, for many salespeople, a job is a job. Like a journeyman reliever who pitches for a dozen teams in his career, salespeople know that they're going to be selling *something* to *someone*. That's what they do. It's just a question of what and where. It was impossible for an applicant not to want in on a gig where commissions were calculated against deals with so many zeros in them. Consequently, a lot of zeros lined up in the lobby to apply for the job.

It doesn't matter what you sell, or how much it costs; customers are a huge pain in the ass. Just ask a waiter. It's equally hard to sell a phone as it is to close a mortgage deal. If the sales process is invariably going to be tough, regardless of the product, you might as well sell something expensive. What better product to sell than money to addicted gamblers? If you're going to sell stuff for a living, if you're willing to put yourself through that anyway, why not sell to lottery winners? At least they had multi-million-dollar payment streams off which a salesman's commissions would be based.

Typically, lottery winners are the bluest of blue-collar folks. But blue collar doesn't mean ignorant. Lottery winners are street smart, and sometimes in direct-to-consumer sales, street smarts make for a much tougher sale than book smarts. When you mix our guerrilla sales methods with jaded, distrusting, financially unsophisticated lottery winners, your sales environment ends up being more cockfight than chess match. Our sales process wasn't always beautiful or squeaky clean. Lottery deals got rough and dirty more times than I'd care to admit. But the sales method itself was complex, organized, and highly effective. Yes, our reps made a lot of money . . . a lot of money. But, my God, did they earn it!

Nothing came easy in lottery sales. There was too much competition and too many ways for deals to go sideways. The stress of closing a deal, coupled with the pressure to keep it together while naysayers and competitors picked away at it day after day, was a lot for any rep to handle. Moreover, it took a certain kind of person to stomach the sale itself, not to mention work with lottery winners on a daily basis.

When we met an applicant who exhibited certain character traits, we shied away from giving him a job. The type of salesperson we hired was different than one would assume based upon the financial components of our sale. We wanted deal guys, not economics and finance majors. As odd as it may sound, finance guys couldn't get out of their own way when they were working with lottery winners. Certain applicants, once exposed to the sales methods at The Firm, would not make it. Even our best reps could barely handle making countless cold calls every day to angry, hassled lottery winners. A lot of salespeople couldn't take it—even if they thought they could coming into the company. Of all the folks who came looking for a sales position, three types of people were almost guaranteed not to make it at The Firm:

GOD GUYS

Not a great fit in the lottery world. This was legitimate work, but it wasn't a kibbutz, either. Half of us kept our hair long to hide our horns. There was not a lot of talk about caring for your fellow man on the floor . . . or in the corner offices. We had a hard enough time making *ourselves* feel okay about what we did for a living. A religious congregation's collective jaw would have hit the floor. A good, God-fearing lottery salesperson was an oxymoron. A *real* person of faith, someone who genuinely put his money where his crucifix was, ultimately found our business repugnant. It's not that I blame such people, or even disagree.

MORAL SCHMORAL

If you had issues selling a deal that wasn't necessarily in the best interest of the winner, this was the wrong place to hang your hat. We made no bones about it during the interview process; ours was hardly a nonprofit, PBS kind of gig.

An interview for a lucrative sales position can make even the purest person say just about anything. That's why an interview is such a crap shoot. But interviewing a salesman borders on performance art. All salesmen are actors—equally creative and nearly as full of shit. Salespeople can bluff their way through an interview. They are professional bluffers. However, convincing me that you can sell during an interview is different from cutting a deal with an edgy winner. And doing it once, doing whatever it takes in order to get a deal sold, was not enough. We needed folks who could do it every day, all day long. We looked for salespeople who *lived* for the chance to get their hands on a winner's money, who relished the opportunity, who would sell a fat deal to their own mother. Those who arrived at our door with a deep sense of morality were never going to last. I respected them. I envied them. I thought enough of them not to offer them a sales job.

Early in my tenure at The Firm, Ben told me a peculiar story detailing the way he'd closed a big deal with a cross-dressing lottery winner. A big winner from the Northeast was desperate to sell some of his prize. He had won almost $20 million in the lottery but still lived in a trailer. His choice of dwellings made him a curiosity; his love of women's clothing made him downright fascinating. How did Ben get the deal done? In a manner of speaking, he seduced the winner. No, he didn't sleep with the guy. But he did his best to make the winner know—without question—that Ben was comfortable with his unique sense of style.

Over the course of a month or so, Ben traveled quite regularly to visit the winner up in his trailer with one message in mind—I'm okay with who you are. If the winner wanted to dress like a woman, so be it. Ben's hip to the whole *do-your-own-thing* vibe. And, just like with any other lottery deal, Ben knew that the key to closing this one was to make the winner feel comfortable in his own skin, no matter what that meant.

THIN-SKINNED

Some of my best salespeople were women. Women tended to do very well selling for The Firm. Still, the lottery sales world was no place for a dandy—male or female. There are few places more jocular than a typical sales floor. We did our best to hire as many women as possible, but the vast majority of our salespeople were still young men. Try as we did, our floor rarely had more than one or two female reps at any given time.

What do you get when you throw an abundance of young males into an extremely competitive environment? A locker room—with all the smells and trimmings. The sales floor looked like *Boys' Town*. Making things even more interesting, we (management) stoked their competitive fires. It only behooved us to make the floor a competitive cage, with little breathing room for the weakest players.

As exacting as lottery sales was, the money kept a lot of reps there long after they'd had enough. Even if you wanted to leave, there was always the problem of the golden handcuffs. Once The Firm got those around your wrists, you weren't leaving on your own. What were the golden handcuffs? They were lottery deals that a rep had signed but were still in the two- to four-month processing cycle. Deals were difficult to sign, and often so lucrative it made quitting with a large commission still due you unthinkable. Therefore, once a rep had a few deals in their pipeline, he was trapped. He may have wanted to get out, but he couldn't, or wouldn't, until he got paid on the deals he was pushing through processing. While he waited, he'd invariably sign more deals, and so on, and so on. The Firm was full of guys who had wanted to leave for years but whose pipeline of deals had kept them there longer than they'd have ever thought possible. Look no farther than me for a classic example.

The Firm's commission-and-override structure created loyalty at gunpoint. Leaving money on the table was tantamount to insanity for a sales rep. Staying in a job that ate away at your insides was a slow burn, but leaving all that money behind was suicide. Management knew it and used the handcuffs to its advantage every day. If a rep was due big dollars on deals that he'd worked on for months—even years—we knew there was no way he was going to quit, so we could twist the management knife that much harder without fear of losing a producer. Just like the salespeople who reported to them, managers couldn't leave, either. Unlike a sales-person who's paid only on the deals that she signs, a sales manager gets a little taste, an "override" of his team's deals. Sales managers had just as much skin in the game as salespeople. An override of all of those fees was potentially worth hundreds of thousands of dollars. Thus, everyone—managers and salespeople alike—bit their tongues and bided their time until their deals funded. At The Firm, the "next deal" was an albatross that never left our collective neck.

Rising through the management ranks, climbing higher up the org chart, meant constantly having to prove that I was the right person to lead the sales staff and, in some ways, the company. My last three to four years at The Firm were spent in the position of vice president and then, senior vice president of sales. It wasn't all roses, but it was hardly a bad gig. I was in control of sales. I was an officer of the company. I was a member of the management com-mittee. In terms of my career, I had more than I deserved. I had a corner office, the largest compensation package in the company, the fancy title, and the power to move the business in a direction that I believed in (as long as the deals kept coming over the tran-som).

But being that high up the flagpole meant a lot of folks had a clear shot at my tushy, and believe me, the bullets flew by all the time. When I assumed control and responsibility for the sales num-bers, the credit for our consistent success may have passed briefly through my office, but the blame for anything and everything that went wrong settled on me like an incurable rash. I ached for someone with whom to commiserate. I loved being in charge, but the toll it took on me was absolute.

From the corner office, I saw everything. I heard everything. I learned all there was to know about the lump-sum industry, its tricks and its secrets. I learned more about the nature of greed and the power of money than I'd bargained for. In the end, despite my success, it wasn't enough to overcome the harsh truths about business, and businessmen. I got sucked into something I wasn't expecting. But I wasn't exactly thrashing about trying to get out of the pool, either.

9

EVERY TIME I TRY TO GET OUT, THEY PULL ME BACK IN

October 16, 1999, Las Vegas

A baker's dozen of degenerate gamblers, foodies, partiers, and dope fiends is in town for the annual Richard P. Green Las Vegas Memorial Extravaganza. It's better known as R.P.G.L.V.M.E, as the acronym allows for T-shirts and other such knickknacks that have become part of the routine, the experience that is the R.P.G.L.V.M.E. Aaron, the onus behind our yearly trip, always has something (dice, flasks, money clips) for the guys to take home with them, the idea being that no one on the trip leaves Vegas empty-handed. We are a gaggle of pudgy, out-of-shape, liberal, upper-middle-class white boys. For one glorious weekend a year, we do what everyone who visits Vegas does: We go ape shit.

Aaron's dad, Richard Green, was a big craps player. He used to take Aaron and his brother to Vegas, where he taught them how to roll dice and generally appreciate the finer things the casinos have to offer the *player's player*. To this day, both brothers are fans of many casino games, but each is steadfastly loyal to craps. Everything else is just garnish.

Richard died from stomach cancer in the summer of 1996. In his will, aside from whatever else he left to his family, Richard carved out a little cash for his sons to take to Vegas, on the old man's nickel—one last time. He wanted them to do it right. Get the suite instead of the standard room. Order the lobster. Get a second bottle of wine, another plate of this, sip of that, puff of the good stuff. Massage? Done. Never tried Kobe beef? *We should do that! Let's get two for the table.* The point was to celebrate life as their dad enjoyed it, at its best, at *his* best, in his happiest place. Thus, the R.P.G.L.V.M.E. was born. We liked it so much, we decided, about two hours into our inaugural flight out to Vegas, that the R.P.G.L.V.M.E. needed to become an annual event—you know, to honor the father. Not one to argue, I've attended with enthusiasm ever since. To do otherwise would be uncivilized.

One of the real coups of the entire weekend is that no one ever has to beg and negotiate with his wife about why the hell he and all of his dipshit friends are headed off to Vegas . . . again. Typically, all hell would break loose if you took ten to fifteen guys at various points in their twenties, thirties, and forties, at various income levels, all pitching their wives that they'd like to, once again, leave the kids and the dog and the diapers and the responsibility and reality back home. News of an impending trip to Vegas is often accompanied by sessions of the silent treatment, the length of which is directly commensurate with the duration of the husband's stay. But this gig is different.

At this point, it would be considered uncouth for anyone to question the integrity of the event. A lot of us had been going on this trip for longer than we'd been married. Many wives have, in essence, married into the tradition. (*Lucky girls!*) Its origins being legitimate, sad, poetic, lovely even, who would dare do anything but offer her hubby a lift to the airport come Columbus Day, each and every year? It's as if we'd created a holiday, our very own Festivus, out of thin air. It may, perhaps, be the greatest scam in which I've ever participated in my life.

This R.P.G.L.V.M.E., our third, we were squeezed into four cabs taking us from the Strip, which I had no interest in leaving, out to a lounge, *well* beyond the Vegas city limits. Vegas is Vegas. The rest of the state is Nevada, and the two are not hard to tell apart. You drive outside of the city of Las Vegas and a door slams behind you. You are now in Nevada. And, what the fuck are *you* doing in *Nevada*?

That night, we were headed to the Legends Lounge, a now defunct live-music venue tucked into a strip mall, some thirty miles outside of Vegas. We were going to all this trouble (leaving the casinos) in order to see Karl Denson's Tiny Universe with DJ Logic. I was far more interested in playing cards than going to hear the band. Still, they were incredible—funky, bluesy, old school, fantastic. They weren't exactly the high-limit slot room at Caesar's, but they sounded great.

It took a solid half-hour for us to make our way out there. The scene was cool. Still, it wasn't long before all I really wanted to do was get back to the neon, the felt, the action. Music is nice and my crew was really into live music, which I love, but not like they did, and definitely not in Vegas. Hearing live music in Vegas is like going to Rome for the Chinese food. I was in heaven and hell. I wanted out.

Once the band gets cranking, I become two people. I am the guy happily dancing along with my mellow, music-loving gambler friends—grooving to the bass, drinking, smoking, laughing, doing my best to look the part. I am also increasingly overcome by my social anxiety disorder. I never really know quite what to do with myself out in public. *Should I be dancing? Is it okay not to dance? Can I just nod along? I'm snapping. Do people snap anymore? Should I lean against the bar while the band is jamming? What should I be doing with my arms while I'm dancing?* Cary Grant I'm not. I'm not even Lou Grant.

The music was loud. We were all giving that fake thumbs-up/head nod we mastered at concerts, pretending to understand each other over the horns. Like an angel, Uri, one of my closest friends, and partner at various casinos around the Pacific Northwest, pulled me aside and asked if I was in the mood to get a cab and partner up on some five-dollar Wheel of Fortune back at The Venetian. *Um . . . yes. Yes, indeed.* Want me to finish that drink for you? Hey, look at that, a cab! *Get in.*

Thirty minutes later, in the safety of all that is wrong with Vegas, we swung wide the doors of The Venetian. We knew just where we were going. It was a walk we'd done a thousand times, as if from home to the end of the block. Heading toward the high-limit slot room soothes any nerves left over from the lounge. I was back in a casino. Here, I was "Mr. U." Cocktails, cigarettes, bright lights, risks, chances—I exhaled. I even loved the anticipation of it, the buildup—sticking a few hundred into the slot's mouth, watching the box light up, coming to life just for us.

We each stuck a hundred-dollar bill into the same machine—going splitzies. At five bucks a credit, the $200 gave us an anemic forty credits on the meter. We had only twenty spins to make this thing fly. Exhausted from all that fake dancing, I leaned back in my chair and lit up a smoke, content to be the silent partner and watch Uri go through the motions with the buttons. He hit a few things, losing more than he was winning, the usual. In no time, he'd knocked our forty credits down to seventeen, a lousy $85. I leaned forward to tap out my cigarette, and suddenly our machine started rumbling, shaking like something really good had just happened. I wasn't yet sure what we'd won, but whatever it was, the special effects were unexpectedly elaborate, even for Vegas. Was it the $3.4M progressive jackpot? Had we just hit the goddamn *progressive*?

What struck me as odd was that the moment we won, it seemed everyone else in the casino won, too. If not, then why all the screaming and yelling? And, come to think of it, why was everyone, *everyone*, sprinting for the exits? Why was my chair suddenly trying to dump me on the floor?

And then, in that strange moment of clarity, it finally dawned on us, two schmucks from back east who knew next to nothing about earthquakes, neither of whom had ever experienced one before, that in fact we were in the middle of our first. My initial thought was, "Fuck, no jackpot." My second thought was, "Wow, an earthquake . . . in Vegas." I felt like a celebrity. It was only when I looked up toward the ceiling that everything got serious. The massive chandeliers, a signature of The Venetian, were swaying back and forth as if attached to a spastic pendulum. When people saw those chandeliers thrashing about like that, fear filled the casino floor. It was universally understood, on a basic level, that everyone had to get out of the building.

Uri and I almost knocked each other over rushing to pry our fat asses out of our seats. I'd known him a long time, and this was the first time I'd ever seen him look worried. That's when I got scared. We were sprinting down the corridor when I looked over and saw that Uri had not only stopped running next to me, but was now charging back toward our machine. *What the fuck?* Perhaps an old lady had fallen in the excitement and Uri was going to save her? Other than that, I couldn't fathom what he might be doing. More stunned than loyal, I stopped to wait for him. In the chaos of the moment, in our first earthquake, when we honestly didn't know if this was *the big one* or something that happens out here every month, making sense of Uri's actions was beyond me. So with the walls vibrating around me I stood there, waiting for my friend.

There was no fallen woman. He'd gone back for the lousy seventeen credits still sitting on our machine. He'd risked his life for $85. And, back in 1999, the casinos had yet to change over to paper tickets in lieu of actual coins churning out of the hopper. So, Uri (and myself by proxy) had to stand there while the machine spit out seventeen large five-dollar gold coins. It seemed like it took an hour. Once he got the coins, Uri sprinted right past me, never imagining that I'd still be standing there, like a dog—waiting for him to cash out. Zipping by, his jeans shorts jingled with the sound of coins.

The earthquake turned out to be nothing more than a good story to take home. No one died, although there were a lot of people standing in the lobbies of various Strip hotels in their underwear or pajamas. Apparently, those with rooms on the top floors got quite a scare. Some folks were even thrown out of bed. They were too scared to get dressed, so they ended up outside in their sleeping attire. It was funny and all, but you had to feel for them. It would be dramatic to say that the earthquake was a life-changing moment. It wasn't. But it cemented something I was already planning on doing. I'd gotten off course with this whole lottery business. I was so lost. The things I thought I wanted to do with my life had been replaced by my obsession with gambling and, therefore, my obsession with selling money to gamblers. It was time for a change. I'd known it for a while, but this time, I was serious about doing something.

Four weeks later, I quit.

The night I resigned, I walked over to Ben's new townhouse, two blocks away from the office. Ben was so busy showing me around his palace, he didn't give me any entry point to start the monologue I had planned on the walk over. Finally, between hearing how expensive a rug can be and seeing for myself just how nice real granite countertops are, I jumped in. The transition was abrupt, at best.

"Benny, I've got to talk to you."

"What's wrong?"

"I'm resigning."

"Sure you are."

"I am. I'm quitting."

"Because I've got granite countertops?"

"No. Because I've got an ulcer."

"From me?"

"It came with the job."

"Do I stress you out that bad?"

"Is that news? Have you *met* you?"

"It's news that you'd let it stop us from making money."

"We're not *us*. At the bars, we're *us*. In the office, it's just me supporting you. The only difference is I get paid more than the rest of the cast."

Then he shut down. He wouldn't let me see it bother him, so he turned off every ounce of emotion, just like that. He was sounding a little too interested, disappointed, vulnerable. And for a man like Ben, that didn't fly. Instantly, it was all business—as if we'd just met and he was late for a meeting. As if we hadn't become who we were in that place—together.

"Okay," he said, tossing his arms up in exasperation, reminding me of the men I'd met and haggled with selling djellaba robes in the bazaars of Casablanca. "Have you told anyone else? HR? Ethan?"

"No, just you." (I'd already told my dad, but I was sure that wasn't what he meant.)

"I'll let HR know in the morning," he said dismissively. "You won't get much in the way of severance money."

"How stunning."

He didn't like that line, not one bit. "Fuck you, Ed." He was relieved to get angry, as it masked his disappointment. The words—"FUCK YOU"—snapped out of his mouth, as if propelled by springs. "You walk into *my* house and quit the best job you'll *ever* have and you expect me to cut you a big check, too? How about a hand job? Wanna fuck my girl while you're at it?"

"No thanks. *(True.)* And I don't want the money. *(A lie.)* "I just want out. That's payment enough," I gulped.

"What are you going to do? Do you have another job?"

"Yeah, in my spare time, I went out and found a job! No. I have no idea what I'm gonna do. I just can't keep doing *this*."

We were both becoming a bit unglued. Ben, because he was losing his loyal ace and closest friend in a company full of sycophants and back-stabbers. Me, because I was beginning to realize that I actually had *no clue* as to what I was going to do once I left the company.

The following morning, Ben pulled me into his office. I knew to shut the door. He slid a folder in front of me. Inside was a single piece of paper. Its title read:

"PROPOSED COMPENSATION PACKAGE FOR EDWARD UGEL, EFFECTIVE JANUARY 1ST, 2000."

"This is what you're giving up. You've got till lunch to change your mind," Ben growled. He wasn't exactly passing out the warm fuzzies, and I was in no mood for his mood. Still, the number at the bottom of the page was quite an olive branch.

He'd obviously been up late putting together a whale of a reason for me to reconsider. I wished that I *had* been bluffing. Had I just been after more money, a position I was often accused of taking over the years, this would have been quite a payoff. He didn't double my package, but he pushed it over in that direction. I was sure he hadn't cleared this with Ethan. You could always tell whether Ethan had seen your comp plan yet. Every angle, every out, every caveat was covered. His prints would be all over it. This plan was pure Ben. I found it hard to read with drool dripping down my chin.

Showing me next year's comp plan was a savvy move on Ben's part. Talk about knowing your audience. After a few years of chasing lottery deals around the country, I'd developed a taste for money. Not to mention, Ben was well aware of my proclivity for gambling. He knew I wasn't sitting on a big bankroll, at least not as big as it should be. Ben figured I'd spend the night questioning what I'd done. I'd quit my multiple six-figure job last night. Yeah, I had a few questions for myself. Coming into the office and seeing the comp plan was a reprieve from the governor. Still, I'd made it through the long night in one piece. I wasn't going to change my mind. *How intense does the office bullshit have to be for a twenty-eight-year-old guy to walk away from that kind of money?*

With the document in hand, there was little reason to stay and chat. There wasn't a real "hangout" kind of vibe in Ben's office, anyway. In fact, it was tense as hell in there. Apparently, this was a read-it-by-yourself kind of memo. We both wanted me to leave his office. I took the folder and scurried out the door. It was just past 9 A.M.

I spent the next few hours making myself crazy breaking down the compensation plan, piece by piece. I closed the door to my office and got lost in the comp numbers. Boy, was *that* some wild inner dialogue! I was telling myself to stay and go more than a schizophrenic dog trainer. Combine that with the fear and sadness of leaving the company I'd called home for the last few years and you had one confused scene in my office. I kept dividing the base salary by twenty-four to see what I would have received in each paycheck. The numbers were big. I was duly impressed. With the proposed increase in my base, combined with even the most conservative origination numbers, I was walking away from a plan that would put me well past where I was. I'd be all but guaranteed to hit a big number. *All but guaranteed.* That was a hell of a thing, knowing what I was passing on. In a way, it was a real shitty thing for Ben to have done to me. Part of me wanted to stay just to force him to pay me that money—money I would surely not have been offered if I hadn't resigned. Something about that irked me to my core. Why was I worth this much money only if I had one foot out the door?

Seeing the compensation plan right there in black and white, knowing that I could stay, that Ben *wanted* me to stay, that I could sit back and let the business run itself and sleepwalk into a huge year, was tempting, to say the least. Actually, it was nauseating— knowing that number and still wanting out. I couldn't believe it myself. I resented my own stubborn position. Who did I think I was walking away from all that cash? How the hell was I supposed to make sense of it for Ben? Still, I was locked in. I couldn't change my mind. Had I acquiesced and stayed, I'd have lost all my credibility with Ben anyway. Moreover, I had a sneaking suspicion that

Ben fattened up the plan just to twist the knife. He knew I had no intention of staying, and therefore he could afford to show me a padded plan that he never intended to actually implement.

I popped back into Ben's office just before noon. "You're not making this easy on me."

"Why start now? Let's give it another year, and then we'll both get out of here, together," Ben said conspiratorially, keeping his voice down, as if doing me a favor. This was hardly the first time leaving together had been brought up. Getting out from under Ethan's thumb was our favorite topic, especially at the bar. Get a few drinks in us and that was *all* we could talk about.

"Leave with me." The words hung out of my mouth in a bubble, as if I were an insane cartoon character. I couldn't believe that I'd said it, but that's what Ben did to me. He was a huge part of the reason that I wanted to quit, but I was still somehow convinced that we'd make good business partners down the road. Just like a battered woman, as much as I hated the way he treated me at times, I loved how things were when they were good.

"You want to stay the month?" Ben asked, resignation apparent in his voice.

"Whatever's best for you." It gave me the creeps, hearing Ben—*the mighty Ben*—sound so deflated. It was depressing. His mood—as always—set the tone for mine.

"Stay the month."

"It's the twenty-fourth. The month ends in a week."

"Then stay the week."

"Sure."

"How do you want to tell your staff?"

"I wasn't sure I'd get the option." We tended to cut our ties pretty quickly once someone resigned. It was typically a same-day thing. But Ben was going to let me leave with some dignity. I wasn't being run out of town or thrown under the bus. *(That part of the story comes soon enough.)*

"Let's pull everyone into the conference room at 4:00 P.M. You say what you want and then I'll say a few words, okay?"

"Thanks, Benny."

"Thank you, Ed."

He was as gracious as hell. He was, for the thousandth time since I'd met him, unexpectedly gentlemanly. I've never known such a riddle as Ben Keller.

The 4:00 meeting came and went. It was a big deal to me, saying goodbye. Still, it didn't last more than ten minutes. I'd scribbled down some notes but, in the end, I never used them. I just told the staff that I was considering business school and that leaving was a very difficult decision but ultimately necessary if I was really going to apply for my master's degree. I kept the real reasons for leaving out of the meeting. It didn't matter to anyone other than management, and washing our dirty laundry in a sales meeting—when I was graciously being given the chance to leave like a mensch—would have been a terrible and immature thing to do. You never burn a bridge. You never, ever burn a bridge.

Everyone was surprised by my announcement. No one saw it coming. The room was full of emotions. I was really surprised by that. And while I appreciated it, it made me sad. I never cried, but folks could see I was pretty shaken up. Out of respect, Ethan came to the meeting and said a few nice words about me. All three of us played it right—Ethan, Ben, and me. It was kind of them to send me off like that. It mattered. It showed a lot of class. It meant a lot to me. It really did.

Life goes on. My departure was a big deal, but as long as Ben was there, it was no show-stopper. Ben was the glue in that place, not me, not yet. It took maybe an hour for the buzz on the floor to die down. After that, it was back to the phones, business a usual. And, while that was exactly what should have happened, it kind of depressed me. I realized that staying the rest of the week was going to be a tall order. Suddenly, I didn't want to finish out the week.

Being there after I'd told everyone that I was leaving was too much for me to handle. It felt like living with an ex-wife. Nobody knew how to act around me, nor I around them. Ben was decent enough to put me out of my misery. Wednesday was my last day . . . or so I thought.

Eighteen Months Later (July 2001), Upper West Side, Manhattan

For some time now, The Firm had been out of my life. It had been long enough that I'd stopped thinking about the industry, or anyone from that time in my life, on a regular basis. Every now and then, the company or the industry would make its way into conversation, as lottery winners still do for me today. The business and its intriguing clientele have a way of staying with you. Once you're associated with it, it's hard to forget you weren't.

I'd been living in Manhattan with my fiancée while she finished her master's degree in social work at Columbia. (*Any guess as to which one of us is going to hell?*) I'd begun working with a start-up called DirectMD, which one of my friends happened to be launching just weeks after I'd left The Firm. DirectMD was built to sell a web-based triage assessment tool, developed by a doctor in Florida. The company consisted of four individuals, three of whom lived in San Francisco and me—all alone in New York, working out of my $3,400-a-month apartment, hemorrhaging money. Every five or six weeks, I'd fly out to San Francisco for meetings. Other than that, I was on my own in Manhattan with no one to answer to but myself. Just me in the Big Apple, the town where dreams are made. Net result? I gained thirty-five pounds and lost every penny I'd saved while working at The Firm. Good times.

DirectMD never got off the ground. We were close on a few milestone deals, but in reality, we never made a dollar. It was as much my fault as anyone else's—more, perhaps. I was in charge of sales and we never sold anything. Do the math. Eventually, while we continued to try and breathe life into the start-up, I, like my three partners, simply ran out of money. That was as close as I ever hope to get to suffocating. Slowly running out of money is for the birds. It was maddening. After a year or so, we begrudgingly shut the company down.

One morning, not a week after we'd officially pulled the plug on DirectMD and my fiancée and I decided to move back home, my phone rang. It was Ari Klein, the top transactional attorney at The Firm. When I'd worked there, he and I were close. Since then, we'd had dinner a few times when he and his girlfriend were in the city. Still, we'd lost touch over the year and a half since I left, but that was true with a lot of the folks at The Firm. When he called, I knew something was afoot. Ari wasn't one to call just to chat.

Beyond the small talk, two things surfaced right away. First, Ben had left. Had I not heard that news from Ben himself several months earlier, I'd have fallen out of my chair. Ben leaving The Firm was akin to Sinatra leaving the Sands. He'd built the place. Second, they wanted me to come back and run sales—my way. They knew that I could handle the gig and that I was likely the only guy who could come in behind Ben and fill his shoes. There was some question as to how they could bring me back in such a way that didn't make an already fragile situation worse, but they definitely wanted me back.

I spent the next two weeks playing coy, doing my best to seem only mildly interested. I told The Firm that they didn't want me as much as they thought they did. *(They were practically in heat.)* I told them they couldn't afford me. *(They could have offered me a ham sandwich and I'd have considered it.)* I told them that I wouldn't work until 9:00 P.M. anymore. *(They offered me banker's hours.)* Whatever I asked for, I got—short of a big base salary. Still, the base was con-siderably more than I was making in New York as I hadn't seen a paycheck, *not one*, since my last check from The Firm. Eighteen months without making a dime . . . That will get you to reconsider a lot of things, most notably who you will and won't work for.

After a few weeks of downplaying my level of interest, I met with Ethan and his new chief operating officer, Jude Dunn. Jude had come to The Firm a year or so before I did. He was a no-nonsense, hard-working, seemingly loyal guy. He was the nebbish next-door neighbor—a nice, quiet, bookish fellow. We'd hung out socially a few times and, overall, we liked each other. I figured they could have done a lot worse.

Little did I know.

Jude had started as a sales manager in another division, so I didn't know a lot about him business-wise. I *was* surprised that Ethan had pulled him all the way up into the COO position, but a lot can happen in a year and a half. I figured he'd earned the right after Ben left in what must have been a wild scene, the after-tremors of which were still being felt at The Firm. Ethan probably gave Jude the gig because he knew who Jude was, and who he wasn't. Jude is everything Ben is not. If nothing else, Ethan was "upgrading" from a demanding superstar diva to a homegrown local favorite. There's no question who was more talented; Ben outclassed us all. But compared to Ben, Jude was a pussycat. However Jude got there, he was *there* and, if I did come back, he'd be my new boss.

At our first sit-down, I had to pass on a very good compensation plan. More than the money, I didn't like how they were planning on limiting my role when I first came back. In essence, they wanted me to return as a supervisor, and then, once everyone got used to the idea of my being back, they'd bump me up in the org chart. I was dying to make some money, but I'd left The Firm in a higher position than they were offering me upon my return. It was a deal-breaker. Plus, I knew they'd make the necessary sacrifices in order to bring someone back who understood the nuances of the lottery business. I had time on my side. The industry has an intense learning curve for even the most talented sales minds. This game was unlike any other. They weren't going to lose their shot at bringing me back over something as minor as my role and title. They knew as much. I knew as much. Passing on The Firm's offer was just part of the dance, one that Ethan and I understood very well, a boogie we'd choreographed together thousands of times. Ethan wasn't surprised that I didn't take the deal.

Jude, however, was mortified.

Jude never understood sales and negotiating, not in a real-world sense. He'd read every book out there on sales, marketing, management, etcetera, but he was all book. He'd rarely gone out and done it on his own, put it all out there in order to get a deal done—especially a lottery deal. That haunted him at The Firm. He never shook that label. That was always a big deal to the sales staff—answering to someone who'd never been in the trenches himself. And, while you could fill a box with all the things that I lacked as a businessman, you couldn't hang that tag on me.

Jude was perfectly suited for the bean counting—back-of-the-house management stuff. He was fantastic at it, as good as it gets. Had he just stayed in that capacity, he'd have been fine. But he wanted to be a front-of-the-house player, too. Still, how do you tell the new COO that he's well out of his depth when it comes to sales and marketing? It's a dicey trick—even on a good day.

Ethan couldn't help but crack a smile as I passed the offer back to a befuddled Jude. Jude couldn't fathom that I'd pass on that kind of money. He'd never made the kind of income that Ben and I had earned at The Firm. He was just so happy to have a good job with a great title that the mere notion of looking a gift horse in the mouth was tantamount to career suicide. He wasn't angry at me for passing on the offer; he was simply dumbfounded. Ethan, on the other hand, knew what he was getting if he pulled me back into the business. He was just trying to figure out how much he'd have to pay for the pleasure of my company. Jude, aware that he'd been seated at the adults' negotiating table, found the good sense to hush.

In late August 2001, going against everything I'd said I'd never do, breaking a promise to my fiancée, I signed on with The Firm for a second tour of duty.

10

OF ALL THE GIN JOINTS, IN ALL THE TOWNS, IN ALL THE WORLD

"It's difficult to get a man to understand something when his salary depends upon his not understanding it."
—UPTON SINCLAIR

FROM AN EARNINGS STANDPOINT, my first few years back at the firm were a success. Margins were up, and virtually every metric we used to measure ourselves was well ahead of where they'd fallen in my absence. When I'd left, business suffered. When I came back, business rebounded. Even I was surprised by the difference in the numbers. *Did I do that?* Yes, at least some of it, but Ethan and Jude weren't dying to give me the credit for the turnaround. Credit would have to equal compensation. And the idea of renegotiating my package was little better than a boot in the groin to Ethan and Jude. I was, shall we say, difficult to deal with when it came to the sense of value that I thought I brought to the firm. Eventually, I got a bump in my comp plan, one I thought was too small and they thought was too big. No one was happy—a sign of a fair deal.

Still, it wasn't all paychecks and happy hours. Those first few years were tough, but nothing in comparison to the way things would end. The *last* two years, toward the end, were bad for all of us. I aged ten years. I honestly did.

On the surface, The Firm without Ben was a more mature, less Shakespearian environment. I was in charge of sales, and at The Firm, sales was the burning bush. I relished being out of Ben's shadow, yet in a way I missed him. I'd trusted Ben more than any-one else in the industry. He was tough—a bruiser. A guy mean enough to beat the shit out of you but smart enough not to have to. (Yet probably still tempted to kick your ass just to amuse his friends.) He had scars on his knuckles, with a real story attached to each one. The lottery business was a street business—very raw, very blue collar. Ben was born for this market. These deals, no matter how large the fee, were cut by guys who knew as much, and never forgot it. Ben was eminently cunning, a master manipulator of people and opportunities. He didn't have to cheat you. He could play it straight and win just the same. He was that good.

I missed the Ben who'd inspired me, who'd challenged me intellectually. (Intellectual stimulation wasn't a big draw with the salesguys. Out on the floor, Zig Ziglar was more than likely the only author we all had in common. You'd mention David Sedaris and someone would ask you in which state he'd won the lottery. I once brought up John Updike in a sales meeting, and was promptly informed by one of the sales reps that they were pretty sure he'd already sold his prize to another company.) So, yes—I missed Ben. I missed the guy who loved movies and books as much as I did. I missed the Ben whose world changed after I bought him a copy of *What Makes Sammy Run?* Sammy Glick was an epiphany to Ben. The book defined him, gave him a model, someone to aspire to be. He had a new literary id. They were very cute together, Ben and his id—a real riot at happy hour. No, I didn't have someone like Ben this time around. I had friends, but nothing like Ben. I wouldn't have come back if he were still there. Yet the fact that he was gone was what I missed the most.

The Firm without Ben was like *Fantasy Island* without Mr. Roarke. It's creepy enough on that island. You *need* Mr. Roarke to keep everyone's shit together. Now, I come back and Mr. Roarke is gone. And, oh yeah—*I* was supposed to be Mr. Roarke now. But I had no tricks, no illusions, nothing up my sleeve. Everybody believed in Ricardo Montalban. Who the hell was supposed to believe in me? *I* barely believed in me. Still, pretending I was properly cast for the part, I put on the white suit, grabbed a fruity drink, and yelled, "Places, everyone!" People seemed to buy it. They had little choice, really. Plus, they were on the island too. They *knew* things got weird without a Mr. Roarke around, even an understudy. In the end, I could sell the cast and crew, but I couldn't con myself. I was winging it. I wasn't half bad, but I was no Ben.

I was better at my job when I was working with Ben. I just couldn't work *for* Ben. Could I be better than Ben? What would that take? If I ever would be better than him, this was my shot. He was gone and I was in charge of sales. He was a legend, but a legend in retirement—not nearly as intimidating. I had been his protégé. It was time to step up and do this without him—better than him.

Early on, Jude and I developed a great working relationship. He was running the day-to-day operations, and all senior managers reported to him. But when it mattered, Ethan was the guy to see. Still, we'd humor Jude, deferring to him on some sales decisions. Giving Jude the "*Aye, aye, Cap'n*" horseshit was no different from filling out an expense report or putting paper in the copier. It was just part of your day, the grind, the job.

Sometimes, I'd need Jude's signature on twenty different things a day. Most of the issues involved approving cash advances going out to winners at assorted levels of crisis, interest, deal status, panic, anger, gambling craving, etcetera. I loved giving cash advances to lottery winners. Live checks made out to needy winners were a happy pill, a cure-all. A well-timed cash advance was like mother's milk to cranky lottery folk. We should have delivered the money attached to a nipple. It could solve just about anything. How many problems *can't* be solved with a bunch of cash driven to your door? The idea was to get as much product cooking out in the world as possible. Get winners spending, for whatever reason, and they'd need more. When they did, we'd sell them their money—retail.

That was the vicious cycle of the lottery business. Get them cash. Get them using it. Offer them more. Rinse. Repeat. Name a company that sells a product whose business plan is any different. It's the model for every bank in the world.

The place was full of action. A deal staying together or ending up with us rather than a competitor typically hinged upon a phone call, an impulse, an impression, a six-figure decision—made in an instant. We'd have money going out the door all day long, five days a week. We'd advance deals that were signed last week, two months ago, a year ago—more. We'd almost always have a live check while traveling to sign a new deal. All we sold was money. We didn't have much else to offer, so we'd use it, leverage it, sell it—gamble a little. Work was a high-energy, big-stakes carnival of offers, pricing, pitching, negotiating, selling, and closing. On a good day, that floor would buzz like a beehive. It was electric. I lived to hear that buzz. It meant we were making money. It was intoxicating, a high unto itself. But, like so many other highs, this one was hard to sustain.

Meanwhile, during my first two years back in the industry, Ethan drove us hard. He was a tough, demanding owner, as well he should be. But he saved his A-list tough-love management for a small group—the three or four folks who really ran the company. When he had us alone—when there was an issue or problem—he could put on some show. His management philosophy was predicated on the concepts of making you fear for your job and the old standby—divide and conquer. If Jude and I were too close, that spelled trouble for our Machiavellian owner. So, stir a little shit, make a little trouble, get us to question one another even in the smallest matters, and . . . *voilà*, there goes the power base. It was all so unnecessary. It should have been called *The Firm 90210*. Still, despite the drama, Jude was needlessly uptight with me a lot of the time. He was often the biggest tight-ass in the city—just the way Ethan wanted him to manage me. That's what having a boss like

Ethan does to you. To Jude's credit, he'd fight for what he believed in—at least he did in the beginning. I always respected that about him.

A lottery deal could fall apart and come back together ten times during a single phone call, which was nothing compared to the insanity, the swings, the excitement and tension that came with a face-to-face deal meeting. When a panicked salesman would call from the table, those calls, desperate for you to fix what they'd just broken—they had to be taken right away. Save a salesman's dying deal and he was as loyal as bees to the queen. If you could close one of his deals for him, out of the training room, extemporane-ously—live, when the deal was on the line—you had a friend for life. Keep your cool there, don't choke, close the deal—that mo-ment, that phone call, was my Super Bowl. That's where I earned my money. That's where Ben had shined back in the day. That's where I focused my attention, too.

Imagine, then, in the midst of whatever real-time-deal issue was on the other end of that phone, having to skip off to find Jude so he could bless decisions you were paid to make. More-over, imagine how borderline psychotic, how perfectly apoplectic, I would get to find Jude all too relaxed, in one of his thirty meet-ings per day, with his door closed—locked, even—as if God forbid someone should sneak in and secretly join his weekly IT update. Jude was the leash that Ethan put around my neck to keep me on the reservation. He'd learned his lesson with Ben. While it worked, that dog collar often felt like a noose, choking my creativity and distracting me from getting deals done.

One afternoon, well into my second tour, Jude called and asked me to come by his office. Jude didn't need to set up many meetings with me, as I'd show up enough on my own. I'd come barging in throughout the day, interrupting his scheduled meet-ings, fully believing that my needs, *deal needs*, put me at the head of the line. It always came across as rude, or, if nothing else, presumptuous, for me to interrupt his meetings. But I was always juggling timing issues on deals, working with a thousand variables an hour. I *had* to interrupt. So the rare call to come into his office usually meant something serious—that, or he wanted to talk about going to Atlantic City to play craps.

I never got used to Jude having Ben's old office. Walking through that same door, sitting within those same four walls, at the very same desk no less—was a surreal, somewhat hollow experience. The room was haunted by my past. It may have been Jude's office, but it was Ben's room.

I walked in and as usual, Jude was scribbling notes on some Excel spreadsheet. Whatever the report, he was devouring the data as if he'd broken the code of the Rosetta Stone. The poor bastard loved schlepping around a pile of spreadsheets. To a guy like Jude, spreadsheets were the lifeline of sound management. *Oy.* The only time I willingly used a spreadsheet was during my fantasy football draft. Jude's spreadsheets and reports were like Linus and his blanket. Try to separate them and all hell would break loose. He wished I loved data the way he did. So did Ethan. I did not. The fact that I had never fully embraced sales reports and metrics didn't help my long-term standing at The Firm. But at that point, I was wholly unaware just how soon this would become *the issue* surrounding my employment.

For once, *this* meeting was not about reports. It was about Ben.

"Hey," I said, chewing on my red felt-tip pen.

"I don't know if this comes as a surprise to you or not, and I don't want you to get . . . how you get," Jude began.

Get how I get? What was *that* supposed to mean?

"Ben's coming back," he added as casually as he could. He wasn't from the great performers.

I thought he meant that Ben was coming back to The Firm. I almost threw up in my mouth. "Here? *When?*" My voice cracked.

"Not *here*. Jesus! He's opening up his own shop—in town."

We sat in silence for a few seconds, the news seeming more real to him now that he'd said it out loud.

"What's Ethan saying?"

"He asked if you already knew. . . . *Did you?*"

"Do you have to ask?"

"I *have* to ask."

"Is that Ethan asking, or you?"

"*We* are asking."

BANG . . .

That was it. Everything changed—right away and forever.

Ben, the most dynamic mind in the industry, had been in hibernation for the last two years, the same amount of time he was legally obligated not to compete with The Firm. Time was up. The bear was hungry.

At first, Jude thought, or at least pretended to think, it would be business as usual. He said that we'd always had competition, hard-core competition in the industry—that Ben would be just another competitor. He thought Ben wouldn't be able to put together the financing to fund deals. And, if all else failed, he thought there was no way Ben would be able to put together a good database. He was wrong.

Jude's a bright guy. Book smart. He knows a lot about finance—and how books recommend you manage people or act as a leader. If that's your thing, he's your guy. What he lacked in natural talent, he made up for by reading and studying the science of the art of leadership. But Jude could live in the business section of the library and there would never be, in all the management and leadership books he scoured through, any tips on how to deal with *this*. He didn't know Ben, not the way I did. And he didn't know the history between Ben and Ethan, not to mention Ben and me—not the crazy stuff. He had no way of knowing how far off course Ethan would take us while he chased Ben's shadow all over the industry for the sole purpose of seeing whose dick was bigger. No one, not even Ethan, saw that coming.

Jack Welch, former CEO of General Electric, says that "if you don't have a competitive advantage, don't compete." Ben agreed. Ben wasn't the kind of guy who'd come back to dabble in this industry. If he was coming back, it was because he was armed for bear. He was coming after us.

Ethan just couldn't help himself when it came to Ben. Ben put Ethan into a lather. He just made him crazy. Ben *did* that to people. How can I be so sure? Because he'd made me nuts for years. It takes a nut to know a nut. Jude, meanwhile, had no idea what he was up against having both Ethan and me so amped up about Ben. If he thought he had his hands full dealing with us before—watch out. Jude had the owner of his company and his top manager going bonkers at the sound of Ben's name. At least I'd try to hide it. Ethan didn't give a shit. Walking around the general office he was all smiles—the consummate host. But behind closed doors, away from the staff, when the big kids talked, the guy would practically pop a blood vessel every time someone said Ben's name.

From the moment we heard that Ben was opening his own shop, no one in sales got a moment's peace. My staff could sign five deals in a day but if Ben's company signed one, no matter the size, tension would fill the hallways. It was ridiculous. I'd have laughed at the entire situation if it wasn't ruining my life. As much money as we made, as many deals as we signed, as solid as our numbers looked on a consistent basis, once old Benny came back, nothing mattered. To Ethan, we couldn't—*I* couldn't—do anything right. Anything I ever said or did again, any victory, any defeat, any marketing piece, any mail campaign—A-N-Y-T-H-I-N-G—went through a new series of questions, suspicions, issues, and paranoid doubts.

I was responsible for the deals we brought into The Firm. Whatever the results, the buck stopped with me. I was fine with that. It was what I'd signed up for. But suddenly, I was also responsible for the deals Ben's company signed—the ones we'd missed. Perfect. It was hard enough knowing why *we* signed a deal. Now, like Kreskin, I had to know why we *didn't* sign a deal. Moreover, I had to know why Ben's team *did*. Ben's success was my failure. Can you imagine? *My* former boss-friend-enemy-mentor-confidant-hero-nemesis was not only back in the game but somehow, I was accountable for his wins and losses.

The poetic irony? I felt like I was reporting to Ben once again. I dealt with him as much now as when I'd worked for him, and working for him was why I'd quit in the first place. He was everywhere—circling around deal issues, causing me stress, beating my guys on a deal, making me work harder than I wanted to, making me think more, try more, want to win more ... this guy was still my *fucking boss*. We hadn't laid eyes on each other in years, yet somehow, because the universe has a sense of humor, he was in my life, every day.

While waiting out his non-compete clause, Ben had created an arsenal of new business concepts—stuff we'd never even thought of before, really smart material, along with beautiful marketing pieces. The guy could always make the phones ring, but this stuff was different. Now he had winners lining up to do business with him. Ben's new marketing and sales tactics came out of nowhere. They were beyond what any of us had anticipated. The industry was not prepared for this fight. Apparently, neither was I.

At first I played it cool. I told Ethan not to worry. I told my staff the same. Now that I was running my own sales group, I was sure I could handle anything Ben threw at us. In the beginning, I welcomed the chance to mix it up with Ben. To be the best, you've got to beat the best. I *wanted* to compete with Ben. I wanted to go head-to-head. I was sure I could beat him in a straight-up game.

For the sake of pride, competition, and keeping my job, I was ready to roll up my sleeves and get busy.

But competitive intentions aside, it was as if Ben had eyes and ears in the place. When things were bad at The Firm, he would twist the knife just so. In no time, he proved that he could run circles around us with his marketing. He had us chasing our tails trying to keep up.

Ben's stuff was so cutting edge—so successful—we were particularly interested in seeing the marketing pieces he sent out. We had a handful of *friendly* winners who would send us our competitors' mail. But here's where Ben was maddening—beautifully maddening. We didn't have to euchre winners into sending us his marketing pieces. *He sent them to us.* He had his marketing people include seven or eight of us in each mail drop. Once a week or so, Ben's marketing pieces would arrive, addressed to each of us. We tried to act like it didn't bother us, but it did. It killed me. It also made me laugh. This guy had balls I'd never dreamed of owning. Sending his marketing directly to us was his way of telling us that we'd already lost the race. Ben blew right by us. I also knew, in the back of my mind, that Ben was tickling my ribs, the business equivalent of goosing me. While we hadn't talked in years, we communicated all the time.

Early on, there was talk that we could make a legal case against Ben competing with The Firm. We tried. We failed. We couldn't stop Ben—legally or strategically. So, when you can't beat up your enemy, who better to turn on than each other? Sometimes, when I'd have to tell Ethan that Ben's crew had just signed a good deal, Ethan would look at me as if I were a poorly chosen fishing guide—still tied to the dock while the other captain had fish jumping into his boat.

Like everything else, the once shocking idea of Ben competing against us soon became normal. It was what it was. Ben was in the business. And my standing with Ethan and Jude started an irreversible nose-dive. While I never got past it and the way it changed the dynamic at The Firm, I got used to it. Dragging that boulder around the office was exhausting, but what else was I to do? Months became quarters. Quarters became years. I was so wrapped up in the business, so completely obsessed with our numbers, with hitting our goals, that I barely noticed time pass.

Those two years after Ben came back were a blur. They are simply lost for me. I was so obsessed with deals, with competing against Ben, with appeasing Ethan, I forgot to live my life. We had our daughter during that stretch. I was barely plugged into the reality of becoming a father, a family. I was so upside-down, I thought I deserved a medal for turning off my cell phone in the delivery room. Frankly, I'm lucky my wife let me come home half the time. It was—*I* was—a terrible mess. My job, impossible before Ben, had become something different altogether.

To say the least, Ben's reappearance on the scene shed an unflattering light on my shortcomings as a businessman. It suddenly dawned on Ethan and Jude that, perhaps, I wasn't nearly as good at this job as anyone thought—even me. For years, I was the best in the building and everyone just assumed that meant my methods were good enough. They were happy to have me back after Ben left, and my results were perceived to be good, or good enough, so no one bothered to look behind the numbers. My strategy was *the* strategy. Before Ben, we really believed that the sales moves we made, the marketing pieces we created, our total approach to the business, were so far ahead of our competition that, ironically, no one really bothered to prove it. Ben's resurrection changed all that.

Now, Ethan wanted every metric, every moment of the sales group's day tracked, categorized, and evaluated—as well he should. Moreover, he was infuriated that reports tracking such data didn't exist in the first place. He was right. We had done so well winging it, managing by the seat of our pants, being reactive, being deal hounds, that we—shockingly—never thought to use, much less create, these essential reports. And when Ethan finally asked for them, the fact that they didn't exist, that fact in and of itself, sent my value plummeting in his eyes—the only ones that mattered. It was unbelievably embarrassing.

The components of my job that I hated, where I was weakest—spreadsheets, critical analysis of data, reports, metrics—I'd been able to ignore because we signed so many deals. My answer to any opposition was my track record. Until Ben came back, results were all I needed to bring to any meeting. Results *were* my reports. I brought in the deals, and deals satiated the crowd. However, those days were gone, as was my autonomy—my ability to run the place my way, without interference, the treasure I'd earned and cherished. My days were a never-ending litany of meetings to fix what, for so long, we didn't even realize was broken.

I seethed with resentment.

Late in the winter of 2005, I received a meeting scheduler from Ethan's assistant. The meeting's subject was "competitor court orders." The scheduler meant we finally had the reports showing which companies were signing deals in the marketplace. The attendee list was intimate: Ethan, Jude, our general counsel, the VP of marketing, my sales managers, and me. Attached to the scheduler was an Excel spreadsheet listing all the deals for which each company in the industry had successfully obtained a court order over the past twelve months. While the data was not entirely accurate, it was close enough. At any rate, the last thing you wanted to do was go into *this* meeting arguing that the data was skewed—not a good starting point. Regardless of what was missing or inconclusive, the numbers were the numbers. Once and for all, the report would show us who was signing more deals in each lottery state over the past year. The meeting was scheduled for the following day, from noon to 3:00 P.M. Lunch would not be provided.

Minutes after receiving the scheduler, I gathered the sales

managers in my office. We spent the next day and a half franti-
cally reviewing the data, trying to understand what happened with
each deal that we had lost to a competitor, namely Ben's company.
There were plenty to choose from. I'd known all along that Ben
would be successful; I just had no idea *how* successful. None of us
did. The numbers were stunning. And there was no hiding from
what the activity notes in our database revealed: Plenty of winners had signed deals with Ben's company whom we hadn't even
been speaking to when they sold their payments. Not good. Even
worse, a lot of activity notes, which are automatically time and
date stamped, showed that our reps were talking to some winners
at the exact time Ben's reps were signing them into a deal. Even
now I can't tell you which is worse. Both scenarios are unbelievably bad—ridiculously indefensible. And I was responsible for the
results.

The small conference room was located next door to my office. If there was a silver lining to attending the meeting, it was
that I didn't have far to walk. That was about all I had to look forward to with this meeting, a short walk. But even when you know
you're beat, you still show up and take your lumps.

The sales managers who reported to me were hand selected—
savvy and dependable. They saw this whole thing unraveling before
their eyes. Once the data came in, they knew it was time to put a
few feet between their loyalty to me and their obligation to themselves. I didn't blame them. They had families and mortgages, not
to mention ambitions. I knew they felt the same way when none
of them sat next to me as we settled into our chairs.

I had done my best to prepare for the meeting, but I was merely covering the windows with plywood before the storm hit—not
trying to beat it, just weather it the best I could. The meeting
was really a referendum about me. It lasted over two hours. It was
worse than I'd imagined. The IT department had set up the over-
head projector so the database could be displayed on the movie

screen against the far wall. The lights were shut off so we could all see the activity notes together. There was a gloomy feel to the room. We could have been watching a movie about puppies and it wouldn't have helped the vibe.

In the meeting, we took the court-order report that identified that Winner X signed a deal with Ben's company on whatever date and cross-referenced that signing date with our database to see what the sales notes said leading up to the time we knew the winner sold his payments. It was embarrassing. We saw deals that had signed on a certain date and in the weeks, months even, leading up to the closing, there were *no notes* from our sales staff. Even worse, there were some leads with notes that said the winner "wasn't interested" the very same week they ended up signing with Ben. It was just awful.

I can't say how many deals were signed in which state. I have no recollection of the exact numbers. Numbers like this you get out of your head at the earliest possible moment. But let me sum it up like this: I did not walk out of that meeting with the same standing, respect, responsibility, or future at The Firm that I had when I walked in. The meeting sealed my fate, which had become decidedly rutted of late anyway. I wasn't being scapegoated. Ethan and Jude didn't have to spin the data to make it look like it was my fault. It *was* my fault. Sure, there were other people who shared culpability, but none of them had my title, my role, my responsibility, nor my compensation package.

After the meeting I was mad at the world. Ben? A little. Ethan and Jude? Sure. Myself? Always. But soon enough, I had a revelation. I was angry at my salespeople, too. I don't mean to imply that I was mad at the *exact group* of salespeople who were working for me at the time I went through all of this. To the contrary. This was an issue long in the making. Lottery salespeople—the ones who mattered, the ones who'd been there a while, who'd seen some success—knew the secret, the same secret I knew. The same secret that kept me from forcing my staff to bang away on the phones, cold-calling lottery winners all day long. The same secret that kept me from manipulating my staff and pushing them to excel the way Ben had always pushed me. What was the secret? Lottery deals, like winning lottery tickets, come at the strangest time, when you least expect it, and ultimately, a lot of it depends on luck rather than hard work. I wanted my staff to work smarter, rather than harder. At least that's the way I saw it. I didn't believe that our database was big enough to handle cold-calling a small pool of winners day after day. So, I fought Ethan and Jude every time they all but begged me to turn up the heat on the sales group. I dug in—time after time. I wasn't willing to be like Ben. I should have been. I was wrong.

It occurred to me that my salespeople, like myself, like every-one associated with this wild industry, were one part lazy, one part gambler, and one part too smart for their own good. Working smart (rather than hard) had paid off too often for them to change, no matter how good the *rah-rah*s were in my weekly sales meeting. My salespeople didn't hit the phones like they could because the best ones knew that they didn't always *have* to work very hard and I knew, or thought I knew, that they were correct. Like lottery win-ners who had done nothing of consequence to earn their money besides purchasing a ticket, my salespeople had seen time and again that a more relaxed calling effort often paid off with big deals that had major fees attached to them. They believed that they needed to be smart and lucky, rather than cold-calling machines. Looking back, I know they believed it because *I* believed it. As long as they handled the few really sexy deals that fell in their laps every so of-ten, as long as they maximized the best opportunities, they didn't have to crush the phones. I suffered from that erroneous belief and because I did, the salespeople suffered from it, too.

Ultimately, we shared the same hope/luck/blind faith men-tality that many winners have. My salespeople, like their boss, were lottery winners through osmosis. And while we never actually *won* the lottery, our similarities to winners were apparent in our relationship with money, our sporadic work ethic, and our compulsive, self-destructive behavior. At some point, when you've seen so many wild deals come out of nowhere and get done, when you've seen your colleagues make tens of thousands of dollars off a deal that they didn't have to cold-call in order to get, deals that simply fell into their lap, money begins to have no meaning. We were all desensitized to the impact of money—what it meant, what it was worth, what we had to do to earn it.

Many winners suffer from the false sense of security that comes along with winning. Some believe that once they win, once they're "rich," they're foolproof. That sense of infallibility was shared by my sales group, and myself, making big paydays without necessarily giving the commensurate level of hard work. Why call every lead in your database when you know that if you wait long enough, a deal will likely come to you? Whether you get your money by picking the correct six numbers in the lottery or by selling the lump-sum option to winners, this kind of money—big money, found money—*is* money for nothing. Money you get by doing nothing is money you are less likely to respect. And when that kind of money keeps coming, whether through annual lottery checks or from various unearned deals that periodically fall into your lap, you start to believe that it will never stop, that you can blow the cash you have, that you can do foolish things, that you can keep underperforming in your job, and that somehow, magically, the money will still find its way into your hands.

So, yes, in addition to being let down by myself, I was let down by my staff. I was never mad at them. I was mad that the facts were what they were. I was mad that I couldn't, or that I didn't, make them work harder for the right to work in a place that legitimately offered *this* kind of money to be made. I was let down that they could get away with not calling all their leads and still make the type of incomes that so many of them did. I was let down that, in the end, I wasn't nearly the motivator, the inspirational leader, that I'd assumed I was. I was mad at them because they helped prove Ethan right. My staff's work ethic, their call results, were right there in the database for anyone to see. And the database told Ethan that he was right about me, that I wasn't who he thought I was, that I wasn't Ben.

I was no longer the right person for this job.

What do you do with a high-profile, popular senior manager who makes more money than anyone else in the company, whose star had fallen to a place out of synch with his compensation package, who is, for the first time, completely disposable?

Correct.

11

SENIOR VICE PRESIDENT OF MY BASEMENT

"When they run you out of town, get out in front and make it look like a parade."
—Father Tom Walsh

I WAS FIRED ON a sunny Tuesday morning, Valentine's Day 2006. Ethan wore red. I knew I was getting fired. I knew it was happening that morning. I did not shower.

I didn't feel any pangs of nostalgia driving in. I had a smoke, which I never did in the morning. If the trip was remarkable in any way, that was it. By then, it was all over anyway. They just needed to make it official. They knew I knew—but we all still had to play out the hand. None of us was looking forward to this. Firing anyone stinks, it really does. But firing me, after everything we'd done together? I didn't envy them, not one bit. Despite all the problems, all the anger—it was still me. As silly as it sounds, we were happy once. We had intense history together. Not all roses, mind you, but seven years—seven years' worth of life, all of it. In the time that I worked for Ethan I'd gotten married and become a father. Both of the men who were about to fire me had been at my wedding. Ethan and I had been at Jude's wedding. We were, in that backwards, hard-to-explain, office way—friends . . . *good* friends. I cared about them. I knew these guys better than 90 percent of the college friends who were once so dear to me.

I felt bad for Ethan and Jude. I understood what a lousy situation it was for them—even that morning. It was a miserable day for all of us. Still, there were things that needed to be said—formalities, truths, half-truths. Plus, there was the elephant in the room: severance. I'd been there, doing very well for them, for over seven years. *Seven years.*

I'd be fired, probably, before I had a chance to get a cup of coffee. I felt like a criminal showing up to start serving time. It was peculiar. As I pulled up, I got a wave of fear. I started to panic. This was going to be embarrassing. One of the real bosses was getting fired. That's big news around the break room. I did not want to go upstairs.

Not listening to myself beg, I drove into the garage and, ironically, pulled into the same spot that I had some four years ago—on my first day back at The Firm. I turned off the engine, closed my eyes, and got into deal mode. I was being fired, but there was still a deal that needed closing. "Focus on the deal," I told myself. "Focus on the deal."

"I am King *Kong!*"

"I am King . . . *Kong.*"

"I am King *Kong?*"

"*Am I King Kong?*"

I felt like Curious George.

I got out of the car and hopped into the elevator. I was ready.

It was weird, getting fired. I'd never been fired before. Still, I'd fired so many folks over the years, I knew the routine. If I wasn't the guy *getting* fired, odds are I'd be the one handling all of this. The whole scene was odd—as if they were prepping a meal for me in my own kitchen, using my tools, my recipes. Like a cow recommending the most humane slaughter method to a butcher, I almost felt obligated to help out.

They were ready. All the little touches were in place. This wasn't some harebrained idea they came up with last night. You don't fire a senior guy without having done considerable planning beforehand. This one had been in the works for some time. Still, I couldn't help myself. I felt compelled to go over the checklist in my head:

Had IT tinkered with my computer's permissions yet?

Was the staff in an "impromptu" meeting in the conference room, thus allowing for fewer spectators?

Were Ethan and Jude tucked away in Jude's office, getting their story straight?

Was Jessica from HR in her office, ready to intervene at a moment's notice should things get out of control?

I *was* curious to see how they did it, what they finally agreed upon, what they decided would be the best way to fire me. In an odd way, I was looking forward to it, at least for the spectacle of it—the conclusion of our soap opera, dragged out over so many months, so many conversations, so many memos, so many arguments. This scene had been years in the making. It shook me at my core—being fired from a company I'd helped build. Still, it was time. We'd been on a bad loop, falling in love and breaking up fifty times a year. We were all tired of the melodramas, the petty tab-keeping and settling of scores, the sycophants, the plotters, the games, the pretending. More than anything, firing me would allow all of us to stop pretending—pretending to still want to work with each other, to still trust each other.

I had to stop pretending.

I sat there in my office, waiting for the call from Jude. Sitting at my desk, I had a view of the entire sales floor. For everybody else, it was just another day. Most of my staff was in by now, other than the guys who worked West Coast hours. You could see and hear everything from my chair. This morning—my last—the random chit-chat, the laughs, the jokes, the everyday hum of the office made me sad. The floor didn't know yet. They were simply doing their thing. An office full of people is like a cruise ship out on the open water. In reality, so many folks on that boat are just floating along—oblivious to the boat's course, or what, for that matter, is even keeping it afloat.

People were coming in and out of my office, asking questions or getting my signature on one thing or another. I was melancholy, seeing all these people—likely for the last time. Granted, I was oozing with falsely inflated nostalgia. This was an office, not an orphanage I grew up in. But so much of my history was tied to this place and these people—it depressed me, the thought of not seeing them again. As much as I hated what my job had become, I loved my co-workers. Forget about the fact that a lot of folks reported to me. I could have been the janitor and still gotten a kick out of having some of these folks in my life. Did I like being their boss? With my ego . . . you bet. But more than that, I loved that I mattered, that I actually made a difference in their lives. Almost all of them—the salespeople, the supervisors, the managers—were better off as a result of working with me, and I with them. I was proud of that. I miss that.

The phone rang and snapped me back to reality. It was Jude. I answered, "Yeah," trying to sound busy and unintimidated. (I was neither.)

"Got a minute?"

"Sure."

"Wanna come down?"

"Sure."

I could tell by his tone that Ethan was in there. So much of the way this whole thing played out could be summed up the same way—Jude was afraid of Ethan. If he'd stood up to him long ago, none of this would have happened, not like this. Would I still be there? Who knows. But I surely wouldn't have been fired from the place—not me, not now, not like this. If the tables were turned, if Jude reported to me, I'd have protected him like a lion does her cubs. A guy with my track record . . . I would have shielded him from anything that came his way. Jude never did that. As a result, at 9:19 A.M., I was summoned to his office for the last time.

Jude didn't look at me.

Ethan, however, didn't take his eyes off me, as if he wanted to make sure I didn't steal any silverware on my way out the door. He did all the talking, which made sense. By now, this was really between Ethan and me. Fittingly, Jude was relegated to the sidelines, a witness once again, there only to document the moment, a passive observer. *My fearless leader.*

The meeting was brief. The silver lining to this whole thing was that we could finally stop pitching our tired arguments to each other. You can't get *more* fired. I was fired. It was over. There wasn't a whole lot of sense in saying much more than I had to. And I surely wasn't interested in hearing Ethan spin this as a good thing for me. He'd decided that getting rid of me was good for business, and that's all that needed to be said.

I fully supported his right to make that call, too. It was Ethan's company. It had always been Ethan's company. They knew how I felt. That's why they were firing me in the first place. How I felt *got* me here. How I felt was written in a dozen memos addressed to them. They didn't need to ask and I didn't need to tell them. We knew where everyone stood. I wasn't winning this fight. I'd lost it long ago.

Even as I was getting canned, I could feel the weight lifting off me. Being fired was devastating. Still, being able to let go of all the baggage, all the bullshit I'd been carrying around for so long, already felt good—really good. I could get used to it, in time. But I was a long way from gone. There was still the issue of the folder.

When Ethan gave Jude the nod, he slid the folder to me. Inside was my release agreement and, if I agreed to the terms . . . my severance package. The folder was burning a hole in my hand I was so anxious to read it. Still, I didn't open it in front of them. I told them I'd look it over and get back to them with a response. And, while we had to go back and forth a few times, we got it done. We all had the same goal—getting me out of the building.

For legal reasons, I can't divulge the details of my severance. Truth be told, for whatever reason, I'm barely allowed to tell my own family what's in that document, much less everyone else. I'm still not sure why it's such a big goddamn secret. It hardly makes for interesting reading, except for my lawyers doing so on billable hours. To them, the document became more interesting each time they read through it. And, after seeing my bill, I figured they must have read it a few hundred times. I think I'm prohibited from giving the details of my severance because The Firm didn't want anyone else to think that they'd get the same deal if they got canned. Still, like every other compensation issue we'd ever had, The Firm thought they'd given me a lot of money and I thought they should have given me more. They took care of me, though. To be fair, they took care of me.

As soon as we had a deal on the severance, Ethan and I pulled the extended sales group into the conference room to break the news. I wanted to get it over with and get out of the building. My nerves were shot. I was heartbroken, nervous, and completely off my game, but I didn't let it show. We pitched it as a mutual decision, a long time in the making, one that we'd discussed a lot over the past few months. I guess it was a decent thing for them to do, saying it was mutual. I doubt anyone really bought it, but that's what we were selling. Ethan thanked me for everything I'd done for the place and we shook hands in front of everyone to show our "no hard feelings" position. His hand was clammy; that's all I remember.

After the meeting, I headed back to my office. It was still my office—at least for a few more minutes. I felt like Nixon, post-resignation, waiting for his helicopter to land on the White House lawn. Typically, when The Firm fires someone, he's gone within minutes. But there were politics all over this situation. They didn't want it to seem as if they were running me out the door. Meanwhile, they couldn't wait for me to leave, and rightfully so. Were I in their shoes, I'd feel the same way.

In the end, I took one thing: my chair. It had cost me nearly two grand and I wasn't about to leave it for the poor schnook who'd replace me. *That'll show 'em.* I'm not entirely sure what else I left behind except for the three glass "tenure awards" I'd received over the years. The awards were a big deal to a few folks—especially the managers—who displayed them like they were Academy Awards or something. I'd never taken them out of the little blue boxes they came in. I guess I never wanted to admit that surviving in this place for as long as I did was worthy of a trophy, much less three. Groucho Marx once said, "I'd never join a club that would have me as a member." I think it's sort of like that. I left the pieces of glass for the new guy.

Not ten minutes after we closed my last meeting, I wheeled my chair toward the elevator. I was going home. Some folks tried not to notice. Some stood up. A few old friends got up and helped me to my car. Someone threw my chair in the back of my truck for me. Someone else lit me a cigarette, one last time. We didn't talk. There was nothing to say. Still, I knew that within a week, they'd barely remember me. It is what it is.

Soon enough, the phone calls and text messages fade out. Everything goes on without you—everything. It used to be, not a day went by where I wasn't completely tapped into what was going on at The Firm—the subplots, the rumors, the red herrings, who was out sick, doing well, happy, looking for a job, being fired, promoted, sleeping with each other. These days, there's none of that. These days, big news in my world is that my kid just said, "yellow pepper."

Just like a lottery winner, if I didn't know who my friends were when I had the money and the high-profile job, I sure do now. These days, I really only hear from Jason. Jason always calls.

Everyone should have a friend like Jason. He should come in a box. They'd sell millions.

Ironically, if it weren't for Ben, I would likely still be in the lottery business. And, while my accountant would prefer that I was making those paychecks, my friends and family are eternally grateful that he resurfaced when he did. Life is richer now, despite what my bank account says. Before Ben reentered the field, our numbers consistently beat those of our competitors. So, who could argue against me? I was one of The Firm's prized employees. Everyone believed in me. Even *I* believed in me. With Ben out of the business, I walked on water. Until Ben came back, there wasn't a pair of hands strong enough to knock me off my high horse. Ben changed all that. When he came back, I lost the credibility I'd earned over all those years—just like that. But, as humbling as my fall was, it was entirely necessary and largely deserved. I wasn't the best choice to run that place. Getting fired was the best thing for me, and truth be told, the best thing for The Firm, too. They did the right thing—for both of us.

Ben is a far greater business talent than I'll ever be. I'm very good, but he's better. I knew that a long time ago. I was, however, taken aback by how quickly he reestablished his dominance upon his return. I thought I could give him a run for his money. I was wrong. That did little for my self-worth and surely didn't do me any favors with Ethan. It's a lot easier to acknowledge Ben's skill now, sitting in my basement, than when my job was to beat him and the yardstick by which I was measured was based exclusively upon how my results stacked up to his.

Ben always had the one thing I wanted more than everything else—self-confidence. In the office, I had the reputation of someone overflowing with confidence. I was in sales; I could play any part. But Ben wasn't acting. In his core, he doesn't give a damn about failure, or what the guy next to him thinks. Me, I'm *obsessed* with what the guy next to me thinks. The guy next to me has haunted me throughout my life. When Ben came back, I had to fight an unwinnable battle on two fronts—against him and against the powers at The Firm. Still, I owe him a lot. I owe him for getting me into this crazy business and more so, I owe him for getting me out of it . . . once and for all.

I resented Ben for years. I held a lot of things against him. Some he deserved; some were merely the grudge I've perfected the art of keeping. It wasn't Ben; it was me. Ben was just a great villain. He was a natural. The fact that Ethan and I had Ben in common was kismet. It kept us in synch—for a little while longer.

Having been out of the industry for over a year now, one thing's for sure: I don't hate Ben. Mostly, I think, I was simply jealous. In a nostalgic way, I even miss him—like the way I miss my roommate from freshman year, just enough to think fondly of him and wish him well . . . but not enough to call.

I have a theory. If on the day they won, lottery winners were told that they had to somehow *earn* their lottery check, rather than simply wait for it by the mailbox, lottery winners as we've come to understand them would be the exception rather than the rule. If you were handed a thousand dollars, if you won it out of the blue, what would you do with it? *No lying.* Yeah, I'd blow it, too. Now, if you were made to dig a ditch or paint a house, or do *any* job for a day or two in order to receive that same money, what would you do with it then? *Exactly.* Me too. Bills are bills.

Earned money is more valuable than found money because it is more *valued.* Earned money is used to invest, to pay our bills, to insure a better life for our families. Found money, money we seemingly get for free, is the money we tend to squander. Earned money is money you respect. If you've sacrificed for it, no matter whether that sacrifice was an eight-hour shift at Taco Bell or as chief surgeon in the ER, work makes you want to keep what you get in exchange for your time, your freedom, and your skills.

I worked hard and sacrificed a lot to keep deals coming in the door. Still, the fact that lottery deals could be so lucrative, and come out of nowhere, coupled with my taste for the casinos, made me think too much like a winner and a lot less like a senior executive in a finance firm. There was, somehow, always a hole in my pocket. Like a winner, I had cash flow. Like a winner, I spent major cash. Like a winner, I figured that I could catch up *next* paycheck, next override, next year. Not coincidentally, it wasn't just me. Many of the salesmen at The Firm blew right through their commissions. And like me, so many of them seemed to waste their money in the casinos. I signed their commission sheets. I *know* what these guys were making and when they were supposed to be flush with cash.

I'd sign a salesman's commission sheet for ten grand, see him get paid, and days later have the same cat in my office begging me for an advance on future deals. Where'd all the money go? Somehow, despite the fact that lottery salesmen made substantially more money than anyone else in the company, they were often broke. Just like winners, the lottery sales group drove the nicest cars and had the latest toys—iPods, fancy watches, cell phones, etcetera. My sales staff drove more BMWs than the German embassy. Random big checks coming over the transom, an odd feast-or-famine relationship with money, a group of people suddenly receiving and mismanaging a lot of money they'd never expected to make. Sound like anyone we know?

Our salespeople *were* lottery winners—we just never bought tickets. We knew how to sell to winners, we understood them, because over time, we'd become so similar to them. We were no better than the winners. If we *were* better, we'd have been doing something other than this for a living. We knew it. Maybe we didn't say it to each other, but you could put lipstick on the industry for only so long. Before The Firm, none of us were such world-beaters that we were used to cutting deals with this many zeros. We were *new money* finance guys, in the same way winners were new money. Some of us fit the profile better than others, but we all fit. We were mainly smart, tough, talented, and personable. But we weren't doing *anything* like this before we found The Firm, or it found us. Having access to potential customers with this kind of money attached to them for *this* group of salespeople was unique and unexpected. We had that in common with winners—being in a unique and unexpected financial position, one we couldn't really explain, much less fully understand whether it was a blessing or a curse.

Looking back, we were a troubled lot. I was the tip of a broken spear. There should have been mandatory training to teach salespeople how to handle coming into this kind of money for the first time. Senior management always wanted to downplay the discrepancy between the sales group's compensation and that of, say, anyone else in the company. Politically, of course you downplay the disparity between sales and everyone else. But, good politics aside, minimizing the sales compensation issue never allowed us to pay any serious attention to what guys were doing with all that cash.

Just as the state lotteries know what new winners should expect, so, too, did The Firm when it came to big commissions going to young, sometimes ignorant, salespeople. Any sales-based company is better off if their sales group makes *and* spends a lot of money. Broke salesmen hit the phones, make a lot of calls, and sell their pants off. Broke salesmen are hungry. There's little need to give them the *rah-rah* speech during the morning sales meeting. They know what's at stake. They manage themselves. Salespeople sitting on a legitimate savings could get lazy or, even worse, realize they no longer needed to suffer the heartburn of this industry. Broke lottery salespeople, like broke lottery winners, are very good for The Firm's bottom line. Could the argument be made that salespeople in general are not the most level-headed, responsible group when it comes to saving their money? Yes. Yes, indeed. Still, the nature of lottery deals—their randomness and their life-changing potential—made each of us, in one way or another, more prone to believe too much in fate, in chance, in luck, words not commonly associated with a dedicated savings plan.

What a slice of poetic justice! The lump-sum industry flourished because many lottery winners were impulsive, poorly educated, broke, and receiving little or no guidance from good advisors. Concurrently, The Firm relied upon those same characteristics in their salespeople to keep them doing its bidding with winners all over the nation. Were the sales group better equipped to handle the commissions they were suddenly earning, they'd be less likely to stay in the industry for the long term. Perhaps salespeople would have given that same insight to winners—who needed the guidance twice as bad.

EPILOGUE:
THE GAMBLE IN ME

"All the things I really like to do are either illegal, immoral, or fattening."
—ALEXANDER WOOLLCOTT

TELLY SAVALAS RUINED MY life.

He did commercials for the Players Club International in the eighties and early nineties. Players Club International gave you VIP treatment at the major casinos. It was the universal casino comp card before there were comp cards at every casino on earth. One day I saw Telly on the telly asking if I enjoy being treated like a king, like the VIP that I truly am. *"Well, yes . . . yes, I most certainly do, Telly. I'm interested in your theories, and I'd like to subscribe to your newsletter."* That very night I went to Atlantic City for the first time. I was nineteen. When I got there, a switch went on in my brain. I've never turned it off. I knew right there that I was hooked. I've never done cocaine, but I'm sure this feeling is the same one some people experience snorting their first line. Before they're even high, they know they like it too much already. I knew. I loved the action. I needed the action. What followed was fifteen years of playing, losing, winning, going broke, and loving and hating every minute of it. "Who loves you baby?" Fuck you, Kojak.

It's remarkable, the ease by which an underage kid can get into a casino and gamble. Do you really think that a casino, with more cameras per square foot than the Pentagon, doesn't know that there are minors playing at the tables or feeding the slots? Back then, when I didn't even have the legal right to gamble, when I was off limits to them, the casinos rolled out the red carpet for me. Here they were, sending mail to my parents' house, giving me free meals and rooms, somehow unaware that I was a minor. Bullshit. Now, I'm sure that if I'd have hit a big slot jackpot, and the casino suddenly owed *a minor* $4,000, they would be *shocked* to discover my age.

When you ask why I spent the better part of my career working in the spider's web of lottery finance, the explanation always comes back to my gambling. The last seven years of my life were spent buying lottery prizes from winners to pay for my own casino losses. The lottery finance business is intense. It's high stakes and, ironically, the asset itself is born from gambling. My job at The Firm was analogous to gambling in so many ways. I was paid to take risks, to make bets. Work gave me the same feeling, the same rush that I'd get in a casino. I could gamble at work . . . for work.

I took a job working with lottery winners because it was offered to me and I needed money. Why'd you take your job? I stayed because I was making piles of cash, almost right away. I found a way to spend most of it. Selling to the winners was like selling to myself. A gambler is a gambler is a gambler.

Gambling is all about living for right now. Gamblers don't live for tomorrow. For a serious gambler, there is no such thing as a savings account. You want to visit your money, you go to the green felt. That's where you left it, there with everybody else's future. Now your money is stacked in rows of colored chips, twenty high. Your money belongs to Caesar's, or Bally's, or in your bookie's pocket. It's anything but yours.

Gamblers gamble for the rush, for that immediate high, that feeling that we need *right now*. That escape from reality, from all our troubles, our pain, our mistakes, our bills. The casino rush is so immediate, so absolute, it might as well come in a syringe. And it doesn't leave marks, impair your ability to operate a motor vehicle, or make your breath smell. Gambling is a covert addiction. There are no physical signs. It doesn't hurt your skin or rot your teeth. It's the most wonderful, disgusting feeling I have ever known. I wish I'd never felt it before. I wish I could turn back time and have someone whisper in my ear not to start.

The only time in my life that I feel completely alone, completely lonely, is when I'm in a bad tumble at a casino. When I'm just dumping money from the ATM right into their pockets. I *know* they are watching me, always watching me with the cameras, the fake pit bosses, and dealers, always seeing the dollars add up. Never once have they asked me if I might want to walk it off or take a break. Instead, they give me a line of credit I can't afford and "comped" rooms and dinners. They even pay for my cigarettes.

I fell for all their marketing tricks. I wasn't their guest; I was their mark, their meal ticket, their meat, their dinner. They are happy to see you because they know that if you stay long enough, with the little bullshit freebies, you'll dump out your bank account right there, once more, like you've done so many times before. It's a helpless feeling.

The trip to a casino is a lot different from the trip home. The trip up is full of excitement, nervous energy, and hope. No matter what happened the last time, this trip—the trip you are about to take—*could be* different. No matter what you did to secure your bankroll, no matter the credit-card debt, the quiet bail-out from Pop-Pop, the bullshit you told yourself to justify betting the rent money, once the bankroll's in pocket, life is good. The trip to a casino is never the time to think about how you weaseled the cash from yourself. You got it . . . mission accomplished. *Go gamble.* Go to confessional after you've sinned, not while it's going down. *Go.* Have fun . . . you *deserve* it. Deal with reality tomorrow. Hell, you might even *win* tonight. Most casinos are built using contributions from folks who think the same way.

There is a wholly different vibe on a plane ride out to Vegas versus the return. The ride out is a frat party. The flight home is the hangover. No one is ever in a good mood on the way home, not even the winners. For big gamblers, winning in a casino is more relief than pleasure. It's like celebrating after the firing squad misses you. You've really bought just enough time to get a few more drags on your smoke. While you are exhaling, the firing squad is busy reloading. The casinos know you'll be back. They know they'll get what you won and then some. In the meantime, how about a free steak?

It's on the way back from a gambling trip, on the long road home, where it often dawns on you what you just did. That's when reality hops into the passenger seat. On the way home—that's where gamblers want to kill themselves. I can't count how many times I've driven back from Atlantic City, or worse, flown back from Vegas, filled with the self-loathing and, moreover, fear—actual fear—as to what I'm going to do about the money I just lost. Still, what's even more deranged is that I've never returned from a losing trip and not seriously considered turning around and going back for more.

That's the upshot with gamblers. We don't learn from the past, and we have little hope for the future (other than long shots on the ponies or the NFL). That doesn't leave a lot of wiggle room in your real life. Winning and losing are important, I guess. But, when it comes right down to it, *playing* is what matters. Feeding the beast. If you told ten gamblers they could go to Vegas tonight, gamble all night long, and then simply be back at work the next day, but they were guaranteed to come back losers, most would still sign on. Winning would just be a bonus. Losing doesn't really matter until you're broke.

Sometimes, when I'd get paid a nice commission check, I'd drive the cash up to Atlantic City to give it to the casinos. I didn't want to lose, but it didn't bother me the way it should. I developed a tolerance to it. I needed to lose a lot to even feel it. I made too much money. I'd been losing for too long. Losing in and of itself is a high. It hurts, but the pain is intense, exciting, familiar. Sometimes I just need that intensity. Losing gives it to me. Winning is nice, too.

On the bright side, I can get tickets to any show in Atlantic City or Vegas, as long as it's a weeknight—and it's not too crowded.

The First Night

Jason Ibrahim is one of my closest friends. Jason is Egyptian. I'm a Jew. We are the upshot of the Camp David Accord. Jason runs the back of the house at The Firm. As much as I hate attorneys, I love Jason even more. Other than my dad, he is the most honorable man I know. Jason is both an attorney *and* a human being. It's confusing but true.

Jason in a casino is like my two-year-old sitting in the bath. There's a lot of excitement, pleasure, and cooing, and you run a fifty-fifty chance that someone is going to pee on themselves. Still, there is nothing better than bath time or a rare trip to Atlantic City with Jason. Both are worth the risk.

At the time of this trip I'd been pretty broke for awhile, and consequently, I'd stayed away from the casinos entirely. Any money I have coming in the door is guarded by my wife for silly things like the mortgage and our daughter's diapers. Jason's broke, too. We don't have a grand between the two of us. In the old days, we wouldn't even have bothered coming up with such a small bankroll. Frankly, it's embarrassing. But I haven't been up here in five months. I *need* this trip.

In the last few weeks, I've developed a bad case of cabin fever. Having spent so many weekends at home, I've been getting huge, wonderful doses of my wife and kid. But, as much as I love the daddy thing, I've been dying to hang out with someone with a penis. You know things have gotten bad when my wife all but begged me to go gamble.

Typically, when I was sitting flush with cash, I'd take a few grand up to Atlantic City. Plus, I'd have a $7,500 line of credit. The goal is to not use the line—which is easier said than done. The line of credit allows you to get a marker from the casino without so much as leaving the blackjack table. All you have to do is ask; you don't even have to say please. Now, in the middle of the night, with a few cocktails in you, and the desperate, uncontrollable need to keep playing and get back what you just lost, you can convince yourself that it makes perfect sense to take out a few grand on a marker. The gambler always leaves a mess for himself to clean up in the morning.

With a $7,500 line of credit, if you lose your cool, and your bankroll, you can find yourself in debt to the casino for just south of ten grand before you have time to think about what the hell you just did. It can happen in an instant. *Everything* in a casino happens in an instant. There's a scene in *Snatch,* where Benicio Del Toro loses it and goes on a mad gambling binge. There's an amazing photomontage showing him shooting dice, laying out stacks of bills, reacting to every moment, living and dying a hundred times per minute. That's how it feels to really let it all go in a casino. The first time I saw the movie, that scene gave me goose bumps.

The casinos make it so goddamn easy for you to keep dumping your hard-earned cash into their tills. If you are addicted to this stuff, the chips are truly stacked against you. It's impossible to win. It's often not until you're on your way home that it dawns on you that not only did you lose the money you came up with, but, as an added treat, you have two weeks to send the casino a check for what you borrowed in a daze at 3:30 in the morning. There is nothing more ridiculous than being in debt to a casino.

The drive to Atlantic City, normally three and a half hours, takes us just under three. We are on familiar ground. We are headed to our favorite place, to do our favorite thing. The miles roll by unnoticed. When we get to our room, it seems obvious that someone made a mistake. We are in a *huge* suite. Obviously, Caesar's did not get the memo regarding my termination. They are betting that I'm the same guy that's been coming up here and blowing his paycheck for the past decade. I'm not. I have no choice in the matter. I'd like nothing better than to bleed away ten grand with Jason over the next two nights. By the looks of the suite our host gave us, Caesar's is all for it. They are going to be disappointed.

Jason is one of those guys who takes two different stomach medicines before he eats anything and still heads right to the bathroom when he's done. Therefore, it's not surprising that it took him five minutes to decide which toilet to use. We have three bathrooms. Doesn't everyone? We may not have a lot of cash, but we are not so broke that we have to share toilets. *This isn't the Depression.*

9:45 P.M.

What to do first? Traditionally, we'd each go shove a few hundred dollars into the high-limit slots. It's a good, quick way to get the blood flowing—like walking into a bar and quickly ordering a shot and a beer. After just a few minutes on the casino floor, you'd know where you stood for the evening. No sense in delaying things any more than absolutely necessary. Get in, get dirty, get gambling, go broke. Tonight we are already broke, so we are trying to show some control. *We've yet to leave the suite.* It's safer in here. We are both trying to put on a happy face despite the fact that it's *killing* us that we have no real bankroll. We don't do "broke" very well, not here.

We can't just head downstairs and lose what little we have. That would ruin the trip. It's a very dangerous proposition being here with a paper-thin bankroll. We are both so callused, so used to gambling, to losing, that we have to play against type and show control here. This is a delicate situation.

If we can't gamble, we will do the next best thing; we'll drink.

10:19 P.M.

The handle of vodka I bought this afternoon won't last the night. Jason went down the hall for ice and mixers but came back empty-handed. It seems the soda machine is broken and the ice maker is producing the smell of burning hair combined with some sort of barking noise. He wants me to come see for myself. I take his word for it and call room service. We aren't interested in eating; we're going to the noodle bar at Bally's. We order $65 worth of mixers, which on a casino room-service menu equals six Red Bulls and a few bottles of club soda. Sixty-five dollars! They *did* have to take the drinks onto the elevator. We are on a "diamond comp" this trip, which means that the casino is paying for everything, including the Red Bulls and club soda. If not, I'd have told the waiter to take them back to the kitchen. I think nothing of making a $400 bet on a hand of blackjack, but I'm not paying six dollars a pop for mixers.

10:36 P.M.

We pour a drink, and then another. But so far, we can still see the elephant in the room. Being in a casino and not gambling is like going to Disney World and doing a crossword puzzle. It's just not why you came. Not having won or lost, not having gotten into any sort of action, is maddening. We didn't drive three hours to be even. I swear, I'd rather be down a few hundred than sitting up here in the suite wondering what will happen once we hit the casino. Also, I'm starting to feel like we had better give our host some action to justify this god-damn suite. It's the *Rain Man* suite. I'm waiting for Dustin Hoffman to sit down and watch *Jeopardy*. What was Caesar's thinking?

10:45 P.M.

Two quick vodka Red Bulls takes the edge off. We're ready to walk the short block on the boardwalk to Bally's for the noodle bar.

Bally's is a real dump, even by Atlantic City's standards. It's one of the casinos that really caters to the bus crowd and poor old people that come up to nurse the penny slots with their social security checks. I get depressed looking at them. I see what I could be in forty years if I keep it up. Goddamn depressing. They are not exactly the life of the party, either. But, for us, for this kind of trip, for the noodles alone, we are happy slumming it at Bally's. I just want some soup.

10:52 P.M.

The boardwalk is warm and breezy, with a light mist rolling off the shore. I'm stunned that it's so empty. Yes, it's Thursday, but where are the rest of the people? It's the beginning of the season and the weather is perfect. We walk past the spot where, last summer, a seagull took a dump on my head. It's a lot funnier now than it was at the time. However, after the bird crapped on me, I went on a mad winning streak. I was up a few grand within an hour. My buddy Keith, a casino mush, who sounds like Demi Moore would if she were a man, was convinced that the bird shit brought me good luck. So what does he do? He goes out to the boardwalk, on a Saturday afternoon, in the middle of July, and starts screaming at the top of his lungs at the birds, "Come on! Poop on me!" over and over again. He even tried to balance French fries on his head as an inducement for the gulls to shit on him. Whatever works. Believe me, if I thought the bird shit was the secret, I'd raise them on my roof. I'd squeeze hot sauce down their throats and wear them like hats. It's not the bird shit.

10:55 P.M.

Jason manages to have two cigarettes en route to Bally's. It's about a hundred yards, but Jason can really smoke when he wants to. I try to tell him the bird-shit story but I can tell he's not listening. Daytime Jason has checked out. In his place—gambling Jason. *This* Jason is insanely fun and a danger to those around him.

10:58 P.M.

We arrive at the noodle bar. The drinks have hit my mood and I'm feeling relaxed, calm, at home.

11:04 P.M.

I see a black guy wearing overalls and no shirt spit onto the carpet by the nickel slots. No kidding. He just spit right on the floor. He looks completely unfazed by the act. There's no guilty looking around to see if anyone was watching; nothing. Perhaps he has mistaken the place for a barn. He may be on to something.

11:09 P.M.

We are finally seated. It turns out, to my delight, that our spitting friend wants noodles, too. He is seated at the bar, directly to Jason's left. I'm thrilled. Jason is mortified. He'd like to go. Waiting for our soup, we watch the spitter try to negotiate two extra shrimp into his soup bowl with the waiter. Soon the cook joins the discussion, which is largely being mimed out, as the spitter does not speak Chinese. He's using the "air quote" sign to represent the bonus shrimp he is trying to win. To his credit, he cuts a deal for one extra shrimp. The cook laughs. The waiter fumes. The spitter smiles. I'm impressed with his sales skills. I didn't spit on the floor and somehow, I'm getting fewer shrimp than *this* guy. If I still had a job, I'd seriously consider hiring him for a sales position. The overalls would have to go. I tell Jason that we should buy the spitter his soup as a toast toward his salesmanship. Jason reminds me that we're broke. The spitter is on his own.

11:48 P.M.

One hour on the floor and I am down only $40. I am ashamed to be staying in that suite. They didn't put us in that room for me to be down forty bucks. They are looking for me to make individual bets, twice a minute, that are three times that amount. I'm often up or down $1,000 or more after my first few hours in a casino. The night is young. Bad things may still happen.

12:27 A.M.

I slip $100 into a slot machine whose theme has something to do with eating cheeseburgers and milkshakes. I guess I'm still hungry. The machine is exceptionally loud and every time I hit the spin button, the noise makes everyone in my row of slots look at me wondering if I hit a jackpot—and secretly hoping I didn't. I'm immediately self-conscious because of the noise. Feeling like a schmuck the entire time, I lose the money and awkwardly walk away.

12:35 A.M.

I move over two rows and stick another hundred into a new Frank Sinatra slot that beckoned with a few lines from "Luck Be a Lady Tonight." Just as I sit down, the lady next to me hits the bonus round. Suddenly Sinatra appears on her video screen, blowing on a pair of dice, wishing her "his kind of luck." I don't know what that means, but I'm quite sure it would be fun to have anything Sinatra gave you, except perhaps the clap. She wins some big bonus prize and Frank is absolutely *thrilled* for her. The two of them break into a duet of "Three Coins in a Fountain." Now, I'm *dying* to hit the bonus. I, too, want Frank's attention. I'm a big fan. Does that count for anything?

Apparently not. As soon as Old Blue Eyes welcomes me to his slot, he quits singing and focuses on crushing me. It hurts even worse coming from him. He is clearly in cahoots with Telly Savalas. There is no bonus, no singing, no walk down memory lane. There is only the dwindling credit meter in the bottom right corner. I'm down $200.

Being down doesn't feel nearly as comfy as I had recalled. I get that goldfish-in-my-stomach feeling. It's unsettling. It's familiar.

My throat is starting to feel the effects of the cigarettes I promised my wife I wouldn't smoke tonight. I think I'm getting sick. Where's Jason?

2:36 A.M.

I haven't seen Jason in two hours. Normally, that bodes ill. He is either upstairs in the bathroom or he is on tilt somewhere among the maze of slot machines. If he's down here and hard to find, it's because he doesn't want to be found. We know how to find each other in here. We've done this a time or two. Maybe he's chasing his money, trying to make it back in one hit. Sometimes, you get lucky. But when you're running bad like that and you're all alone—that's when the ugly stuff happens. I do one more exhausting lap around the slot loop I know he likes. However, he could purposefully be somewhere I'd never look, like the nickel Betty Boop slot area. Sometimes, up here, you just need to be alone.

4:43 A.M.

I walk out to the boardwalk to get a signal on my cell. Phones rarely work on the casino floor. I'm convinced they purposely jam the signal so gamblers are that much more removed from real life. You know, from things like the wife or the boss calling—little things like that. The second I get a signal, the text messages start flowing in from Jason. Is he down? *No.* Is he ill? *Shockingly, no.* Does he need bail money? *Still, no.* He's been looking all over for me. *He's winning.* Apparently, Jason put $20 into a quarter slot, just to kill some time. After a few spins, he hit for $1,000. Ever since, he's been up in the suite, guarding the vodka. I text him that I'll be right up. But, on the casino floor, there is no such thing as *right up.* I stop and try my luck one more time before going to the suite.

5:04 A.M.

I make a nice run on the slots. I pulled $800 out of a video poker machine with some sort of tie-in to the World Series of Poker.

We are hungry. I call room service and place the order. Fried dumplings, buffalo wings, and a hot fudge sundae comes out of my mouth before I give the time of day (daybreak) any thought. What did you expect us to order, yogurt and fresh fruit? I'm embarrassed to be ordering ice cream at dawn, but I quickly get over it. I go to bed after breakfast.

The Second Day

10:15 A.M.

I feel like I'm at the eye doctor. The sunlight is blinding. Jason broke the electric window curtains last night. He tried to close them, forgetting that they were automatic. He yanked the curtains, expecting to pull them across the length of the windows. There was a long blue spark. It made a disquieting, hissing noise. Jason looked like he was holding a lightsaber. We were too tired to pretend to know how to fix electric curtains. Jason laid the whole mess in the Jacuzzi. We are lucky to be alive.

10:19 A.M.

Today's Friday. I wanted to sleep in. The casino will be full of amateurs all day anyway. It will be a scene, full of monkeys who don't know what they're doing—generally just clogging up the place. But, with the sun blasting in and the casino just eighteen floors below, I can't sleep. I get up for a shower.

10:21 A.M.

The entire bathroom is sand-colored tile with gold trim. It screams "trying too hard." The shower is also, apparently, a steam bath. Meanwhile, I can't figure out how to turn on the water. It is perfectly maddening. The shower is too complicated for me. *Good morning, dummy*. After a few minutes of wiggling knobs and pressing buttons, I abandon trying to summon the steam. All I want is a regular, hot shower. Now how the hell do you turn on the goddamn water?

There is a mini shower head directly at penis level. After three minutes of turning the four different knobs every which way I can, the penis shower starts begrudgingly spitting out lukewarm water. Nothing else works, but suddenly you could eat off my groin. Here I am, in the nicest hotel room I've ever seen, and I'm seriously contemplating washing my entire body under this two-foot shower head. I decide to give up and turn everything off. Inexplicably, water starts flying out of four different shower heads. There's water pulverizing my head, my butt, up, down . . . there's even steam. It is the greatest shower I've ever taken. I am blown away.

There's a bench inside the shower. I sit, breathe in the thick, wet air, and try to meditate while the steam works its way into my lungs. I've been trying to meditate more, as my wife is convinced it will help me relax (like *I* need to relax). So I meditate in the shower. Basically, I sit there and breathe . . . and breathe . . . and contemplate masturbating. After fifteen minutes, I've had enough. I hop out and get ready to head downstairs.

10:30 A.M.

I get out of the room without waking Jason. I leave him a note saying that I'll be in the casino. This is our thing when we are here or in Vegas. I wake up early and head down to the casino for some morning action and Jason sleeps until happy hour.

Gambling-wise, this is a pivotal time for me. I'm up almost $400 from last night, and a swing in either direction would be huge. If I get lucky and make a few runs, I'll be sitting pretty for the rest of the day and tonight. I'll be able to gamble more—and loosen up a bit from the pinch of having such a small bankroll. Plus, if necessary, I can put a few hundred into Jason's hands, too. He could need it, and when we gamble, we share our winnings.

10:38 A.M.

Once I hit the casino floor, I see a $25 blackjack table just starting to shuffle the cards for a new shoe. Even better, there's only one other guy sitting at third base. He's got several huge stacks of quarter chips and an impressive pile of black ones, too. I count close to three grand neatly organized in front of him. I sit down, giving him a knowing nod, doing my best to look like I'm not going to fuck up his game by making a bunch of stupid calls because I "felt the mojo." He stares back at me. *Not to worry, my friend.* With me you get one thing at a blackjack table—perfect basic strategy, nothing more, nothing less. Plus, I'll pass you an ashtray. I'll even listen to your bullshit, if that's your thing. You can be the chatty mechanic from Detroit, or the quiet cowboy from Denver. I could care less. You want to talk? Fine. Mind my own business? Sure. Just do me one favor. Play your cards the right way, every time, or fuck off.

10:40 A.M.

I order coffee from the waitress and wait for the dealer to finish shuffling. There is no cup of coffee or cigarette better enjoyed than the one you just poured or are about to light. Wherever you wake up on any given morning, coffee and a smoke are one thing you can count on—that and a pee-pee boner. This cup of coffee will go down with all the hope and optimism of a born-again Christian. Brand new day, brand new table, extremely clean penis. I'm in my special place.

10:41 A.M.

It's amazing how you put $300 in actual paper cash down in front of the dealer and she turns your cash into a short stack of green chips about the height of a poorly made Reuben. The whole concept of chips in a casino is the greatest single marketing idea I know. If I played with paper money, I'd nervously bet $20 at a time. Chips *are* make-believe, aren't they? I give the dealer, Roberta, my cash. She gives me green clay, and asks, "How ya doing, honey?"

I respond with a spirited, "Haya," meaning it more than normal. I *did* meditate this morning. I lay out $50 in my betting circle, doing my best to make sure the pit boss sees my action. I'm betting twice the minimum out of the gate so he'll rate my play for the session right away. Playing $50 hands with a $300 bankroll is dangerous. You're talking about six hands worth of chips. Many would say, and rightfully so, that I had no business sitting down with such a little amount and betting $50 minimum per hand. If I start off on a bad run and lose a few hands in a row, I'll be up from the seat well before my coffee arrives. That would be bad. I need the coffee and I want to gamble.

Just as Roberta reaches for the first card in the shoe, an old Chinese guy sits down in the middle seat. Mr. Chips and I give each other the "oh no" eye roll, as a wild card has just joined the fray at the last second. If he can play blackjack, he's welcome. If not, we are not pleased. When he reaches into his pocket and pulls out two handfuls of green, Mr. Chips looks at me and winks. When our Asian friend reaches into his other pocket and pulls out a messy salad of black, purple, and *orange* chips, we know things are about to get interesting. Black chips are worth $100. Purple chips are worth $500. Orange chips are worth a cool $1,000. Mr. Asia has something like $15,000 in front of him. Suddenly, my $300 buy-in is put into perspective for everyone—including the pit boss. I'm definitely not the most interesting thing going on at this table. Even *I* don't give a damn about me right now. What have I just stumbled into? I'm set to play a fresh shoe with two guys who have about $20,000 between them. They *should* know what they're doing with that kind of cash in front of them. At the very least, I'm excited to watch Mr. Asia play with a mad pile of money in front of him, even if he makes bad plays.

"Checks play," Roberta quips, letting the pit boss know there is real weight being bet at our table. He's well aware. The bosses have a sixth sense for big chips approaching their pit. Perhaps I'm important by association? I feel like a kid, rather than the fifteen-year casino vet that I am. Now, I'm worried that *I* will screw up the two *other* players' hands with my silly $50 plays. *Well, I was here first, so there.*

Roberta burns the first card, letting us see it. It's an ace, my ace. Shit. The next card out is mine, also an ace. Mr. Asia gets a ten, Mr. Chips draws a queen. Okay, so far, so good. But, with the law of averages, I'm sure that the next cards will be worthless fours and fives. No. After Roberta deals herself a hole card, the next three cards come out—nine, king, ace. Twenty, twenty, and a blackjack for Mr. Chips. The dealer has a seven showing and turns over her hole card, also a king. She has seventeen. Winner, winner, winner. Each of the three players gives that "just settling in" exhale. Now we are playing some cards, boys. I light a smoke just as my coffee arrives.

Things get real good right away. It's almost embarrassing. My two best friends, Mr. Chips and Mr. Asia, are good players and they're both making increasingly big bets—as am I. Roberta is starting to look uncomfortable. I imagine someone upstairs is watching her deal winner after winner and the data is going directly in her employment file. We now have two pit bosses watching the action. I feel like a celebrity. Although I'm hardly the story of the table, I've quietly doubled my stack. I, too, am more interested in Mr. Asia's $500-to-$1,500-per-hand bets but, still, little old me is kicking ass. I wish Jason were here to see this. There's nothing like being up in a casino. It's a fleeting feeling. Gamblers keep chasing it, but it never lasts.

11:07 A.M.

I'm doing well. The other two are going nuts. Caesar is getting fidgety. Mr. Asia is up a cool $5,000. Mr. Chips has made close to $2,000. I've run my $300 up to a respectable $800. I'm still the little fish here, but the $500 profit I've made basically doubles my bankroll. I take the five black chips that Roberta has been paying my winnings with and put them in my shirt pocket. I make sure the boss sees it. He does, and makes some mark in his notes. I imagine they'll ding Roberta for paying me in black chips rather than the green ones I've been betting. The casinos know you are more likely to keep your black chips than your green ones. Black chips have a power over gamblers; the green ones just don't compare. When I put the $500 in my pocket, Roberta looks right at me and discreetly nods. She reminds me of my nana. She knows what she's doing. She's been paying me with the black chips on purpose, in exchange for my green-chip bets, so I'll put the things in my pocket while the getting's good. I love Roberta. I look for a ring.

Once I realize what she's doing, I put a green chip up as a bet for her. I've been tipping her all along, a nickel here and there, but, for what she's doing, she's earned some green action herself. My table mates seem to be catching the same insider vibe from Roberta. She's dealing us all winners *and* she's going that extra mile, sort of cashing us out along the way, a big-time dealer no-no. Suddenly there are green bets going up for the dealer as tips almost every hand. As I was the first of the three of us to bet a $25 chip, I feel somewhat responsible for Roberta's good fortune. I'm downright proud of the generosity I've inspired. Perhaps she will tell her family about me later tonight over dinner. At one point, Mr. Chips bet $100 for her after a blackjack that paid him $1,500. She lost but was thrilled to get the action. Roberta must have shoved $400 into the tip box attached to the table next to my knee. This is one of those runs where everyone is making a lot of dough, even the dealer.

We are one happy family: Mr. Chips, Mr. Asia, Roberta, and me. But the love fest comes to an end. The bosses had seen enough. They'd seen enough of the overly friendly dealer, of the three players using solid basic strategy *and* getting great cards, of the chips uncharacteristically flowing out of their rack into our greedy little hands. They pull a dealer off another table and send Roberta packing. Roberta, the love of my life, the most important lady in my world, very nonchalantly claps her hands together, rolls her wrists left and right for the cameras watching from above, and demurely whispers, "Thanks, boys. Good luck." And, just like that, Roberta is gone. Did she even exist at all? Does she want my contact info? A hug? Something? Roberta . . . Hello?

11:31 A.M.

Our new dealer is a priggish little fellow named Davis. Davis is everything Roberta is not. He is disinterested, unimpressed, and overall, a general pain in the ass. I hate him. I hate his name. I hate the gap between his teeth. I hate the way he's tucked his Caesar's button-down shirt deep into his pants. It makes him look like a gym teacher. He seems to enjoy the fact that the pit bosses brought him in to cool off the table. To me, Davis should take this as an insult, not something to feel smug about. Right away, Davis starts taking big bets back from the table, specifically from Mr. Asia.

For whatever reason, Davis scooping up $1,000 bets from Mr. Asia is bothering me a lot more than it seems to affect my man from the East. Asia is shockingly untroubled by Roberta's departure. He's surprisingly unsuperstitious. In a casino ripe with superstitious people, Asians tend to lead the pack. Normally, they are more freaked out by something like a sudden dealer change than anyone else. Not my Asian. He is firing purple bullets like it's the last chance he'll ever have to gamble. Within six or seven hands, Davis has whacked Asia's monster chip stack in half. I'm furious. Asia doesn't blink. The guy just made and then lost nearly $10,000, all within the span of fifteen minutes. This table is not for the faint of heart. Not needing to be hit over the head with a hammer, I decide it's time to go.

In no position to lose the profit I've made, I push my chips toward Davis, motioning that I'm ready to cash out. For effect, and to make sure the pit boss gets my play into the system for my comps, I pull the five black chips back out from my pocket and add them to my stack. Davis, seemingly annoyed that he won't get a shot at my money, begrudgingly stops the game to color up my chips. He quickly counts out a pile of four greens, and then another, and another, and so on. I'm quite impressed with myself. When it's all said and done, I've got $1,450 in chips. I made a $1,150 profit. To my table mates, this is small time. But this morning, with my bankroll being what it is, I've just hit the mother lode. I was up $400 when I left the room a mere hour ago. Now, I'm suddenly sitting on a profit of $1,550. Plus I've got my original bankroll, so I'm looking at just about $2,000, out of nowhere. I'm the happiest kid in the casino.

12:05 P.M.

Jason finally calls my cell. I answer, "You missed it!"

"What flavor?" he asks with a combination of jealousy and rage.

"BJ, first base, $25 minimum, $300 buy-in, two or three sick runs, good players, big cash at the table, great dealer, Roberta, we're in love. I walked with almost $1,500."

"FUUUCCCK!" says my loyal wingman. "Where are you now?"

"Sitting at a one-dollar poker machine, waiting for your fat ass to get up," I said. "You hungry?"

"So hungry!" says my attorney. "Come up for room service."

I'm not that hungry (too juiced from the casino), but I want to give Jason details and I'll always eat. Plus—*diamond comp,* the food *is* free. I decide to play my video poker game out until I run out of credits or I win over $100. Just a few hands later, I'm dealt a lousy pair of sevens, which I hold. I draw three cards: seven, seven, jack. I hit four of a kind. Unreal. I'm waiting for Allen Funt to come up with cameras and tell me to give the money back. I'm still running on adrenaline from my blackjack triumph, and now this? The four of a kind pays $300. Jesus, my bankroll is a remarkably comfortable $2,400. I'm basically up $2,000. Being up $2,000 is always great. But being up this much, having started with only $500, is really something.

3:16 P.M.

Jason's watching soccer, so I crawl into the bedroom for a nap.

6:46 P.M.

I sleep like a bear but wake up to strange voices that don't belong to Jason or me. Opening my eyes, I see two men standing in the Jacuzzi. That's never good. Thankfully, one of them is not Jason. What the *fuck* . . . oh yes, they're here to fix the blinds. Thank God. For a second there, I thought these two guys were some sort of "gift" from the casino. Wrong room. Jason is still watching soccer. When he sees that I'm up, he makes us both a drink. We have dinner reservations at Morton's in two hours.

9:00 P.M.

Dinner at Morton's. We always eat well in Atlantic City. But, tonight, we are taking the "diamond comp" to the next level. We have oysters, scallops wrapped in bacon, and a Caesar salad, then the Cajun rib-eye. The food is excellent. The wine flows. Even better is the $2,400 safely resting in my back pocket. With the meal fully comped, we run up a $400 tab and never dent our bankroll. A few espressos later, we're off. It's time to gamble. Each of us seems content to wander off in a separate direction, and that means someone's bound to lose a lot of cash. There are some things in a casino for which you don't need witnesses.

10:44 P.M.

The casino is overflowing with neophytes. The Saturday-night crowd is heaven for the house and hell for real gamblers. You can barely find room on a table and when you do, odds are that it will be full of monkeys making bad plays, killing winning hands, and generally making you want to choke anyone with that *just here to go clubbing* vibe. I want to play at the tables, but even *I* refuse to wait in a cattle line for the opportunity. Knowing that the scene will die down just past midnight, when normal people tend to head up to their rooms for the night, I decide to kill some time at another slot machine, content to chew on a toothpick, nurse a drink, and wait for the tourists to retire.

The $2,400 is burning a hole in my pocket so I head over to the high-limit slot area, recently renamed the "Palace Court" by the marketing folks upstairs. The room is elevated from the rest of the casino. The raised environment is meant to accomplish two things. First, it sections the riffraff away from the heavy hitters who really keep the casino in the black. Second, within those four walls is everything someone might leave a casino floor to get, right there for the player. Need to use the bathroom? No reason to schlep across the casino like everyone else. Use *this* private bathroom instead—it's even got a gold sink. Hungry? There's a lady who does nothing but walk around handing out little quartered sandwiches with the crusts cut off. They are lousy ham and American cheese on Wonder Bread, but the crusts *are* cut off and the lady gives you a napkin. There's little to complain about. When you've been gambling for the last six hours with no nutrients entering your body but the lime juice you've been squeezing into your gin and tonics, those sandwiches are heaven. They know their market. Most of the people in the Palace Court are out of their tax bracket, anyway. The only court they've ever been to before involved an arrest for urinating in public. The ham and cheese on white is a real crowd pleaser.

I know just the machine I want to play. It's an old favorite, one that has gotten me out of a lot of jams over the last few years. It's a five-dollar *Wheel of Fortune* machine, the third one from the left, in a row of four identical machines against the far wall. I've played each of the four machines. But, this one, *my* machine, is special, different. We have a general understanding with one another. I don't take advantage of her generosity, reserving our interactions only for particular occasions. The machine, "Vanna," appreciates my loyalty and tends to pay off in kind.

Just as I'm about to settle into my chair, I realize that I haven't urinated in hours. I decide to take advantage of the Palace Court's exclusive bathroom, making a beeline for the door. Upon returning, I see an old lady nestling into my chair. Vanna and I look at each other. Her look is cold, hard. I know what's about to happen. Vanna knows, too. I can barely watch. There's nothing either of us can do at this point. The lady shoves in a $100 bill and like the pro that she is, Vanna springs to life. The granny waits as the credit meter climbs up to twenty. At two credits a pull, she'll have ten spins, *my* spins, to make hay.

I find myself hating someone's grandma. Yes, hardly rational, but as visceral as if Hitler kicked my dog. The first spin, nothing. The second, nothing. *So far, so good.* The next three spins come and go without so much as a cherry hitting the board. She's already down $50, halfway to getting her ass off Vanna's lap. Still, I could just feel it. Vanna was about to bust. It was like watching someone kiss your wife. On the next spin, Grandma hits the coveted bonus symbol, earning a spin of the wheel, guaranteed to win anywhere from $125 to $1,199. The fake crowd goes wild, screaming, *"Wheel . . . of . . . FORTUNE!"* Giddy with her *"oh, would you look at that"* mock surprise, she spins the wheel and coos with wrinkled delight. The wheel starts to spin, clicking exactly the way it does on the TV show. It lands on the big prize—$1,199. I taste bile. Why $1,199? Why not $1,200? Because Uncle Sam gets a bite of any jackpot over $1,200. The casino throws the gambler a bone by keeping the tax man out of the equation. Again, casinos know their market.

11:23 P.M.

I haven't seen Jason since dinner. And while I'm steaming from that lady winning my money on the slot in the Palace Court, things are decidedly worse for Jason. I didn't lose; I just could have won, if it weren't for my childlike bladder. Jason has actually managed to lose what little bankroll he had. Undeterred by the swarms of players jockeying for seats at the blackjack tables, Jason slid into a spot at a $25 table in front of the doors leading to the boardwalk. This area, cleverly named "The Party Pit," is the epicenter of chaos, especially on a Saturday night. Knowing better, he sat there and played among the worst of the worst gamblers just in off the boardwalk, and steamed as they made one bad decision after another.

He knew he was in trouble when the guy at third base split two jacks against the dealer's "five." Making matters worse, the genius won both hands and forced the dealer to bust, making him the toast of the table. Jason actually had to suffer the indignity of returning a high-five from the player to his right, in celebration of the winning decision made by the moron at third base. Rather than getting up, he dug in, wanting the seat more than the better odds of winning elsewhere. Consequently, Jason is down—a lot. He's got that ATM look in his eyes. I suggest he panhandle on the boardwalk. Perhaps he'll spit on the floor?

11:56 P.M.

Jason is not the only idiot. We tend to travel in pairs. I just gave back everything I earned today. Who helped fleece me? Vanna.

I take back everything I said about her. She is a mean, heartless bitch. I sat down in the seat still warm from the old lady's tushy and proceeded to fill Vanna's belly with my bankroll. I head up to the suite to lick my wounds. I feel like a schmuck because I thought I'd overcome my demons up here. I thought I'd be able to nurse a few hundred bucks and protect the winnings I made over the last few days. No.

In the *hollow victory* category, we decide to stop the bleeding. Neither of us goes back down. Jason doesn't hit the cash machine. I don't make matters worse by losing my original bankroll. My "profit" now sits comfortably back in the casino cage, where it was likely to stay. I was just holding it for a few hours.

Why was I good at selling lottery deals? Because I am a gambler. I played the lottery every day; I just didn't buy tickets. Like winners, I can smell something for nothing, just around the corner, in the next roll of the dice, the next flip of the cards, the next spin of the wheels. Like winners, I lived too much for today, for the moment. Fun on credit is no way to live. It tends to catch up to you.

ENDNOTES

1   NGISC, p. 1.

2   NGISC, p. 2.

3   John Morgan and Martin Sefton, *Funding Public Goods with Lotteries: Experimental Evidence.* Discussion Papers in Economics #185, Woodrow Wilson School, Princeton University, June 1997.

4   NGISC, p. 2.

5   Charles T. Clotfelter and Philip J. Cook, "On the Economics of State Lotteries," *Journal of Economic Perspectives*, vol. 4, no. 4 (Fall 1990), p. 105.

6   NGISC, p. 3.

7   NGISC, p. 3.

8   Calculations based on an estimate from Terri La Fleur, publisher of *La Fleur's Lottery World*, a monthly trade magazine distributed to lottery executives worldwide. La Fleur estimates that overall, 1.1 percent of lottery sales go toward advertising costs. Thus, 1.1 percent of 2002 U.S. lottery sales ($42.4 billion) is about $466.4 million. Sources are as follows: (a) Suzette Hill, "POP's A Winner for State Lotteries: These corporations spend $400 million a year on advertising while balancing profitability with public policy issues," *Point of Purchase* magazine, online article, Copyright 2001, Kopel Research Group, Inc., March 31, 2003 (July 7, 2003); (b) The North American Association of State and Provincial Lotteries (NAASPL) online, Fast Facts, "FY01 & 02 Sales and Profits," July 7, 2003.

9   Clotfelter and Cook, *Selling Hope: State Lotteries in America*, p. 11.

10   Illinois House of Representatives, "Report and Recommendations," p. 123.

11   *Chicago Tribune,* August 12, 1987.

12   Clotfelter and Cook, *Selling Hope: State Lotteries in America*, p. 37.

13   Clotfelter and Cook, *Selling Hope: State Lotteries in America*, p. 7.

14 NGISC, p. 3.

15 Tyler Bridges, "Push underway to legalize video gambling," *The Miami Herald*, October 30, 2002 (June 5, 2003).

16 NGISC, p. 3.

17 Charles T. Clotfelter and Philip J. Cook, "On the Economics of State Lotteries," *Journal of Economic Perspectives*, vol. 4, no. 4 (Fall 1990), p. 112.

18 NGISC, p. 4.

19 Peter Keating, "Lotto Fever: We All Lose!" *Money*, May 1996, pp. 144, 147.

20 Keating, "Lotto Fever," p. 147.

21 NGISC, p. 5.

22 NGISC, p. 1.

23 NGISC, p. 6.